Texas Guinan

Texas Guinan

QUEEN OF THE NIGHT CLUBS

by Louise Berliner

UNIVERSITY OF TEXAS PRESS   AUSTIN

Copyright © 1993 by Louise Berliner
All rights reserved
Printed in the United States of America
First edition, 1993

Requests for permission to reproduce material from this work should be sent to Permissions, University of Texas Press, Box 7819, Austin, TX 78713-7819.

♾ The paper used in this publication meets the minimum requirements of American National Standard for Information Sciences—Permanence of Paper for Printed Library Materials, ANSI Z39.48-1984.

Library of Congress Cataloging-in-Publication Data

Berliner, Louise, date
    Texas Guinan, queen of the night clubs / by Louise Berliner. — 1st ed.
      p. cm.
    Includes bibliographical references and index.
    ISBN 0-292-78111-3
    1. Guinan, Texas. 2. Entertainers—United States—Biography. I. Title.
PN2287.G75B47   1993
792.7'028'092—dc20
  [B]   92-1720

In memory of Maxwell E. Lopin and Patricia Lopin Berliner

September 19, 1931

Dear Texas,
 ... *My great wish is that those who are fortunate enough to see or hear you will feel the spark of the real you. To most of the world, you are a lady of legends, the brilliant blond Queen of New York's Midnight Madness, the Lucretia Borgia, who stabs 'em to death with a wisecrack. But this part is your foreign legion. The real you is a stranger. That is why little dogs bark at you. The real you with your breadth of vision, your compassion and your understanding is as big as the state from which you took your name. If life is service, you have lived and are now living. And if we get out of life only the happiness we put into it, then, dear Tex, your next venture will be a joyous mirror, reflecting back at you the countless hours of enjoyment you have given to others.*

Earl Carroll

Contents

Acknowledgments	ix
Author's Note: We Meet	xi
Introduction: Hello, Suckers!—A Glimpse	1
Waco: Home on the Ranch?	6
Did She or Didn't She? (An Author's Aside)	19
There's a Sucker Born Every Minute	26
Marie	38
Everything West of New York Is Just Bridgeport	45
Texas Guinan—Quack, Actress, or Saleswoman?	66
Never Jilt a Woman Who Can Shoot	76
Birth of a Hostess	90
Where the Bread-and-Butter Men Roam	108
On Trial	131
Homecoming	150
Fifty Million Frenchmen Can't Be Wrong: We're Too Hot for Paris	168
Tomorrow and Tomorrow	181
After Words	190
Notes	197
A Bibliographic Note on Major Sources	207
Bibliography	211

Films of Texas Guinan, 1917–1933 215
Index 217
Photo section following page xvi

Acknowledgments

Many people gave something to this book, whether it was their memories, advice, research assistance, or a chance remark that set my mind ticking. I would like to thank you all. Among the many I would like to specifically thank:

Ivan B. Berger, Ellen Kuniyaki Brown, Irving Caesar, Maryann Chach, Allen Churchill, Nancy Ciezki, Samuel Cimman, Spencer Clark, Chuck Davis, Geraldine Duclow, Erica Duncan, Ed Eulenberg, William Everson, Wendy Schacher Finn, Ben Finney, Betty Fussell, Mrs. W. Harrison, Aubrey Hastings, Frances Schwab Hewick, Emilie Jacobson, Ruby Keeler, Kent Keeth, Mrs. F. A. Kling, Herman Kogan, Audrey Kupferberg, Elizabeth Lawton, Claire Luce, Laurie Lisle, Edna McClean, Virginia Ming, Vivian Perlis, Lou Rigler, Patrice Amati Runyon, Joe Russell, Nanon Sanderson, Rebecca Spears Schwartz, Evelyn Sharp, Emily Sieger, Mrs. A. Cowper Smith, Patrick and Connie Smith, Kathleen Spivack, Bob Summers, Mark E. Swartz, Lowell Thomas, Anthony Thompson, Laurie Trail, Doris Vinton, Marc Wanamaker, Meyer Weintraub, Frankie Westbrook, Fred Wittenmeier, Charlotte Wright.

A special thanks to Elaine Durbach, whose unique ability to wonder and care about Tex enabled her to live the book with me, offer invaluable editing support, and still remain my friend.

Also thanks to my family, who believed in me, and to John and Sylvie for their patience at the end.

I would like to acknowledge the following people and institutions for their permission to use material in this book:

Donald Gallup, literary executor for Thornton Wilder, for his permission to use the quotation on p. 184 from Thornton Wilder's letter of June 21, 1933, to Dr. Moulton, Chicago.

Hollins College Archive, for allowing me to use the material from their Texas Guinan file.

The Ossabaw Foundation, for granting me time and space to work on my manuscript in the spring of 1982.

The Shubert Archive, for permission to use material in the archive.

Laurie Trail, for permission to use quotes from Julian Johnson's letters.

Patrick Smith, for allowing me to quote from Michael Guinan's and Tex Guinan's correspondence.

This project has been made possible, in part, by a grant from the Youthgrants in the Humanities Program of the National Endowment for the Humanities, a federal agency established by Congress to promote research, education, and public activity in the humanities.

Author's Note: We Meet

> *I like noise, rhinestone heels, customers, plenty of attention and red velvet bathing suits. I smoke like a five-alarm fire; I eat an aspirin every night before I go to bed, I call every man I don't know Fred and they love it, I have six uncles, I sleep on my right side and I like carrots. I eat a dozen oranges every day and I once took off thirty-five pounds in two weeks. I guess that settles my personality.*
> —TEXAS GUINAN, DALLAS MORNING NEWS, NOVEMBER 6, 1933.

Texas Guinan was a night-club hostess—funny, magnetic, loud.

The meaning of "night-club hostess" has altered through the years. When Tex first made it up it meant ringmaster, comedienne, mom, and meddler. It meant staying up all night long, stone sober, watching over crowds dizzy with liquor, and keeping them happy till dawn.

This was risky because the Volstead Act had made the alcoholic action in night clubs strictly illegal. However, the risk added to the charm of the place, and everybody who was anybody—and many who weren't—went to Guinan's. She became known for her generosity, her sharp wit, and her knack of saying the wrong thing at the right time.

The twenties, in New York City, were a time of loud jazz and the sneaking of alcoholic drinks when the Feds weren't looking. In the spring of 1928, the guests at the Salon Royale Club weren't sneaking with enough care, and the Feds closed down the joint, arresting, among others, the Queen of the Night Clubs herself. Charged with "maintaining a public nuisance," i.e., working at a club that sold liquor illegally, and thus being a partner in crime with those who sold the stuff, Tex was forced to look for a lawyer. After a long search she found my grandfather, Maxwell E. Lopin. Years later he recorded the story of the trial, and after he died, I found his manuscript.

So I have always had the illusion that I inherited Tex, like a parcel of land or a family heirloom, or that we were somehow related and Tex a great-aunt ten times removed.

At first I didn't know much about her, but I admired her spunk. I was seventeen at the time, enamored of the twenties, and liked the idea that someone could be arrested as a public nuisance. (I had no idea what that meant.) Tex sounded like fun. I thought when I got older, I'd edit my grandfather's manuscript, do a little research, and tack on a biography at the end. A quick and painless path to fame and fortune.

I later discovered that Tex hadn't left any of the proper clues. She hadn't kept a diary or written letters, and if she'd written at all, it had been on postcards, scribbling most of the message off the edge. Occasionally, she'd sent telegrams, but she had liked the telephone best.

What Tex did leave was a blazing trail through New York's daily tabloids. Scarcely a day passed during the twenties when Tex didn't appear in somebody's column. Her witticisms were quoted, her nightly antics described, and her life story printed in serial form. What a character! I was hooked. Then I began to discover that the biographical details she had fed to the press were anything but accurate. As I sought to untangle the truth from the fiction, trying to understand why Tex had tampered with her past, a picture of the real woman began to emerge.

During my search I had the good fortune to track down Tex's nephew, Patrick Smith. The days I spent with him and his family, feeling like family and treated like a treasured niece, were exciting and bewildering. They were *her* family, yet they were regular people who ate, slept, watched TV.

I was reminded that Tex was a human being who'd had to deal with the ordinary stuff of life just like everybody else. Unfortunately, she'd left few traces of that in the headlines and memorabilia that outlived her. However, she had left some clothing and jewelry. I tried on her fur coat, and feeling the weight of it, had a sense of how big a woman she'd been—big. I also put some of her rings on my fingers, a bracelet or two on my wrist, and dressed up in her black velvet frock with the salmon silk lining and scandalously low back. The Smiths must have sensed my attraction. They sent me home with one of Tex's fox furs, and I began draping it over my shoulders as I paced the floors of my apartment seeking inspiration.

Wearing Tex's clothes was only the beginning. Before long I was seeing my own world through her eyes. Mostly I liked her attitude. Though often she'd played the world-weary cynic, she was at heart an optimist. She loved and believed in people. She had the cheeriest advice. "Don't let your soul warp," she'd said. "Don't be a crab. My God, have a good time and enjoy life. Have fun!"

Yes, I liked her very much. I found myself wishing I could go back to the twenties and catch her show, maybe interview the Queen of the Night Clubs in person.

When I finally heard Tex speak I was in a small, dark room in Los Angeles watching *Broadway thru a Keyhole*, her final film. Though her part was small, she was very much herself, but I was surprised by this self. She was not at all what I had pictured. I tried to absorb her voice, the way she moved, her square muscular jaw and tight blond curls. I kept turning back the film and freezing each frame, searching for the true Tex.

It was only when she said "Hello, Sucker!" that I recognized her. The words came out like a laugh and seemed as natural as a sneeze. That laughing "Hello, Sucker!" created this book.

Texas Guinan

"Mayme," at age four.

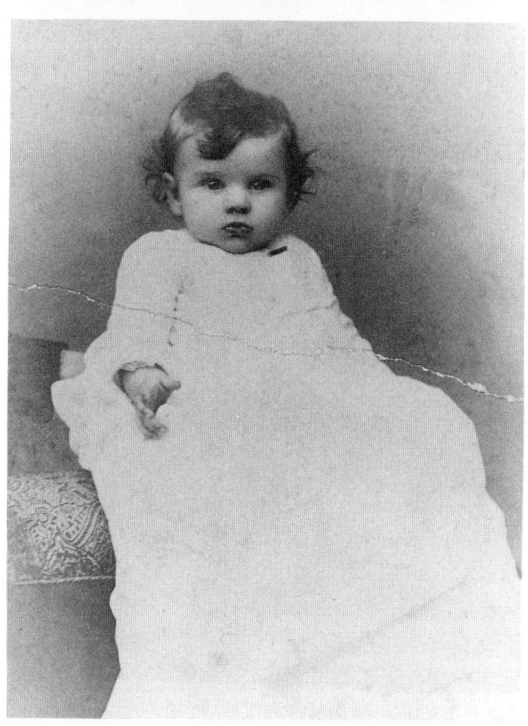

Mary Louise Cecelia Guinan, 1884.

Tex in *The Gay Musician*, 1909.

Left: Julian Johnson.

Below: Tex in *Passing Show of 1912*, 1913. Photo inscribed "To Mama from Her Baby—Texas."

Left: Tex in *Hop O' My Thumb*, Manhattan Opera House, 1913. Theatre Arts Collection, Harry Ransom Humanities Research Center, The University of Texas at Austin.

Below: Tex, musical comedienne, ca. 1915, possibly in *Whirl of the World*.

Left: Publicity postcard from Texas Guinan Productions, 1921.

Below: Tex as silent western heroine, 1921.

From the back of the menu for the "Texas" Guinan Club: F.P.A., Julia Hoyt, Johnny Dooley, Gallagher and Shean, Barney Gallant, Rose Rolando, Avery Hopwood, Hugo Riesenfeld, Dagmar Gadowsky, Ann Pennington, Eddie Cantor, Earl Carroll, Peggy Joyce, Dick Barthelmess and Mary Hay, Bebe Daniels, Gloria Swanson, Harold Lloyd, Jack Barrymore, John Murray Anderson, and the artist, Wynn Holcomb.

Front cover of menu for the "Texas" Guinan Club.

Left: Tex, Bessie, and brother Tommy, 1927. Camera portrait by G. Maillard Kesslere B. P.

Below: Tex and some of her "lil girls." Theatre Arts Collection, Harry Ransom Humanities Research Center, The University of Texas at Austin.

Tex and Aimee Semple McPherson, 1927. *New York Journal American*. Courtesy Harry Ransom Humanities Research Center, The University of Texas at Austin.

Tex, probably 1928. Pinchot, photographer.

Tex, 1928. Pinchot, photographer.

Tex and attorney Maxwell E. Lopin, 1929.

Tex interviewing Mae West, 1930. *New York Journal American.* Courtesy Harry Ransom Humanities Research Center, The University of Texas at Austin.

A page from the program *Too Hot for Paris*: more of Tex's "lil girls."

From the program *Too Hot for Paris*, Tex's bus, Whoopee on Wheels.

Tex with telegram, 1930s. Theatre Arts Collection, Harry Ransom Humanities Research Center, The University of Texas at Austin.

Introduction:
Hello, Suckers! — A Glimpse

> *But O Egg Man, the personality!*
> —ASHTON STEVENS, CHICAGO AMERICAN, OCTOBER 20(?), 1929

"Hello, Suckers!"

She was here! The queen, the magician, the ringmaster, *the queen.* She was here. Now they could have some fun.

"Hello, hello, hello."

They had been waiting all evening in the Club Intime, in the basement of the Hotel Harding at Broadway and Fifty-fourth Street—millionaires, movie stars, rumrunners, and college boys. The night club was one of the many that had mushroomed in the wake of the Eighteenth Amendment, which had gone into effect on January 16, 1920, outlawing the manufacture and sale of beer, wine, and all liquors.

After the initial groan of gloom, America had gone underground to drink. Racketeers and entertainers alike began to prosper, supplying booze and good times to countless speakeasies and night clubs. Liquor sales were much more profitable now that the stuff was contraband, and the profits from night-club markups even better. Apparently, Prohibition could be good business. Without it, all kinds of people would be out of a job, from the many diligent government agents who sought to uphold the law to the rumrunners they hunted. But the government didn't see it that way. It would stop the merriment at any cost. In the name of the law, the Feds spent thousands of dollars sneaking agents into the basement rooms of hotels and brownstones—rooms sardine-tight with people. And Americans continued to do as they pleased.

Of all the night-club attractions, and there were many, one continued to draw the government's attention: Texas Guinan. "La

Guinan," as the reigning journalists of the day had fondly christened her, was known along the Broadway Main Stem for her famous greeting, "Hello, Sucker!" and her equally famous expression, "Give the little girl a big hand." She was also notorious for her ability to escape prosecution on nuisance charges—violations of the Prohibition laws—and emerge, as the *New York Times* put it, "better advertised to boot." After a long and colorful career of singing, acting, filmmaking and attention seeking, Tex was one of the best-loved and certainly best-known hostesses on the Main Stem. She knew how to exploit the madness of the twenties and still give everybody what they called a "good time."

Her noise was amplified by the artful scribblings of Walter Winchell, Heywood Broun, Mark Hellinger, Louis Sobol, and countless other columnists for the daily tabloids. Their diligence and Tex's endless bouts with the law filled her treasured scrapbooks with clippings, kept the public interested in her career, and packed her clubs with customers. Tex also fed the press glorious stories about her past.

The most complete collection of these stories appeared as her autobiography in April and May 1929 in the *New York Evening Journal*.* Of what was printed, much turned out to be true, some only half-true, and the rest, just good night-club copy. But even family and friends were fooled. (In fact, years later, Tex's secretary/manager, John Stein, wrote a biography based on many of these newspaper inventions.) The stories did serve several purposes, though. They formed a protective fence to keep the world out and guard Tex's private self. The stories also entertained the public and strengthened Tex's popularity. The truth and fiction ultimately formed the legend known as Texas Guinan, Queen of the Night Clubs.

The newspaper people, too, invented much of what they wrote, and Tex didn't seem to mind. She said, "I don't care what they say about me, if they only say something," and with her help, they said plenty. She was shameless in her thirst for publicity and once went so far as to stage her own suicide just to advertise a new club. Those who knew about the gag said Tex had hired a look-alike to act as if she were going to throw herself into the pond at Central Park. Tex arrived just in time to "identify herself," as she put it, and to pose for pictures with the "suicide."[1]

---

*Henceforth, "memoir" or "autobiography" in the text will refer to this specific collection in the *New York Evening Journal*, also known as "My Life—AND HOW!"

The media had indeed helped Tex create herself, as had the twenties.

World War I had set the stage. By the late 1910s, patriotism had overridden most other concerns, and national idealism was high. But once the armistice was signed by President Woodrow Wilson in November 1918, Americans quickly tired of great causes. Nothing seemed to matter. Perhaps they had begun to feel the growing pains of their rapidly industrializing country. These pains manifested themselves first as restlessness, and then, as the Jazz Age.

The Jazz Age, also known as the Roaring Twenties, the Lawless Decade, and the Era of Wonderful Nonsense was America's first shot at "playing." Certainly there were enough new toys on the market, from the radio to the Oriental game Mah-Jongg. There were also shorter skirts, bobbed hair, and dozens of scandals and romantic photoplays. However, Americans didn't want to play just a little bit; they wanted to play hysterically. Tex understood that.

Tex understood that restless feeling, the itchy uncomfortableness that paced through American consciousness like an anxious teenager. What Americans needed, judged Guinan, was a place where they could escape. So she set up her clubs, and between the hours of 10:00 P.M. and 6:00 A.M., customers were free to do as they pleased.

So on any night in any year in the mid-to-late 1920s, impatient night-club guests awaited Tex's arrival. Take this typical night in the basement Club Intime, some night in 1929 when Tex was at the peak of her night-club career. As usual, some customers had been foolish enough to arrive as early as 10:30; others had been there only since midnight. As the hours accumulated, everybody sat expectant and bored, elbow to elbow, ankle to ankle, watching the ever-increasing number of tables devour what little dance floor there was. The smartest of the spenders tipped the waiters huge amounts to get what they thought would be ringside seats. The smarter ones tipped better, promised more later, and were seated in front of everyone else.

In the early part of the evening, long before *she* arrived, guests tried to supply their own fun. They fumbled around in the suitcases or brown bags they'd stored carefully under their tables and poured themselves drinks from flasks that bore their initials. When the strolling musicians were resting, there was other live music to dance to. Once in a while, a brave couple challenged the rapidly disappearing dance floor with a short tango.

Many of the guests—most of whom were smart enough to keep their seats and leave the dance floor alone—were old friends. Some knew of each other only through the society columns of the *New York Graphic*, the *Sun*, or the *Post*; others became acquainted through long nights spent here, at the Club Intime. They came from the theaters, from other clubs when they closed, from society parties, or from out of town. Many were fabulously wealthy or lived flagrantly beyond their means; others had reputations as big spenders, fortune hunters, sugar daddies.

Part of the thrill of visiting the club was to see who else might be permitted to walk through the well-guarded doors. Perhaps lady-killer Charleston dancer George Raft would stop by, or General W. W. Atterbury, president of the Pennsylvania Railroad. Maybe Jean Acker, Rudy Valentino's ex-wife, would arrive surrounded by admirers, alongside Metropolitan Opera star Frances Alda, Ed Riley, noted Brooklyn criminal lawyer, or Walter Winchell, columnist.

Somewhere the cigarette girl, Ethel, was making her way through the tangle of tables and chairs. She offered packs of cigarettes, ten in each, for the outrageous price of one dollar. Other customers paid more than twice that for four cents' worth of ginger ale.

There was a moment, near 1:00 A.M., when some of the guests had had enough of waiting. It was easier to have a good time if someone else supplied the jokes. Then a murmur went through the crowd, and the word *Texas* became a chant, a cheerleader cry for the home team, for Broadway's own. She was here. She was home.

And there she stood. Her blond hair was straight out of the peroxide bottle, but the enormous smile was her own. "Hello, hello, hello!" she laughed to her friends. Hands reached out to touch her as she made her way through the bodies and tables. Sequins and red-cloth petals hugged her abundant dimensions, coaxing her curves into the image of a long-stemmed red rose. She wore red stockings and shoes with rhinestone buckles to match, and diamonds just about everywhere else. The diamonds all but overshadowed the modest string of pearls and the live red rose pinned to the strap of her gown.

Finally Tex reached the stage. She climbed onto a chair and sat on the back of it. "Hello, Suckers!" she bellowed. She gave a nod to the band, then led the crowd in a shouting version of "California Here I Come," while tossing wooden noisemakers and endearments to some of the regulars. "You all feel good now," she shouted, "but wait till your check comes!" Laughter. A group of young girls dressed in tight-fitting shirts and silken shorts ran onto the tiny dance floor. "Give the lil guurrls a great big hand!" urged Tex from her perch. The girls began to perform a favorite number known as "Cherries." Regulars from Tex's former clubs recognized the number, not for its originality or tune or even the talent of the fourteen-year-old carrying the basket of fruit and singing, but for the opportunity it provided, to be part of the act. If a male guest was lucky, a delightful young thing might pop a fresh cherry into his mouth, and another might muss his hair or if he had no hair, kiss his bald head.

Soon the girl with the basket began to make her way through the crowd. "Cherries!" urged the chorus. "Cherries!" shouted the waiters. Ethel, the cigarette girl, added her voice, as did the maitre d'. And the guests. "Pick me, pick me," they pleaded. "A cherry," some demanded. The small room was loud with voices, but one rose above all others—Tex's.

Her voice was loud, metallic, audible over the noisemakers. She used it to draw you and your neighbor into the act, to make Broadway your neighborhood, her club your home. Nobody ever felt left out in Tex's club. She remembered your name, maybe shook your hand. If you were lucky, she singled you out for one of her jokes. Nobody quite knew what she did when the customers went home for breakfast, but who cared. While she held court, Tex was the sparkling mistress of Broadway. No wonder she was known in New York as the "Queen of the Night Clubs," and in Chicago as "the National Weakness."

Tex herself had originated the role of night-club hostess back in 1923—and they had said it was by accident!—three years after the Eighteenth Amendment had reared its head and bitten the jugular vein of nightlife on the Main Stem—Broadway. But there were no accidents. Texas's timing was perfect. She'd begun way sooner than 1923. She'd begun by being born in the somewhat sleepy frontier town of Waco, in Texas, on January 12, 1884, almost thirty-six years to the night before Prohibition became law.

Waco: Home on the Ranch?

> *Perhaps no other autobiography ever written carried the incongruity of this one, with the Queen of all "night hawks" describing in her Broadway vernacular the quiet home life of her Irish immigrant parents and their struggle to bring up four children and manage a 50,000 acre ranch.*
>
> *And, when her story is finished, you may have a new mind picture of the night club hostess who, according to a jury, spends her life showing people a good time and is not a public nuisance.*
> —ADVERTISING FOR TEXAS GUINAN'S "MY LIFE—AND HOW!"
> APRIL 1929

"**M**y age?" The Little Cowgirl of Broadway was perched atop her red piano scratching her head with a wooden noisemaker. She laughed. "Don't you ever read the newspapers? You can figure out for yourself that my childhood days were pretty nearly frontier days in Texas." She let out another whoop, hit the noisemaker on her left knee, and threw it in the box beside her.

"Kids, in my day, Waco had no Checker cabs and nobody had ever heard of an automobile. When you wanted to get anywhere, you mounted a pony and rode across the hot plains."[1]

That's right, customers were thinking, no Checker cabs back then. Just Tex, astride a bucking bronco. Just Tex, astride her red piano. Though most of the crowd had already read Tex's story in the *New York Graphic,* the *New York Evening Journal,* and various interviews from her early stage career, they enjoyed the telling, almost more than the tale itself. It was part of the evening's entertainment, a way to have fun while the girls changed for the next act.

Suckers, my father's ranch stretched over 50,000 acres—at least several times the size of New York City—and boy, life on a Texas ranch in those days was a rough and tough proposition. Like other Texas kids, I learned early to ride and shoot. Before I was out of my teens, Buffalo Bill Cody, who was visiting my father, remarked one day: "Guinan, I'll bet that little girl Texas was born in the saddle and cut her teeth on a six gun."

He was nearly right. My father used to laugh when he told the story that, instead of a teething ring, I used to bite on the trigger guard of his gun. Maybe he exaggerated a little, but I'll swear that a revolver seemed like just another household appliance to me.[2]

Tex turned to signal the bandleader, and the story was lost in the next phase of the floor show. Everyone knew how it ended, anyway, but few suspected that the ranch Tex grew up on was located in her head and not in Waco at all.

Of course, why question Tex's background? She was from the Wild West, wasn't she? She rode horses in silents, didn't she? And what about that name? If some suspected that she was stretching the truth, they forgave her. Because even if her story wasn't altogether based on fact, the childhood of the cowgirl fit. That wild spirit of the frontier days, the "Little Tex" or "Tomboy Texas" she told about, who played with horses, not dolls, who hunted rattlesnakes with her brothers and could rope a steer with the best of the cowhands—all that belonged up on the stage with Tex. It was how she wanted to be seen.

Joseph Guinan, Tex's grandfather, came to the New World from Ireland during the potato famine of the late 1840s. Settling down on a farm outside Richmond, Quebec, he and his wife raised Michael, Tex's father. As Michael grew, ambition slowly swelled within him, ambition to be something other than a farmer—to make money and his own way in life. There was a popular form of gambling in those days called "pioneering." When he turned twenty, Michael kissed his parents good-bye, put on his walking shoes, and headed south via Detroit, Michigan, to try his luck. Documents say he crossed the border on May 2, 1877.

Meanwhile, his future wife, Bridget "Bessie" Duffy, had been growing into a strong and stubborn woman in a town near Richmond called Sherbrooke. Her father, Richard Duffy, had also left green Ireland for the freedom and fertile acres of the New World. Once there, he had married Canadian Mary McCabe and together they raised a family. As their daughter Bessie grew, she developed a sizeable measure of curiosity and ambition in her, just as Mike had.

However, this curiosity was not as appropriate for a young woman as for a man in those days, and the family was relieved when she chose to accompany her sister to join other relatives in the mining town of Idaho Springs, Colorado. Eventually Mike and Bessie would meet and marry in Georgetown, Colorado, on June 18, 1881.

In the late 1870s, much of the United States was still considered uncharted territory. Promises of rich farmland, grazing lands, and precious metals had been wafting eastwards across the Great Plains, and the beguiling phrase, "Go west, young man," had drawn countless eager settlers to the unclaimed reaches of the new frontier. In Texas, where Mike and Bessie eventually set up house, white settlers displaced the Indians and began to build towns to support their trade and their "civilized" habits. Railroad tracks began crisscrossing the plains and valleys, and with the aid of the trains and the freight they carried from the coast, the frontier became more than a temporary campsite. It became home.

These dream-chasing pioneers were a strong lot. They had to make up their lives as they went along. The tall tales they heard in eastern cities had said nothing about tornadoes and dust storms, droughts, starvation, kids dying fresh from their mothers' bellies. On the frontier, the land was rich but wild; to tame it took all the pioneers' strength, creativity, and courage.

But the pioneers were inventive. They had several means for taming the wilds, other than their stout hearts and broad backs. They had God, for one thing. And the family. And the rigid principles of the Victorian era. These helped contain the unknown and bring order into frontier chaos.

In its most extreme forms, however, such order stifled the creativity that had led the pioneers west to begin with, and out of this contradiction both Prohibition and Mary Louise Cecelia Guinan were born.

For Mike Guinan, stories of Texas, the heart of the Wild West, whispered one essential word: *cattle.* When he arrived in the bustling, booming town of Waco, he was surprised to learn that although there were still ranching lands on the outskirts of town, no one seemed as interested in livestock as in corn and other cash crops, particularly cotton. Most of the cattle business had moved further westward, and the once-extensive grazing lands had become farmland.

Back then, cotton was on everybody's mind. Wacoans built a cotton palace and crowned cotton queens. In October 1884, the year

Tex was born, the *Waco Daily Examiner* sighed, "Cotton bales constitute the ornamentation of a live town. They are bewilderingly beautiful." A week later it proclaimed, "Waco Boometh."

Indeed, Waco was fast becoming an important trade center. If settlers were not enticed by cotton or the city's rapid growth and business opportunities, they came for the curative thermal waters and mild winters or to take advantage of the abundance of fine schools and universities. By 1881, the first phones were installed, and by 1886, permission for electricity was granted. In 1885, the invention of "Dr Pepper," a digestive soft drink, put Waco indelibly on the map. Mike had certainly brought his new wife to live in the very heart, the "Athens" of Texas.

If you walked along the unpaved streets of this young Waco, you might notice the firm of Eaton, Guinan and Company on the corner of Mary and Fourth streets. That was where Mike and his partner J. C. Eaton worked. Mike's incredible drive and ambition—the same ambition that had gotten him off his father's farm and down to the new frontier in the first place—had moved him from clerk to partner in Eaton's wholesale grocery and had quickly earned him a respected place in the Waco business world as well as special mention in the *Immigrant's Guide to Waco*. In fact, what the *Immigrant's Guide* said about Mike could easily have been said years later about his daughter: "He is a wonderful example of what ability and energy can do in Texas without capital. He possesses fine business ability but his indefatigable industry is the striking part of his character. He is business all the way from the time his eyes are opened in the morning till they are closed at night."[3] (Night-club hostess Tex was "business all the way" from the time her eyes opened in the evening until they closed at dawn.)

Mike had come a long way since he had left his father's farm, and all in a very short time. When the adult Tex decided to tell her life's story, however, she had another idea of what would be interesting and impressive. Certainly, she would never let on that her father had been just a grocer.

Tex wanted to establish her family as an adventurous, pioneering *American* family living out the American dream; finding success—and many acres—in the West. Out of pride in her Irish roots, she sometimes said her parents came straight from Dublin: "My father's name is Michael Guinan and he was born in Dublin, where you can get rock and rye, real Scotch, or all the stout you can drink, without any stool pigeons, Prohibition agents or any other kind of snoops to bother you."[4] Otherwise, her standard story made her a fourth-generation Texan. Tex was proud to be an American (and what's more American than a cowgirl?), and her adopted first name was a tribute to her state.

Tex explained in her *New York Evening Journal* memoirs:

> I want you to understand the kind of life I was bred to and realize how all these events helped shape my later career. I want you to know how the wild freedom of my youth influenced my life after I had said good-bye to the plains and set out to seek wealth and fame in what we laughingly call civilized cities.
>
> And you know I was a tomboy. You may say I was a roughneck. But give me a break, because it's hard for a girl to be gentle and ladylike out there in the great wide open spaces where men are men and women are safe—in books.[5]

As the celebrity Tex fed the hungry masses visions of Tomboy Tex taming broncos, the town of Waco was feeling both pleased and dismayed by the publicity. For years, Wacoans had wanted to claim Tex as their own because she was famous, but they weren't quite sure about her. In fact, they were not sure about Tex in the same way the town's mothers hadn't been sure when Tex was growing up. Then she was a wild, harum-scarum tomboy who climbed trees with the boys and played pranks on the townspeople and on the nuns at the convent where she went to school.

Townspeople couldn't quite forget that back when Tex was growing up and Virtue, Duty, Self-Denial, and Sobriety still reigned, the word *actress* was somewhat synonymous with *prostitute*. From press accounts, they had a picture of Tex as a hard-core, brassy, night-club personality. This image they shared with most of the population who had never met the queen or visited her clubs. Chances were that she smoked cigarettes, drank hard liquor, and mixed with all sorts of unsavory characters. Hadn't she been married too many times for a good Catholic girl?

The Guinans had seemed a decent enough family while Tex was growing up. Mike and Bessie weren't the sort to make it into the social columns of the gossip weekly the *Artesia*, and they seemed to stick to themselves. They were respected, even though they were outsiders *and* Catholics in a Baptist town. In fact, in the eyes of a townspeople who were fiercely nationalistic, their emigration from Canada stamped them forever as foreigners.

Though Tex chose a ranch as the setting for her childhood, Mike and Bessie raised their children in town, first, at 1436 Washington Street, later, at 604 North Fourth. Their first child, William, was born in 1882, and Mary Louise Cecelia followed on January 12, 1884. That was Tex, though she wasn't called that till much later. Bessie had five more children, but only Pearl (born in 1887) and Tommy (born in 1891) survived.

Mary Louise, nicknamed "Mayme" (or "Mamie"), was a crossbreed of a strict upbringing and frontier ingenuity. She was properly trained by a concerned Bessie in all the womanly arts: to cook, sew, and realize that above all, neatness counts. She was taught to be gracious and polite to guests and all adults, and was schooled in making others, especially menfolk, feel at home. In effect, she learned what it meant to be a good wife and mother, though she took this training a step further when she became a famous nightclub hostess.

Mayme adored her mother, and her early life revolved around the noble aspiration to be Mama's little helper. Bessie, in turn, grew to depend on her eldest daughter, and the two were so close that the family nicknamed them "Big Mayme" and "Little Mayme."

Despite the responsibility and trust that Bessie gave her, Mayme felt a constant need to earn her mother's attention, even if her methods resulted in a spanking. At age one, Mayme had been thrust from center stage after the birth of brother Walter Harry. Even though Walter died, she was constantly being ousted as new characters joined the Guinan cast. Poor Mayme would do anything to regain the spotlight. In her *Evening Journal* memoirs, she would write, "For a while it seemed as though I got a licking every time I had a chance to invite one."[6]

In many ways, Bessie represented the values of the era: stability, virtue, devotion to the family above all. She believed in the spanking and was determined to instill practical sense into her children, teach them right from wrong. Thus it would seem that playing the good girl would be the shortest road to Mama's good graces. Yet Mayme had a wild laughing streak in her, a prankster side, and Bessie didn't seem to mind.

Perhaps Bessie saw her childhood dreaming self in Mayme, the adventurous self that had left the family in Canada for a new life on the frontier. The child was certainly more entertaining than William, her staid older brother, and Pearl, her younger sister. Mayme had a way about her that made everyone her friend.

Despite being a prankster, Mayme became enamored of the church. In this, she was influenced by her mother. Bessie, a devout Catholic who was never without rosary beads in her pocket, drew great pleasure from her visits to St. Mary's Church of the Assumption.

For Roman Catholics in a Baptist town, church events carried great significance as social events. At these gatherings, the Guinans could meet, mingle, and gossip with other Roman Catholics. For Mayme's curious little-girl self, the church was also a place of great theatrical events, full of pageantry and mysterious stories—as well as a place to see others and be seen. From childhood on, the church would play a strong role in Mary Louise Cecelia's life. Later it would be apparent that the philosophy of serving others, of generosity and kindness, were the tenets of the church Mayme had taken most to heart. When she grew up, her main concern in show business would be to serve others, to make sure everybody had a "good time."

In Waco, there were forty-five churches serving a population of twelve thousand by the time Mayme was born. Aside from churches, the only other places in town serving the equally important function of meeting place and political forum, and that could hold large crowds, were the saloons. In addition to the "lowlife" bars, there were several elegant and civilized saloons in Waco that operated much like men's clubs, where lawyers and local leaders congregated and good food was served. But these were few compared to the many less-reputable bars.

For, despite the fact that Waco was a Baptist stronghold, there was much drinking amongst both the locals and people passing through. Waco was the largest town within a radius of fifty or sixty miles, and many travelers on their way further west stopped there for provisions and rest. They populated the less-fancy saloons along with the cowboys who rode in from the range for booze and supplies.

This was the frontier Waco Mayme grew up in. Cattlemen really did still walk the streets, and men carried six-shooters. The Code of Honor still reigned, and duels and shootouts were not uncommon. Some held drink responsible for the violence.

The saloons formed a curious contrast to the high moral tone set by the strong presence of the many churches in Waco. In fact, the mere existence of the saloons awakened hostility in the hearts of the local teetotalers, causing the question of temperance to be broached. While Mayme was growing up, these early murmurings were echoed in cities and villages all over the U.S. and would eventually spark the Prohibition movement.

One of the first recorded protests about alcohol occurred in the 1770s, when a Quaker rose in meeting and complained about the smell of rum on the breath of several of the men around him. By 1808, the first temperance society in America was founded. Moderation was advocated and promised to be popular, but it didn't catch on. Eventually, the movement proposed total abstinence.

Following the Civil War, the moral crusade against alcohol became political. In 1869, the Prohibition Party was founded, a political party aimed at nominating a presidential candidate who would sympathize with the "dry" cause. Then in 1873, the Women's Christian Temperance Union (WCTU) added its powerful voice. The WCTU was to have an impact on the children (future lawmakers of the 1920s), whom they reached in school, through the law they helped effect making temperance education compulsory.

In Waco, the discussion about temperance was stormy. There were plenty of teetotalers among the Baptists and the Methodists, but abstinence from drink was not in the background of many of the settlers who had come from the plantation-supporting states of the deep South. Many had their own stills on the plantation premises and drank whiskey every day "to kill germs." They kept a jug around the fireplace and passed it around to all the family—including the kids.

"Ardent Spirits" had accompanied the colonists to the New World and had always been considered a gift of God as well as an enduring link to the old country. A keg was always present at weddings, wakes, christenings, the founding of the town church. And sometimes the clergy drank more than anyone else.

However, the settlers knew that too much drink could be a danger on the frontier—it kept men from doing their work and kept them from protecting their families. It made them careless, loud, apt to fight, and apt to beat their wives and children. Early temperance and Prohibition propaganda reaffirmed the belief that excessive drinking stood in the way of social harmony and mental and physical well-being.

How did all this touch the Guinans? The Roman Catholic Church was historically uninvolved and uninterested in the cause of the "drys" (those in favor of abstinence). However, Mayme grew up with a strong opinion about liquor: Texas Guinan, as far as anyone knew, refrained from ever trying it.

She explained in her syndicated column that appeared during the height of her fame, "I have never touched a drop of liquor in my life. It doesn't appeal to me. Some people have never eaten caviar. They maintain they do not like it, despite the fact that they have never tried to eat it.

"And so with me and the liquor question.

"I have heard many prima donnas sing, 'Drink to me with thine eyes.' After drinking, you may not have any eyes.

"Man frequently drinks to forget. And about the only thing he forgets is when to stop."[7]

Though seemingly incongruous with her adult role as the spirit against Prohibition, Tex's teetotaling made sense, at least at the club. For, like bartending, hostessing and drinking did not mix. Her friends agreed that she never touched a drop herself.

Of course, Tex didn't care if others drank. That was their business. She didn't judge others' habits and believed in freedom of choice.

She inherited this attitude from her parents. Though later in life both parents might have been uncomfortable with Tex's chosen career, they never said a word about it in front of others.

Mike sometimes took this relaxed attitude a bit too far. He adapted a hands-off approach to parenting and let Bessie do all the disciplining. Also, Mike tended to be more of a dreamer than Bessie. He liked to speculate, though his wife said there was a better word for it—*gambling*—and took chances. Mayme inherited her sense of adventure and her overactive imagination from him.

Although Mike's career had gotten off to a promising start, he did not remain just an ordinary grocer for long. When Mayme was almost five, Eaton, Guinan and Company went bankrupt. December 1, 1888, marked Mike Guinan's first splash in print. "The Great Bankruptcy" declared the *Evening News*. "Business Troubles," whispered the more discreet *Day*.

The bankruptcy turned out to be the result of a slow winter and bad collections, but Eaton descendants have speculated that Mike did something with the assets. As one of the Eaton granddaughters told it, Eaton, who was in charge of the bookkeeping end of the business, fell ill early in the winter of 1888 and was out of the store for quite some time. While he was absent, the business "took a turn for the worse, and the assets, so we've heard, turned into diamonds for the Guinans."[8] When Eaton returned to work, the store's finances were beyond rescue.

There is no evidence that Mike misbehaved in this case. Later, however, he began taking risks by concocting some shaky business deals. Tex, too, would become attracted to taking risks, but she seemed to be more levelheaded than her father and generally more successful at her attempts.

For a while after the bankruptcy, Mike Guinan was a jack-of-all-trades, while continuing to maintain connections with the grocery business. Mike's jobless years—as far as public records are concerned—between the bankruptcy and his next appointment seemed not to have affected the family's financial situation all that greatly. For instance, they continued to live in their house on North Fourth Street. However, the instability of the family fortunes was felt throughout the household. When Mike had money, he was quite generous. In a good month, he went out and bought his family the finest clothes in town. In a bad month, meals were scanty. When his pockets were empty, Mike sometimes sent his children on extended visits to their Colorado cousins.

Mike was never cured of taking business risks and had many changes of fortune in the years that followed. Mayme grew up with a deep fear of poverty and the conviction that her father was unable to take care of her mother. As soon as she was old enough, Mayme wanted to earn money to help the family. Later, after she succeeded in the theater, she provided for her parents until her death. In her newspaper memoirs, she once mentioned that because she had her family to take care of, marriage was a luxury she could not afford.

Mike's impression on his daughter was to strengthen her resolve to make her way in the world. This would provide the impetus for her to succeed in her later career. As a child, however, "making her way in the world" translated into creating her own style of doing things. This looked a bit like wild behavior. Bessie attempted to interest Mayme in some of the more peaceful "female" pursuits. She succeeded, to a certain extent, but not in the way she'd envisioned.

For example, Bessie liked to dress Mayme properly in the heavy clothes of the period: wide-pleated dresses with one straight row of shiny round buttons marching down the center, wide belts, big, lacy collars, and hats with ruffles. These clothes might have seemed suffocating to some little girls, but Mayme loved them and enjoyed all the fussy accessories that went with her dresses. What she didn't accept were the rules and regulations that came along with the era that dressed her, rules endemic to a small Baptist town, a strict Catholic household, a world dominated by *shoulds* and *have-tos*.

To her mother's dismay, Mayme began to develop a penchant for tomboy antics. Instead of playing with the girls, she ran around with her brothers and neighborhood boys and preferred climbing trees to playing with dolls.

To tame this Texas tomboy, her parents sent Mayme to the Convent School of Sacred Heart, the pride of Waco Catholics. Founded in 1873 by the sisters of St. Mary of Namur, the school had achieved fame as "the school for the elite." Many of the fifty or so boarders—of whom only sixteen were actually Catholic—came from Waco's finest homes. Others came from out of town or abroad.

Today not much remains from the school except the attendance records. They show when Mayme went to school and who her classmates were. One of those classmates was Sarah Hopkins Muhl. She remembered Mayme for her pranks. In particular, Mayme sometimes ordered large quantities of baked goods from the local bakery for fictitious customers. Other times, she'd try on every shoe in a shoe store, sending the poor clerk up and down ladders to fetch shoes she had no intention of buying.

After Mayme played a responsible child at home, helping her mother with the other children, she was ready for a little fun when she came to school. It seemed a quick way to win friends and attention, and it gave scope to her natural acting ability.

Mayme used the captive audience of classmates to develop her sense of humor and timing. "She liked to startle," Sarah Hopkins Muhl recalled in an interview with the *Baylor Lariat* in 1967, "and she kept things pretty lively for us and the Sisters at school."

In those days, the facts of life were never discussed openly or even whispered about. Mayme, however, had been witness to quite a few births in her short life. She knew where babies came from, even if her classmates did not. Once, after Mayme missed a day of school, Sister Clara demanded, "Miss Mayme Guinan, will you please explain why you were absent from school yesterday?"

Mayme replied, hiding her mischief with the proper amount of hesitation, "I had to stay home and hem diapers for the baby that is going to be born at my house." Sister Clara, along with the rest of the girls in the class, grew red with embarrassment, and some of the boys choked on snickers. What a scandal![9]

Another time, when Mayme was a bit older, she and Sarah went out for a stroll. "The two must have been in their early teens," recalled Sarah's daughter, "and my mother was very naive, very modest, very good. She suddenly looked around and said to Mayme, 'My word, where are we?' 'Oh we're in the red-light district,' answered Mayme matter-of-factly." In those days, passing even close by the red-light district, known as "the Reservation" or North Two Street, was not a matter to be taken lightly. If compelled to walk anywhere near there, all respectable women and girls were expected to keep their glances to the other side of the street until they were safely away. No wonder Sarah, when she heard where she was, gathered up her skirts and ran straight back to the convent, not even stopping to catch her breath. She and the other girls were convinced that Mayme Guinan wasn't afraid of anything.[10]

In the twenties and thirties, Sarah would berate her own daughter for collecting clippings of Mayme-turned-Texas. "She was *not* a celebrity," Mayme's old convent friend would declare. "She was *notorious.*"[11]

Though the local girls were impressed by Mayme, some of their mothers weren't sure they wanted them to play with that wild Guinan girl. For example, Mayme had a crush on Kathleen Gorman who lived around the block in what the adult Tex remembered as the "Gorman mansion." Every school day, Mayme would come by the house to walk to the convent with the beloved Kathleen, but often Mrs. Gorman would send her daughter off in the carriage before Mayme got there. Mrs. Gorman was concerned, recalled Kathleen's younger sister Mary, because she thought Mayme was "tough." But Mayme never forgot Kathleen. Years later, when she returned to Waco as the famous night-club hostess, she asked an old cab driver to take her to the Gorman mansion at 616 North Fifth Street. The Gorman mansion? The cab driver scratched his head and took her to the big, old Victorian house. Staring at it, Tex said, "My God! It has shrunk . . . .!"[12]

Mayme spent a great deal of time playing alone. She had an active imagination and was always inventing situations to act out, sometimes borrowing scenes from books she had read.

Like many girls her age in the late 1800s, adolescent Mayme read adventure books and lived on dreams of "girl saves baby," "girl rescues cat up tree," etc. Laura Jean Libbey, for one, had been busy writing wonderful love stories for young girls and women, all of which had happy endings—even ones like *A Forbidden Marriage* and *When His Love Grew Cold*. Mayme adored the Libbey stories because she could pretend she was the heroine in every book.

Once, however, Mayme got carried away by her imagination. She had just finished reading the details of an incident about a brave young mother who saved her baby from the wicked clutches of her villainous husband by crossing a series of rapids in a leaking boat. At that point, Mayme noticed that the waters of the Brazos, which ran close by her very own backyard, were swollen by the spring rains. The current was swift and would make perfect "rapids." All Mayme needed was a boat and a baby, and she could play the brave young mother in a real river! After rejecting the idea of using her four-year-old brother Tommy, she went across the street to the neighboring Garlands and borrowed baby Hugh. Next, the boat.

It was difficult to find a boat just by asking outright. No one was about to let a little girl out on that nasty-looking river. Mayme finally borrowed a wooden tub from an old washerwoman who couldn't understand what Mayme wanted with it. But Mayme had the whole scenario planned out. She wept and raged at her villainous husband. She told him that she and the baby were leaving. She stepped into the wooden tub. "Don't you dare try and stop me!" she cried. The baby howled. The river roared. Mayme set off for the high seas, to cross the rapids and take her child to safety.

Suddenly the tub started leaking. Why it's just like the story! exclaimed Mayme to herself. Everything was perfect. More words for the villain. The tub filled with water. It was time to do the rescue scene.

Just then Mrs. Guinan and a panicking Mrs. Garland appeared on the shore. Was that a whip Mayme's mother held in her hand? In place of an irate husband stood two fuming mamas, angry at the troublemaker Mayme and fearful for both children's safety. It seems Mrs. Garland had grown suspicious after Mayme had borrowed the baby, and she had gone to the Guinans to check up on him. The ladies had immediately assumed the worst and had run down to catch Mayme in the (her) act. The little heroine and baby were rescued, alas, before they could rescue themselves, and Mayme couldn't sit down for a week afterward. But was she sorry? Not one bit. She was furious. Mother and Mrs. Garland had ruined the story. She refused to speak to either of them for days.[13]

Did She or Didn't She?
(An Author's Aside)

> *As a child Texas branded cattle and rode on the ranch astride,*
> *like a cowboy. At least, she says she did; and as it's quite*
> *likely why raise any doubt at all?*
> —RICHARD MILNE, BOSTON SUNDAY POST, JUNE 14, 1931

Did Mayme really go off in a wooden tub down the Brazos? Fact: the Guinans lived close by the Brazos River. Fact: their neighbors, the Garlands, had a baby named Hugh. End of known facts.

I honestly believed, or wanted to believe in the Mayme who would be so carried away by her own imagination that she would act out an exciting adventure story in her own backyard. When I was a child, most of my games were "pretend" dramas of that type. But that kind of memory leaves few traces behind, and nothing more solid than anecdote. Is it thus unreliable?

When I began my research, I was looking for *the Facts*. (I thought *the Facts* would lead me to *the Woman*.) But often I found what looked more like part-facts, or accounts built around one or two verifiable truths and many dubious details. For someone who swore never to assume anything without proof, such half-truths were unacceptable, even though I felt certain Mayme would have done many of the things the adult Tex described. I knew, for instance, that she had somehow ventured out on the Brazos River in a wooden tub. For Mayme was an exhibitionist and enamored of her role in life as the daring actress. She had a wild imagination and wanted to be a heroine. The spirit of the tale was true to the child I thought Mayme had been.

The anecdote came from Tex's newspaper memoir which appeared in the *New York Evening Journal* in April and May 1929, right after her famous trial for "maintaining a public nuisance." I should have been warned by the title, "My Life—AND HOW!" But I was naive. Besides, hadn't her former manager used the material as if it were fact? Either he too was fooled by her tales, or he was being faithful to Tex by perpetuating the fiction.

Assuming they were factual, I used the names, dates, and events from the memoirs as clues to lead me to my next points of research. Take that idea of the ranch. Why, of course she grew up riding horses. Hadn't I already seen her in a silent western film? I knew she could ride.

I remained a believer until the week before I went to Waco to do research. While perusing a sheet of Guinan family information, I noted, with horror, the list of family addresses. They were located in town, complete with street names and numbers. But hadn't Tex been born on a ranch?

During the next few years I looked for a loophole. Somewhere Tex had learned to ride; somewhere Tex had had access to a horse, a ranch. I even came up with a "semi-ranch" theory. I wanted desperately for her to have grown up on a ranch and been a cowgirl, to have done all the cattle rustling and rope tossing she'd claimed to have done. Perhaps all her acquaintances had also wanted to believe, for apparently no one had ever challenged her tale.

Tax records declare that the Guinans owned their first "mule or horse" the year Mayme turned eleven. Everyone knew how to ride back then, but horses were quite expensive and more of a status symbol than a child's pet. (Tex claimed that when she was six, her father gave her a pet pinto pony named Pedro.) Families tended to hitch their one mule or horse to the carriage or buggy.

To clear up my confusion about Tex's nonranch upbringing, I dove into the files at the Texas Collection at Baylor University in search of dates, names, church records, land deeds. I was relieved to find something as substantial as the deed that noted the year her father sold their house at 1436 Washington Street and moved the wife and kids to 604 North Fourth. I also discovered that these facts were not much use, because the real child continued to elude me. Where was a Mayme equal to the image of Tomboy Texas? Perhaps *the Facts* had nothing to do with *the Woman*.

I searched the daily papers. Occasionally a one-liner would note Mike Guinan's latest business trip to Colorado or Arkansas. But no Tex. No Mary Louise Cecelia.

If only Bessie had been a saver. Was Mayme the type of child who brought home school art for the family icebox?

Looking at the little I knew of young Mayme, I tried to weigh the truth of the anecdotes the adult Tex had written. They were, after all, her vision, her representation of her own childhood. And they did hold little pieces of verifiable truth. This was the Little Tex she wanted us to see. But why that mask? Why rewrite the past?

I concluded that Tex didn't exactly rewrite the past, just re-imagined it, shuffled the pieces a little. This was the childhood that fit the adult, that matched her spirit and what she became. The little cowgirl was never once called Mayme, always Little Tex or Tomboy Texas, a miniature night-club hostess in training. She even gave herself blond curls, though she was a brunette till her forties.

Even if Tex had invented, or elaborated, on the truth, such inventions, as I discovered, were no sin in the twenties. Everyone did it—it was the style. Most stars had highly fictionalized newspaper autobiographies because not only did the stories keep their fans happy, they also preserved the stars' privacy.

Tex had a clear and reasonable vision of a childhood based on "wide, open spaces," "the freedom of the plains," and the happiness she equated with that freedom. Considering the era of rigidity she grew up in and her mother's iron rule, this image of freedom seems out of place. Yet in terms of Tex's adult life and her roles as the spirit against Prohibition, it made sense. She told readers of her autobiography,

> Altogether I had the happiest gayest sort of childhood—between spanks—any young American could have. Roping steers and helping the boys round up the horses were chores which I learned at an early age. I wore pants like my brothers all day long, and except when caught and sent to school I was tearing around the ranch on a horse.
> That active outdoor life is responsible for my unusual good health and endurance at present. A city bred girl would never survive the arduous life I have led, and still lead.
> It was a glorious feeling to lope or gallop my pinto across miles of plains with the hot wind blowing my long yellow curls out in a straight line behind me. And it never occurred to me to be proud of my freedom at such a tender age. It simply seemed natural to ride. It was the life of the Texas plain.[1]

Tex loved the romantic image of the independent pioneer of the wild ranges, a strong symbol of very American ideals. She made her childhood sound like a good western, fully equipped with horses, rattlesnakes, six-guns. There was also the hard, repetitious work of looking after the livestock, but that was the stuff that built character.

According to Tex, her parents cut their promising cowgirl's career short when they sent her off to school. Tex said,

> When my family realized I was becoming too boyish for their idea of a proper daughter, they sent me to a convent in Waco, where efforts were made to turn me into a lady. I managed to get a horse at the convent, and did more riding than praying, so no serious damage was done to my love of sport.
>
> Mother and father did all they could to bring me up a very conventional young lady. I appreciate their conservative efforts, and I know I owe my good health and my level head in an emergency to them—but what a demure daughter I turned out to be!
>
> Entering school seemed like a great adventure. Thinking of it now, I guess my coming was an adventure for the nuns who taught there.[2]

The convent she described was Tex's alma mater, Sacred Heart—and she actually attended school there. After Tex became famous, she looked back on her days at Sacred Heart with great affection. She told her public that she kept a special place in her heart for Sister Clara, who had taught her the ABCs but had omitted instruction in IOUs and CODs. Sister Clara had been notorious for giving the hardest exams at the convent. Tex never forgot the time she took one of those tests with disastrous results. She claimed (in an anecdote of dubious authenticity) that after the test, Little Tex and the rest of the girls in the class met outside to discuss their answers. Soon it was obvious that either the other girls had taken a different exam, or that Little Tex was heading for an "F." She confided her suspicions to a classmate Emma Trout, and Emma told her not to worry. Sister Clara wouldn't look at the papers until the next day, so that gave her plenty of time to think up something.

Little Tex remembered that back home in the barn she had three mice in a cage. At one time she had planned to make them into pets but had failed miserably as a trainer. She had decided to keep them anyway for a special occasion. Well, a special occasion had arrived. Little Tex smuggled the mice into school the next day and put them in Sister Clara's desk. She knew that when Sister Clara opened the drawer she would scream and everyone would rush out of the room. Then Little Tex could steal back her paper, change the answers and pass the test. All went as planned, except for one minor thing. Emma Trout "squealed." Little Tex was spanked and forced to take a new, harder exam. But the story wasn't finished.

The town of Waco was repairing a road on the edge of town, and the workmen had been using an old horse-drawn scraper for leveling the ground. The day after Little Tex was caught at the convent, she ran out of school as soon as it let out, and lay in wait along the road by the scraper, waiting for Emma to come traipsing home from school. As soon as Emma appeared, Little Tex jumped out and pushed the unsuspecting but undoubtedly guilty Emma into the scraper and shut it from the top. Emma remained trapped inside the scraper all night because there was no way to lift the hood from the inside. The search party found her early the next morning. By that time, Little Tex had run away and hidden in the barn. When they finally caught up with her, she took her spanking bravely. Nothing mattered now that she was even with Emma.

In retrospect, the adult Tex saw that incident as "the first time I ever had shown any cold-bloodedness. It is the same instinct that drives me now, I guess, in dealing with the out-of-town buyers who are simply aching to leave their bankrolls behind them when they leave New York."[3]

Emma Trout really was a classmate of Mayme's at the convent, and the town of Waco was in fact repairing many of the roads during her years at school. The adult Texas always built her anecdotes on true characters and threw in enough facts to make her memoirs plausible. But would she really do such a thing to Emma Trout?

Not surprisingly, prankster Mayme starred in many of her school's productions. Her fancy was captured by what she felt was high drama, not the Shakespearean kind, but rather the highly situational and melodramatic. The kind of shows she saw as a child encouraged this fancy, as did the Laura Jean Libbey books. Mayme became convinced that theater was an exaggerated form of real life. She carried this notion with her throughout her stage and film career and was often criticized for it. Knowing this gives a possible explanation for the mix of truth and fiction in Tex's memoirs.

Mayme saw her first stage performance at the Waco Opera House. Many a road show traveled through town, and the Guinans often attended the Saturday matinees. Between times, Mayme wrote skits and organized the family into a troupe of actors. As in other households, home entertainment was especially welcome on long winter nights. However, Mayme didn't know when to stop. She was always acting, her sister Pearl later told her son, around her school chums as well as at home.

The theater in Waco was not a terribly sophisticated institution when Mayme was growing up, and many of the traveling stock shows were built on the talents of one or two good stars and an untalented supporting cast. Although the townspeople flocked to the theater, they were suspicious of it and afraid that it might be bad for their morals. Thus in an early version of Tex's big break in the Waco theater world, she doesn't tell her folks what she's up to, and when her father finds out, he is so angry he comes to the theater and pulls her off stage.

"Those old melodramatic shows in the Waco Opera House went straight to my head," recalled Tex in her memoirs. "I thrilled and suffered more intensely than the actors themselves did—so intensely that one day I broke up the show in my excitement."[4]

That show, in Tex's story, was *The Lime Kiln*, starring Katie Putnam. At the climax of the play, the villain locked the hero into the lime kiln and hid the key in a rain barrel. In came the heroine, searching frantically for the key to the kiln. The first time the fictitious Little Tex saw the show, she was beside herself with anxiety. Katie was moving awfully slowly and if she didn't find the key soon, the hero would bake. Finally Little Tex couldn't stand it any longer. She stood up and yelled, "The key's in the rain barrel, Katie. Hurry up, Katie, and you can save him." Katie and the baking hero immediately lost the spotlight, and the startled audience broke into laughter. There was no way to re-create the suspense, and the curtain came down on the show. Maybe Katie and company never forgave Little Tex, but the adult Tex claimed it was Katie Putnam (who did in fact perform in Waco more than once) who inspired her to become an actress. At least, she provided an opportunity for Tex's first taste of what it was like to steal the show and have the attention of an entire audience—if Tex's story is true, that is.

"The footlight fever was raging in me," Tex later told readers, "and I lived only for the day when I might have a chance to act before a packed house in a real theater."[5]

Soon she had her chance. One day, "Little Tex" just happened to be in the box office when someone from the current repertory company came running in to tell the owner that the lead of the evening's feature had fallen ill. Of course, Little Tex convinced them to let her take her place. She confessed, however, that she turned out to be a terrible actress and lasted only a disastrous three days.

There is no proof that Tex began her acting career in Waco. Nevertheless, the seeds for a budding actress-entertainer were definitely planted there. Young Mayme's need to invent and be noticed, the need to act off the stage as well as on, helped nurture that seed.

In the fiction version of her story, Tex claimed that at this point, when she turned sixteen—an event she said happened in 1906 instead of the true date 1900—she ran off with Hank Miller's 101 Ranch Wild West Show. This was a natural solution for her exhibitionist desires and a perfect marriage of the theater and cowgirl fantasies.

Although it is possible that young Mayme rode in rodeos and certain circus events, acquiring the skills she later exhibited in her silent westerns, she could not have joined the Millers at that time, for Hank Miller did not exist. The eldest Miller Brother's name was Zach, and Hank might have been a distortion of that name. However, the 101 Ranch Wild West show was not due to hold its first rodeo roundup for another eight years. By that time Mayme would be married and living in Chicago.

"Exaggerate the world," Tex counseled in later years. "Dress up your lives with imagination . . . don't lose that purple mantle of illusion. It's worth more than the price of admission to prohibition."[6]

There's a Sucker Born Every Minute

If you ever cease to let the sawdust smell lure you, when the munching of peanuts stops being a joy, when the acrobats and aerialists leave you without thrills, go and give yourself up. There was never a little girl who didn't want to put on a ballet skirt. There never was one who didn't want to ride on the back of a big white horse. . . .
The barkers. The ring generals. Balloons, pop. Animals. . . . A little music, a little dancing and a little clowning. Life is like that. It's a circus. And we all want to perform in the center ring. Life certainly is a quaint gift by someone from somewhere.
Spring is here! Put on your bonnet, Mama. Give me my sulphur and molasses. And come on, let's get to the circus.
—TEXAS GUINAN, "TEXAS GUINAN SAYS," APRIL 5, 1931

And come on, let's get to the circus! "Little Tex" was impatient. All night she lay awake in bed, full of imaginings and desires. She put her head and half her body out the window trying to see as far as the fairgrounds and believed she could smell the horses on the night breeze. She was sure the long night before would never end.

Hank Miller's 101 Wild West Show had come to town, and the Guinans were going. Papa was generous enough to let all the cowhands off from work for the day, and they all saddled up their favorite broncos and headed out to the fairgrounds. Little Tex wanted to go with them and had already saddled her pet horse Pedro when her mother caught her by the pigtail and made her ride in the carriage with the rest of the womenfolk. When they arrived at the show, Little Tex slipped away as soon as her mother's back was turned and went to watch all the warm-up tricks with the rest of the boys. Of this, the adult Tex added,

> Some of our boys gathered outside the big tent and began stunting with their broncos, while I looked on with Dad and a few other men. At first I was satisfied to watch, but after a few minutes, I fairly itched to do some riding myself. And when I itched, I usually started scratching.
> I turned to a big man beside me and said, "I'm going to show these smart cowboys a few of my own tricks."
> "Go to it," he urged, laughing. "Knock on 'em." That was a favorite phrase of cowboys. . . .
> I sprang on Pedro's back and whirled into the middle of that knot of cowhands. For an hour I followed up every stunt they did. Just like a game of stump the leader. Then I did a little leading myself, putting Pedro through all his paces. The boys were delighted. The big man was so surprised you could have knocked him off his pins with a feather. When I quit he strode over to me.
> "Little girl," he said, "you're one of the greatest bareback riders I ever saw. I'm Hank Miller. I own this circus and you can have a job with me any time you say the word."
> "You've hired a hand," I said. "When do I start?"
> . . . Next day I was 200 miles away from home.[1]

Waking up in the middle of the night to the tune of the train whistle, Little Tex was startled. For a moment she forgot where she was. A voice in the mist outside her window shouted Tulsa, and she remembered. On the road. The circus.

Though circus life was full of surprises and excitement and her costumes beautiful and sequin-studded, Little Tex was tired of sleeping on trains and on the ground, tired of not having bathed in days. The food was awful and she'd lost a couple of pounds. Still, the people were friendly, and they had become a new kind of family for her. She never forgot how she'd felt as a kid, standing in the audience wanting a piece of whatever it was that the circus folk had—wanting to run into the center ring and be a star.

And now, when the spotlight was on her, she felt as if she had only just come to life. She discovered that when she was not performing, when she was not with people at all, she lost that feeling. Consequently, she acquired a strong taste for applause and the presence of large crowds.

"The racket certainly didn't breed refinement," Tex told readers of the *New York Evening Journal*, "but I loved it. I had never had a chance to see the country, until Hank Miller gave me a job. Besides, I loved to be where there were crowds of people. The circus crowds, most of them in little jerk towns, fascinated me. The big tent, the smell of the animals, the buzz and roar of the fakirs and the suckers on the midway—all these were like the breath of life to me."

Between acts Little Tex wandered the fairgrounds and studied the way in which the circus folk created suckers out of every small-town man and wife; she watched their willingness to be hoodwinked, their eagerness to part with a nickel or a dime. She began to see that a crowd likes nothing better than to watch someone else get gypped. She soon understood how Barnum had discovered that suckers were born every minute. Years later the adult Tex would quip that the birth rate was double in New York City.[2]

Though Little Tex was enjoying her independence and stardom with Hank Miller's show, by the time the troupe reached Fort Worth she was ready to go home. Before she could, however, the show did the same old parade routine down a street that resembled all the Main Streets she had ridden down before. But this time, as Little Tex sauntered down the road, she noticed something crawling into the path of the oncoming horses. Spurring ahead of the group, she raced her pony down the street and without leaving her saddle, bent down and picked up the baby—who later turned out to be the mayor's daughter—and brought the child to safety. The crowd loved it, and Hank Miller gave her a fifty dollar bonus for the stunt. He incorporated it in the show, and Tex used it years later in her silent westerns.

Little Tex arrived home a heroine and a few dollars richer than when she left, to be greeted by the news that the family was moving to Denver. Her father had speculated unwisely on the cotton market and lost everything. He resembled all the suckers Little Tex had met in her travels, and years later, the adult Tex used her father's experience to illustrate the situation of the New Yorker who gambles. The punch line was, "Stick to your knitting, play in your own backyard, and let other people's rackets alone."[3] Later she followed her own advice faithfully and steered clear of the liquor end of the nightclub business.

It is easy to be swept up into the saddle with Little Tex. What child hasn't dreamed of running away with a circus? The adult Tex was very much at home with the images of the circus and the rodeo because both had been an integral part of her childhood. She was fascinated by the life surrounding the big top, and her favorite memories were of the excitement and "suckering" that went on at the fairgrounds. The midway antics could easily have taken place any night at one of her clubs. In fact, the kinds of lessons Little Tex learned from the rodeo—if she was ever in the rodeo—were perfect for a night-club hostess' education. Tex would later decorate her Century Club like a circus, complete with ringmaster and calliope.

Many facts conspire against the possibility of Tex's circus/rodeo career, at least with "Hank" Miller, but with a peculiar twist. The adult Tex told her manager John Stein that during her tour she acquired the habit of picking up things that belonged to others. Some call this tendency *kleptomania*. She merely collected soaps, teaspoons, small items left lying around restaurants and public restrooms, but they filled her knapsack and came home with her to Waco. Because she made this highly personal confession to her manager, who wrote that only he and her private maid knew about it, the circus incident is harder to discount. Why invent kleptomania? Tex was to continue "picking up" things she had no use for until she died.[4] (Although John Stein took the early details of Tex's life largely from her newspaper memoirs, every once in a while he came up with a surprising fact gleaned from his seven years in Tex's employ.)

According to public records, the Guinan family left Waco and moved to Colorado in 1900. If Mike had lost his shirt on the cotton market as Tex claimed, the family was comforted to know that through his many business contacts in the West, he had a secure job waiting for him in Denver, as a salesman for the public warehouses. In the years that followed, he would change jobs like socks, moving from salesman to broker to real estate agent and back to broker. He installed his family at 1758 Washington Avenue and later, in 1907, settled them at 1373 Marion Street in the well-to-do Capitol Hill area. They remained there until the family left Denver in 1915.

Bessie and Mike were pleased to move to the Mile High City because they both had many relatives in the area, and had met and married in nearby Georgetown. When they arrived in Denver, Mayme and the rest of the Guinan brood were with them, but the fictive Little Tex was not. Little Tex was on her way to the elite finishing school of Hollins Institute, seven miles outside of Roanoke in Virginia. She was fresh off the back of a circus steed and her arrival in the East made quite a sensation. She carried the entire Wild West off the train and onto campus with her.

> Boy was I a knockout! All dressed-up like a race horse. My new clothes had come all the way from Chicago—from a mail order house. Don't try to imagine how I looked, because you can't. Among other things, I wore cotton stockings. Ma had turned thumbs down on silk hosiery. It wasn't decent in those days. And I was on my way to a smart school back East.

There was no reception committee waiting for me when I got there. But you should have seen the way those fashionable girls turned out after word got around that the little ranch girl had arrived. They gathered around me and stared as though I were a freak in a circus side show. And no wonder.

Just imagine a couple of hundred daughters of our best families, well-dressed, beautifully manicured and wise in the arts and graces that make a woman a "lady."

Then picture me, the wild woman from the West. First of all there was my walk. I had the swinging cowboy stride that got me places, all right, but wasn't considered so hot at Hollins Institute. My hands were disgraceful, fingernails broken and torn in shoeing my own horse. Fingers and hands scarred and calloused from handling a rope and a branding iron. Arms and face nut-brown from years of riding in wind and sun. And, on top of all that, the shop-by-mail togs.[5]

In her story, Tex stood out like a sore thumb and had difficulty finding friends among all the starched skirts. Her first days were filled with vivid tournaments of hair pulling and scratching, but finally she found a friend in the unlikely Sarah Cowan, daughter of the rich and famous A. J. Cowan, owner of the B & O Railroad. Sarah took Tex for her first manicure, taught her how to whiten her hands and arms and enter the ranks of those "fashionable girls." The two became such good friends that when Tex learned from her mother that she could not afford a second term at Hollins, Sarah arranged to have her father loan Tex money. Tex later paid him back.

Sarah was the first friend that Tex ever really described in her autobiography in any detail. Though she gave no specific characteristics, Tex did focus on the quality of their relationship, with Sarah as her first guide to the world of fashion and poise. It's a shame that Sarah never had the opportunity to attend Hollins College. But then, neither did Tex.

Sarah Cowen, known to her friends as Sally, was a real person, but there is no proof that Tex knew her. Her father J. K. Cowen, was a railroad magnate, and both were long dead by the twenties when Tex's story came out. In fact Sally's life was a well-known tragic tale. The young heiress had run through her entire fortune very quickly and had died penniless, friendless, and addicted to drugs.

By the date Tex gave for her first term at Hollins, 1906—a date off by six years according to the date the Guinans moved to Denver (1900)—Mr. Cowen was already dead and could hardly have loaned her the money she needed. The A. J. Cowan of the story might have been J. A. Edson, another railroad magnate, whose eldest daughter had actually been a classmate of Tex's at Sacred Heart. Tex could have combined J. A. Edson and J. K. Cowen to reach A. J. Cowan, in the same way she distorted Zach into Hank Miller.

Tex took pleasure in dropping names, even when she didn't get them exactly right. Though her story made it seem as if girls from the West were a rarity at this select eastern school, Hollins' archivist Anthony Thompson points out that at the turn of the century, more students came to Hollins from Texas than any other state except Virginia.[6] Tex was in love with the image of a very special, elite schooling. She also had to explain how the cowgirl had acquired the polish required to lead the glamorous life of a star. She constantly sought to erase the fact that she grew up under very ordinary circumstances.

The adult Tex was heading into dangerous territory because her stories no longer concerned just her family or her personal life but well-known institutions. Her night-club audiences were greatly amused, but the officials at Hollins were confused by her reference to their fashionable college, and alumni all over the country sent letters and clippings to Hollins about Tex's claim. Finally, Hollins' president, Matty Cocke, set out to do some detective work and wrote Henry R. Luce, editor of *Time* magazine. If Luce didn't know who she was, nobody would.

Aug. 14, 1929

Mr. Henry R. Luce, Editor of *Time*
New York, New York

My Dear Sir:—

Can you give us the real name of "Texas Guinan"? We have had sent us several newspaper clippings in which she claims that she was a student in this institution.

If this is a fact, she must have entered Hollins under a different name. Our catalogue records back to 1853, do not show any such student!

This communication is, of course, confidential, and is prompted by a natural desire on our part, to clear up Miss Guinan's statement . . .

Very sincerely yours,
Matty L. Cocke
President[7]

Luce's managing editor, John S. Martin, supplied Tex's full name and it was soon established that Mary Louise Cecelia was not listed in the records. More correspondence followed. One alumna from Texas was asked to interview Tex's mother and investigate in Waco. Hollins was not enjoying the publicity.

Two years later, rumors still circulated. Looking for some gossip, Luther Greene of the Virginia Drama League wrote Susie Blair, assistant professor of drama at Hollins.

March 3, 1931

Virginia Drama League
University of Virginia

My dear Miss Blair,
... The rumor has reached my ears that Texas Guinan is a graduate of Hollins. I wonder if you could tell me if this is true, when she was there, if she graduated, what was her record, and any stories which have lived after her. We want to use the information in a story, for the next issue of the program, about certain notorious and glamorous ladies who have gone to school in Virginia.[8]

Jos. A. Turner, business manager and secretary to the Board of Trustees at Hollins, replied for Miss Blair. (Turner later became so fascinated with Tex's claims that he began the Texas Guinan files at Hollins.)

March 5, 1931

Dear Mr. Greene,
... I would not like to undertake to classify any alumna of Hollins College as notorious and glamorous. ...

In regard to your specific request for information about Texas Guinan, I advise you confidentially that she was never a student at Hollins College. We think it wise not to go into print with a denial and have therefore ignored her claim which has been made with rather annoying frequency during recent years.[9]

After two years, a great deal of discussion and head scratching, Hollins officials decided that neither Tex nor Sally Cowen had been a student at Hollins. Rather than make a public denial of the story, they would continue to ignore it, as such a denial would give both

Tex and Hollins too much publicity. The Guinan file in the college archives remains open to this very day, and once in a while the archivist receives a querying letter.[10]

The real Mayme Guinan lived and grew to womanhood in Denver. The adult Tex rushed to fill those four years with schooling in both the circus and Hollins, but they were in fact quiet years, spent socializing, acting, visiting, and growing up. The invention of a Hollins education to give Little Tex some refinement was unnecessary because Mayme had Bessie. Even before Mayme reached the age of fifteen, Bessie was already thrusting her eldest daughter onto society's front porch. It was time to stop training and grooming and get her out playing the big game in life—catching a man. Bessie believed, along with everybody else, that Marriage was the true vocation of Woman.

Idaho Springs and Cripple Creek were chosen as testing grounds. Several summers before the Guinans moved to Denver, Mayme and her mother visited Bessie's sister Mary in Idaho Springs. There, the two older women sought to launch the young beauty at the local dances. Miss Mayme quickly became known as the life of the party, and her cousin Katy Hoban remembered in a 1945 interview with the *Rocky Mountain News* that Mayme had impressed everybody with her vitality. "She had a premonition that her life was going to be short and so she said she'd make it sweet too, and gay. That was her philosophy . . . She was always full of fun."[11] The summer she spent with Katy Hoban, Mayme became known for hostessing little "parlor entertainments," where she harmonized all evening long with the musicians of the area. How she loved to entertain! Mayme had begun singing at home, when her mother taught her snatches of the songs she'd learned as a child, and she had studied music at Sacred Heart as well as with a private teacher, Mrs. Cochran. In her memoirs, Tex claimed that she also joined her church choir.

Another summer, Mayme and Bessie went to Anaconda to visit other relatives, the Conleys. The Conleys were a well-respected, devout Catholic family, and two of their four offspring were musicians. The visit lasted several months, during which Mayme and her mother became quite well known by the socialites of the mining community. Lowell Thomas even claimed years later that Mayme played the organ at the Sunday services in the local church and that he used to hike over from the neighboring town of Victor just to see her.[12] Church records, though, list the organist as a Miss Mamie Wells. (Thomas also mentioned that she taught Sunday school. He said, "Some years later my demure Miss Guinan metamorphosed into the famous brassy-blond mistress of Broadway's night life.")[13]

Another man to recall the young Mayme's visit was an old miner from Cripple Creek, who included a detailed description of the Guinan manhunting style in his memories of the old mining town.

> Mrs. Guinan, anxious that her daughter achieve popularity, taught Tex the art of make-up ordinarily used by the dance hall girls—plenty of rouge, powder and lavish lipstick; dressed her in the heighth of fashion in such a manner as to attract attention. Tex, as she was soon called, gay and flirtatious, played her part well. . . . She had men from all walks of life trailing her wherever she went.
>
> Tex glorified in her swarm of beaux, and when she became tired of one would flippantly discard him as easily as a woman's glove, and grab another. There was always one obstacle in the way of her suitors, however, for whenever she had a date with a man, Mother Guinan was always on the spot and Tex never left unchaperoned. Wherever Tex went, Mother Guinan went, never leaving the girl out of her sight. It puzzled many as to why Mrs. Guinan should dress her daughter to attract the masculine eye but still keep such a tight rein unless it was to secure a wealthy husband for her. At any rate, Tex was always very much in demand and Mother was always there.[14]

It's hard to know how much of the old miner's story was romanticized by memory. Though Bessie had always dressed Mayme in the most lavish fashions that the fluctuating family fortunes could afford, Mayme was, by age sixteen, strong-willed enough to determine her own style. Thanks to those early years when her mother had paid so much attention to how she dressed, she had grown to feel that clothes were important. Now she took that lesson and added a twist—clothes could help her stand out in a crowd and be noticed. She liked that. In her youth she'd played pranks for attention. Now she used her attractiveness. Bessie went along with her dramatic style as long as it stayed within the bounds of propriety. Later, when Mayme began to spend time with more theater people, she would acquire a taste for the extraordinary.

In her early teenage years, however, the tendency to dress flamboyantly was just emerging. This was noticed and remembered by the *Denver Post* years later: "During the brief period of her life in Denver, Miss Guinan was noted for her devout religious life. To her, attendance at church was an event of major importance in life and she dressed for the part."[15]

The social aspect of churchgoing had taken on new dimensions.

The church became a hunting ground, and every week a fashion show. Denverites never forgot Mayme's weekly visits to the Church of Immaculate Conception on Logan Avenue. Reports in Denver papers say she preferred black lace and frequently appeared in a semiformal evening gown. Sometimes it was not even semi, but wholeheartedly formal: sleeveless, low-necked, with a sweeping train. These outfits were accompanied by dramatic touches: large, black picture hats with plumes, a bunch of artificial violets pinned to the shoulder of the gown. In another article, the *Denver Post* reported, "Sometimes she would appear sensitive of the low gown she wore and would pass much of her time attempting to make it less abbreviated."

The *Denver Post* also recorded that once the Guinans settled into Denver life, the fashionable Mayme, "fortified with a beauty of a fresh brunet type, a strong personality, charm and a decidedly friendly nature, stormed the social fort and gained admission. She was undoubtedly one of the leaders of this set as her presence graced every affair of importance."[16] Regardless of her involvement in the social world of Denver, Mayme kept one name in the back of her head, the name of a man she'd met at her cousin Katy's home all the summers she'd been in Idaho Springs—Johnny Moynahan.

Katy's daughter Charlotte remembered her mother telling about Mayme and the numerous men who courted her back in Idaho Springs. "She was everybody's girl. . . . Then this Johnny Moynahan came along and they said she fell head over heels with him."[17]

John J. Moynahan did not move to Denver until 1902. Until that time, Mayme needed to amuse herself. Local reports say she took up schooling again and began to attend an unnamed female seminary. An account from the *Denver Times* written in 1910, when Tex was making her first successful cross-country tour as a budding prima donna, told how, during one of the school productions, she was discovered by Colonel Peter McCourt, the famous midwestern theatrical manager. He offered to hire her for one of his traveling companies, and she reportedly accepted. Years later, a local paper recalled that she had played the pauper in the company's production of Mark Twain's *The Prince and the Pauper.*

Even if Mayme was not with Colonel McCourt at this time, most reports tend to agree that she was involved in some way with the theater, whether in stock or, as local accounts say, in amateur productions. She favored the wild-western dramas, which were very popular at that time, and this is when the "Tex" part of her began to emerge. "Buckskin Nellie," she later claimed, was her favorite character, and "Gun Girl" was another, according to one of her costars, the famous musician Joseph Newman. There were other rumors that she had once been known as "Flaming Mayme of Gigglewater Gulch."

In her *New York Evening Journal* memoirs, Tex continued the story of Little Tex in the theater, and as before, used several real names and details in her account, overlapping fiction with fact. She credited Johnny Moynahan with the ability to get her her first job in the local stock company—he had clout since he worked as cartoonist on the *Rocky Mountain News*—and she found herself earning eighteen dollars a week. Eighteen dollars was the amount she was offered when she supposedly joined the company in Waco and was also the salary she said she received at her first job in New York.

During this particular part of her story, Little Tex, who by now had grown into quite a "little lady" as well as an actress, was destined to meet her first beau, at least the first to be recorded. His name was John Greenwald, and he was another real character like Moynahan, who became slightly fictionalized.

The real John Greenwald appears in the old directory as a laborer. In Tex's story, he was a wealthy mill owner who fell in love with Little Tex after one of her shows. He proceeded to catch her every performance and started sending flowers. It was a perfect, fairy-tale romance. He had money, looks, and brought her roses. He courted her, he got down on one knee, he proposed. She accepted, and found herself the mistress of a gorgeous diamond ring, her first. Then she started thinking. Marriage.

Tex had played the big game and played it well enough to be setting up the life she—her mother had told her—had always wanted. She would never have to work or worry about money for the rest of her life. Only the idea of being a wife, at least for the person Tex had become, was a little bit frightening. Prince Charming had insisted she give up the stage when she married him. He didn't want to share her with anyone else. She wasn't so sure she liked that.

In fact, she wasn't so sure she liked Greenwald, the man, at all. Sure he was handsome, young, and rich, and so what? Yes, he would help solve the family's financial ups and downs. But what about the audience, the applause, the attention? Who would she act for? And what did he really know of her?

Three days before the wedding, Little Tex went to visit her good friend Johnny or "Jack" as she had begun to call him, at the office of the *Rocky Mountain News*. Somehow she proposed to the fellow and the two eloped.[18]

There is no way of knowing what role John Greenwald played in Mayme Guinan's life, but she did marry John J. Moynahan on December 2, 1904. Although she eloped, Tex still ended up playing the marriage game and trying to fulfill her destiny as a "good" woman. She could never quite erase the years of Bessie's training. Even during the long years of romantic alliances, she would tell the press that her current companion was her husband—just to keep up with public appearances. But she only married once. (Tex's younger sister Pearl also eloped. Pearl's son Patrick said she needed to escape Bessie. If Mayme felt the same, she might have been chafing under her mother's tight rein. Indeed, Pearl told Patrick that when the girls were teenagers, Tex would sneak out the window of their room when their parents wouldn't let her go out.)

After Mayme signed the marriage contract as "Marie," she and her new husband were faced with a big decision. Where to next? In Tex's story, the two couldn't choose between San Francisco and Chicago. So they decided to flip a coin and if it was heads, Chicago, tails, 'Frisco.

It was heads.

Marie

> *This, customers, is the first time I have ever told the story. And it's the first time I ever admitted that I asked a man to marry me.*
> —TEXAS GUINAN, "MY LIFE—AND HOW!", MAY 11, 1929

Marriage, a new frontier.

The year was just about to turn 1905 when Marie (as Mayme was now called) and Jack arrived in the growing metropolis of Chicago. They came without much money and with a suitcase packed tightly with dreams. Although they had known they would encounter the skyscrapers of the Loop scribbling "progress" across the city skies, they did not expect the poetry of Chicago to be written, for the most part, in steel. Somehow they thought that beyond the prairie they would find a clean jewel of a city, standing on the banks of a placid Lake Michigan. Instead they found crowds, noise, dirt. Progress.

"Wasn't that romantic? If it was, all the romance was knocked out of us in the next few weeks.

"We hit Chicago in the pouring rain, with only a few dollars in the family bankroll, and the town looked drearier to me than Denver."[1]

Temporarily camping out in a tiny furnished room on Goethe Street, the Moynahans soon learned that penny-filled cookie jars could not support two grown people—two hungry grown people. One plain lamb chop often disguised itself as dinner for the two of them and was the cause of many an argument. But since the two were newly married, even these small quarrels had a sweetness to them.

"It was tough sledding in Chicago for a while," recalled Tex in her memoirs. "After my life in the open, I found out what it meant to live in a close little flat, cooking, washing dishes, sweeping and making beds while Jack hunted for a job."²

Jack finally found a job as a cartoonist with the *Chicago Examiner*. Soon the Moynahans were able to leave the crowded one-room flat and move to a roomier place of their own at 410 Dearborn Avenue.

While Jack worked days, Marie played housewife. She liked playing according to her own rules, away from Bessie's and all others' watchful eyes. She enjoyed having the time and space to be alone. And marriage continued to look like an exciting new adventure.

Little is known about those years. When Tex looked back at Marie in her memoirs, she didn't dare touch her. Childhood lent itself to fantasy—marriage didn't. Tex mentioned some of the incidents that happened during the marriage, but she barely talked about Marie, Jack, or the relationship itself.

Who was this woman, this perfect homemaker? Was she the same person as Mayme the prankster, the flamboyant and popular personality of Cripple Creek, Denver, and Idaho Springs, the lady who felt she didn't really live if she wasn't the center of a large crowd? Flaming Mayme of Gigglewater Gulch indeed. It was as if a new character had walked onto the stage. Marie.

Marie was not Mayme, and she was not Little Tex. She was not even grown-up Tex, not yet. She was the in-between one, the married one. On the outside, Marie looked calm and housewifely; inside a tug-of-war had begun. On one end of the rope was the tug from the desire to entertain, to be noticed and applauded. The other end was pulled by the desire to love and be loved.

Somewhere in all this there was Jack, or "Moy," as Marie often called him. He was her anchor in life, a hardworking, serious man, practical, yet also creative. Where Marie was flamboyant and in need of attention, Moy was quiet and content to remain in the background. Where she sometimes let her emotions control her, he was solid and levelheaded.

Early in their married life, Moy began to use Marie as a model for his cartoons. In those days, she was a blossoming brunette, more curves than lines. Soon she appeared in the *Chicago Examiner* as the City of Chicago, an American Dowager, and any number of political characters. Playing the Muse gave Marie an opportunity to express herself. It was like acting again.

Sources on Moynahan offer few details about the man. Tex doesn't help much—in her memoirs, she never makes Moy real. For her, he was a background character, the dancer who accompanied the prima ballerina on stage just to lift her at certain points in the performance. This became the role all her men would play.

Not only did Tex downplay Moy's role in her life, but she, at various times, denied ever having loved him. In her memoirs, she married him primarily to leave Denver and go east to New York. "Jack knows I married him to get out of Denver and there are no hard feelings about it."[3]

However, Marie loved Moy enough to move with him to Cleveland in 1906 when he got a job on the *Cleveland News*. Of course, Cleveland was on the way east. They lived at the Euclid Hotel for a short time and by 1907, were listed in the local directories at 2332 Prospect Avenue. Local reports say Marie sang with the choir at church, occasionally performing at a little café behind the old Euclid Avenue Opera House. John Stein's account says, on the contrary, that Tex was her most domestic during that time and stayed away from theater and singing engagements—as singer and as audience member—until the night Moy bought tickets to see Charlotte Walker.

Charlotte Walker was one of the more famous actresses at the turn of the century. Chances are the production in which they saw Walker was written by her husband, Eugene Walter, a well-known playwright and native of Cleveland. Tex later told the story of Walker's performance to Stein because she considered it a key incident in her life.

Before the show, while the Moynahans were out eating their own separate lamb chops, who should enter the restaurant but Mrs. Walker herself, surrounded by a very attentive group of admirers. As soon as she entered, she attracted all the conversations and stares in the room. She remained the center of attention for the rest of the evening.

Marie had not realized how much she missed performing until Charlotte Walker strode in and captured the restaurant. Jealousy and old desires were beginning, growing within her. Diamonds. Men. Attention.

During the performance, Marie watched Walker carefully. She was certainly a step above the frontier stock actresses Marie was accustomed to, but not *that much* better. Marie could be just as good, given the chance.[4]

According to Stein, shortly after the Walker incident, the Moynahans moved back to Chicago because Jack had found a better-paying job. There is no listing for them in the Chicago directory past 1905, and most sources—except Tex, whose memoirs omit mention of Cleveland altogether—don't indicate a return to Chicago. Whether they lived in Chicago or Cleveland, the Moynahans began to grow apart.

Moy now seemed wedded to his job. Often he worked nights and slept days and spent very little time with his wife. As a result, the two began losing sight of each other and the dreams they'd married with. On top of all that, Moy thought Marie had begun to change. She was no longer the Mayme he remembered. She became extravagant and somewhat odd. He told Stein years later how she started with colors,

> the wildest, most dashing colors. She would bend her hat down if she thought it would make her stand out from a crowd. She dreamed fantastic dreams—her imagination was vivid and wild. . . . She was a strange woman, and each year found her a more and more changed personality from the Mayme Guinan whom I had married in 1904. Her methods were anomalous. In the summer when everyone was melting under the heat, she insisted upon wearing furs; in the winter's bitterest cold, she gowned herself in low-necked dresses. If you pointed out that she might attract attention her reply was: "Certainly, I want to be different."[5]

Perhaps Charlotte Walker's restaurant entrance had stimulated Marie's imagination. It's odd that Moy hadn't known of her flamboyant side from those years in Denver. At any rate, the role of housewife had lost its novelty. Eventually, the desire for a career would compel Marie to choose between Moy and the stage.

The choice to trade the security and respectability of marriage for the uncertain life of the actress/singer may not have been an easy one to make. It contradicted Marie's upbringing, her era, tradition. Yet her desire to be in the limelight was so strong that eventually, in spite of her background and a lasting affection for Moy, she chose to leave.

Tex later said people shouldn't marry unless they were willing to sacrifice everything for marriage.[6]

In her memoirs, Tex's first step toward igniting her career was to begin training her voice at the Chicago Conservatory. Her claim is substantiated only by the fact that she had a "trained" voice and must've trained it somewhere. But at the conservatory? If she did go there, the timing of her studies is unclear.

In the early 1900s, Chicago was one of the best places for musical study and performance west of New York. The Chicago Conservatory enjoyed prominence as a leading musical institution and had an enrollment of over fifteen hundred pupils. Not only did the conservatory offer excellent training but the opportunity for its students to make public appearances. If Marie did study there, she would have been affiliated with the Hinshaw School of Opera and Drama.

Before Marie could begin studying voice, however, a new character needed to enter the story, a man named Marshall Field I. By the time the Moynahans had arrived in Chicago, Marshall Field had already established one of the largest department stores not just in Chicago, but in the United States. Tex decided that this well-known man and/or his well-known store would receive the credit in her memoirs for having launched her career. Thus, in all her autobiographical accounts, she assigned him the honor of offering a scholarship for study at the Chicago Conservatory of Music. She then created a contest around this scholarship and proceeded to win it.

"Call it luck, call it nerve, call it determination, a miracle or what have you," wrote Tex to her readers, "but I won that scholarship with a soprano voice that I had used mostly to yell at cowboys and steers.

"The Broadway critics may call it personality, Elinor Glyn may call it 'It.' You name it and you can have it. But I copped the bacon over 800 other girl contestants."[7]

Despite Tex's recollections, neither the store nor the family has any record of a Marshall Field Scholarship. Marshall Field I himself died in 1906, the year Tex claimed the award was won, and the Field historian states that it is unlikely that a scholarship would have been awarded in his name that year.[8] (Besides, she spent that year in Cleveland.) In addition, the conservatory rarely went beyond bestowing an occasional gold or silver medal of excellence upon their better students. Alas, we know Tex's penchant for upgrading her history, and a conservatory education—on scholarship—sounded as impressive as a Hollins diploma.

Along with the scholarship came several versions of how and why it was won. Most of Tex's stories scheduled the contest around the time Marie came to Chicago with Moy, but in several accounts, Tex staged it a bit earlier, when she was still at home in Waco. In one version, Tex described herself as a child prodigy who was sent by her music teacher Mrs. Cochran to enter the contest at the blushing age of fourteen. In another version, she was sixteen and coming home from a semester at Hollins.

"You talk about chance—the very way I made my debut on the stage was merely that. Travelling to Chicago from Virginia where I had been attending school, I met on the train Reginald De Koven, the composer. He suggested that I enter a contest for a year's scholarship at the Chicago Conservatory of Music, and so I did. I was chosen from 800 contestants."⁹

The content of these two stories is not as important as Tex's use of the stories to prove a point. Winning the scholarship illustrated her ability as a singer, her strong determination, and her extraordinary luck. It also gave her something more interesting to do than housework during the Chicago period of her life.

In every version of the contest/conservatory story, there was one common factor, and that common factor was a man named Reginald De Koven, the famous composer of light opera. There were so many ways in which Tex involved him in her story that we could play a game of multiple choice. Pick one of the following. Reginald De Koven was involved in the life of Texas Guinan in that:

a. He met Tex on the train from Hollins to Waco and told her about the contest.

b. He was her neighbor when she lived on Dearborn Avenue.

c. He was one of the subscribers to the conservatory. ("At the conclusion of the course in the conservatory each contestant was to be given a chance in some music production. The subscribers made this possible. I had a letter to Reginald De Koven.")¹⁰

d. He was a judge from the contest who was so impressed with the quality of her voice that he told her to look him up if ever she came to New York.

e. None of the above.

Reginald De Koven was important only because his presence in this chapter of Tex's autobiography will pull Marie into the next. In the newspaper version, Tex said,

"I went right to work at the conservatory, studying, living on the $25 a week they allowed me, and having a glorious time at the operas and concerts.

"I guess I was the cockiest pupil the conservatory ever saw. The committee thought I had a voice. I knew I had vitality, health and ambition and a yen to make Broadway. So I was sure I couldn't miss.

"When my course was ended, I told myself I was a finished prima donna. It was a wonder I wasn't finished soon after that."¹¹

Now it was time to arrange a leave-taking. Marie's continued success in her studies encouraged her to separate from her husband and eventually prompted her to head for New York. In the tradition of fairy tales, she packed her few belongings, kissed Moy goodbye, and set out to seek her fortune.

Thus ended Texas's only attempt at married life. She never married again, though millions thought she had, and Moy himself waited until several years after her death before he remarried. The two remained affectionate friends throughout Tex's lifetime, and she said in her memoirs, "I want to say right here that Jack Moynahan never gave me a bad break as long as I lived with him. My opinion of him can be squeezed into one short sentence. 'He's a great guy.'"[12]

Later it would be said that Tex sometimes thought she was ready to return to the quiet life with a good steady man. Her close friend, journalist Mark Hellinger, remarked in his column in the *Daily News* after her death, "I have listened to her as she swore that she'd quit the whole racket at any time for a guy she loved—and a baby. I never wrote that last item. I was afraid I'd be kidded too much. But, strangely enough, she meant it."[13]

And so, not unlike the many young dreamers who had left home in search of the Broadway promise, Mary Louise Cecelia Guinan caught a train for New York. However, unlike those aimless wanderers who simply arrived in the train depot of their dreams, this woman had a destination. According to her memoirs, Reginald De Koven had told her to look him up if she ever came to Manhattan. Well, she was coming.

Everything West of New York Is Just Bridgeport

> *Texas Comes to Gotham but There's No Brass Band*
> *at the Station*
> —TEXAS GUINAN, "MY LIFE—AND HOW!"
> MAY 13, 1929

> *Anyway, I grabbed the first train to New York and if anybody had been willing to listen to me, I would have told him that Reginald De Koven was waiting for me somewhere, pacing up and down his studio and gritting his teeth in angry impatience because I hadn't come sooner to star in his show. Honest, that's the way I felt about it.*
> —TEXAS GUINAN, "MY LIFE—AND HOW!"
> MAY 11, 1929

Marie arrived in New York in 1907. Though she'd had visions of what she might encounter there, she found the city breathtaking and unpredictable. New sights and sounds hit her in sequence the way credits flash across the screen: New York. Broadway. Those lights.

The sounds of Broadway surrounded her—the high-heel, soft-shoe conversations on the pavement in front of the towering Times Building, the song of horn and trolley bell. For a while, Marie was not quite sure if she had invented the Times Square spectacle or if she were standing on a big stage. Everyone acted as if hired for a grand street scene in a Follies extravaganza. Women heading for dinner at Rector's, the greatest of the lobster palaces, captured the arms of their escorts and admired their newest diamonds as they caught the light from the marquees. Outside numerous stage doors, men stood waiting with flowers in their hands and button holes. One day they would wait for her.

New York's infamous traffic accompanied the crowded sidewalk scenes. Long, open double-decker buses fought their way down the avenue alongside hansom cabs, victorias, and electric buggies. Charmed by the fuss, the complex patterns of the trolley tracks and the noise, Marie took the confusion of the bodies and the smells and wrapped it around her like a costly mink coat. She loved New York City, wanted a piece of it. At last she was *home.*

"Better a square foot of New York than all the rest of the world in a lump—better a lamppost on Broadway than the brightest star in the sky," she would later tell the world.[1] It was love at first sight.

After this ecstatic introduction to the avenue of her dreams, Marie, or should we say "Little Tex," jumped Mayme-like into a cab and headed straight for 42 East Sixty-sixth Street in search of Reginald De Koven. Besides having a letter of recommendation in her hand, she also had the gentleman's word that he would give her a job if she ever came to Manhattan. "I'll bet he often cursed himself for that unthinking moment when he spoke out of turn and told me he would give me a job if I ever came to New York," Tex later told readers of the *New York Evening Journal.* "He probably forgot it, but I didn't. I'm like the elephants, they never forget." There is no way to be sure whether the following incident really happened, but the story as Tex told it later became one of her favorites.

When the cab pulled up *chez* Mr. De Koven and deposited a starstruck Little Tex at the steps of the mansion, our heroine had been thinking about those lights on Broadway. Soon she'd be famous—another Lillian Russell!—and mazda bulbs would brighten her name. She marched up the front steps without hesitation and rang the doorbell of the mansion. Her dreams were soon interrupted by the presence of the large and almost-menacing De Koven butler.

"Mr. De Koven is entertaining guests at dinner," the major-domo announced, with a haughty glance at Little Tex's cheap suitcase. "Is he expecting you?"

"He sure is!" cried Little Tex with enthusiasm, enthusiasm she wished she felt. She followed the butler to the dining room and soon stood in the doorway, searching for the right face. Walking over to the distinguished-looking man seated at the head of the banquet table she said, "Hello, Mr. De Koven, I'm here at last."

De Koven looked questioningly at his butler.

"Don't you remember me?" asked Little Texas anxiously. "I'm the girl who won the conservatory prize in Chicago. I came for that job." Another awkward silence.

"Oh, yes, yes, yes!" exclaimed De Koven suddenly. He could not remember the child. But certainly she had courage. He had better invite her to sit beside him and join the dinner, or else they would never get past the soup.

After the servants set a place by De Koven's right elbow, Little Tex joined the party, which the adult Tex later claimed was made up of artists from the Metropolitan Opera. She also insisted that Caruso, as well as the great Gatti-Casazza, director of the Metropolitan Opera from 1908–1935, had been among them.

Seated at the table surrounded by people speaking in other languages, Little Tex was soon off into her own little fantasy world. She was enchanted by the beauty of the room, by the diamonds adorning the necks and fingers of the women present, by the grandeur and style with which the De Kovens lived. She told herself that now this was all to be part of her life, that it was her due as a "star" of the opera.

After dinner, Little Tex had a short session with her host and was quickly ushered out of the house with the instructions to report in the morning for rehearsals of his operetta, *The Snowman*.[2] (This was, in fact, Tex's first job in New York.)

Most struggling actresses didn't land their first job by collaring a famous man over dinner. In the early 1900s, job hunting on Broadway was a gruesome affair. Roles were plentiful, but since everyone who came to New York was a would-be actor, comedian, or juggler in search of a job, the mere act of arriving at a producer's office in time to grab a chair or a good place in line was hard work. If the young hopeful was lucky enough to get hired, she soon discovered that rehearsals were payless and ran from three to ten weeks. Then she had to hope that the producer or star, both of whom had total control over their casts, wouldn't take it into their heads to fire her. And of course there was always the chance that the show might not succeed.

Even with such trials awaiting her, Marie, soon to be known only as "Texas," could not have arrived on Broadway at a better moment in theatrical history. In an attempt to capture a fickle public, battling theater owners were struggling to outdo each other, creating more extravagant attractions and bigger shows by the month. At the turn of the century, there were already forty-one legitimate theaters in New York, more than in any other city in the world. In and around Broadway, Sixth and Seventh Avenues, from Twenty-third Street to Forty-first ran the Garrick, Empire, Majestic, Savoy, and many more. Their stages were graced by the royalty of theater: the Barrymores, John Drew, Mrs. Minnie Maddern Fiske, Richard Mansfield, Douglas Fairbanks, Raymond Hitchcock, Lily Langtry. The year before Tex arrived in town, Sarah Bernhardt had appeared in *Camille*, Nazimova in Ibsen's *Hedda Gabler*, James O'Neill, father of playwright Eugene, in *The Count of Monte Cristo*. While turn-of-the-century crowds still loved the repertory which emphasized the players more than the play, times were changing and new types of shows came to be offered. In 1907, the Ziegfield Follies was born, the first of the great extravaganzas.

Finding themselves before a smorgasboard of acts and shows to choose from, the public became so addicted to the stage that attendance at the local theater or opera house, once a special outing, became a regular event. This happened across the United States and enabled many shows to take to the road.

This was good news for the striving young actors. They continued their pilgrimage to the big city full of hopes and expectations and soon found that Manhattan was very much like a woman's love, "both the sweetest and most cruel, at once, in the world."[3] Or so thought Tex. Years after she'd fallen in love with the Great White Way, she philosophized that the city "offers the greatest prizes and the greatest obstacles. It cries, I will give you the world! and when you come to take it, lo! It rises against you like some monster and tries to prevent you from taking it."[4]

Tex had always had drive and her rise in the New York theater world was launched by her own consistent efforts. However, effortless stardom has always been a premium, and Tex preferred to attribute her success to her extraordinary luck. Certainly, being in the right place at the right time played a crucial role in her life, but timing and luck weren't everything. Once Tex chose a course of action—in this case, success on the stage—she became driven by that pioneer spirit she'd inherited from her parents and ancestors. Thus she was persistent and tenacious in her climb to stardom. In addition, her imagination left no room for failure. She later gave this recipe for success:

"If you want anything bad enough, go out and fight for it. Work day and night in order to achieve the goal. Sacrifice your time, your peace, your sleep. Sweat for it, fret for it, plan for it. Lose your terror of God or man for it.

"Hold fast to the pillars of faith, hope, confidence, stern pertinacity. Defy cold poverty, pain of body and brain.

"Besiege and beset for it, and you're bound to win."[5]

During those first weeks in New York, Tex encountered the first of her trials as the adventurous heroine: poverty. On the advice of an old-timer, she took a small room down in the notorious, bohemian Greenwich Village at 72 Washington Square and paid two dollars a week for rent and breakfast. She lived on a diet of rye bread and milk and between washing and ironing the same clothes every evening, dreamed of where she would live when she became rich and famous. Years later when Tex owned a seven-room apartment just around the corner on Eighth Street, she kept two of her several cars in the garage that stood where number 72 had been.

Tex could never have lived anywhere but in Greenwich Village. Physically, it was the most charming, most intimate of the city's neighborhoods. Many historians later compared the Village at that time to Paris's Latin Quarter, with narrow, winding streets that sometimes tumbled across old footpaths and occasional streams, streets that bore names more often than numbers. These streets spun out like broken spokes from the central Washington Square Park, in those days quite spacious, green, and genteel. While fountains played and traffic flowed across the cobblestones from Fifth Avenue into West Broadway, the park sat calmly at the base of the fabulous mansion-studded avenue with Stanford White's new monument to Washington at its head. In contrast to Fifth Avenue's mansions, the small, cozy houses of Greenwich Village created a small-town feeling, and with the added attraction of low rent, invited inhabitants from all classes of bohemia. In the years surrounding Tex's arrival, the houses filled with artists and anarchists alike, ranging from rich women like Gertrude Vanderbilt Whitney, who converted a stable on Macdougal Street into a sculpture studio, to the playwright Eugene O'Neill, writer and activist John Reed, anarchist Emma Goldman, and poet Edna St. Vincent Millay. Just down the block from Tex at 61 Washington Square, many of these bohemians painted and versified their way to fame, alongside writers like Willa Cather, John Dos Passos, Max Bodenheim, and Stephen Crane.

Greenwich Village was the symbolic center for creative energy as well as a place for those seeking to declare their independence. Several people have since described the Village as a state of mind, having no boundaries except the imagination.[6] Recalling the Mayme of earlier chapters, it was thus a most appropriate locale for the inventive Tex.

Soon after she arrived in New York, Tex wrote Moy that she had "made it" and that he no longer needed to worry about her. The letter was something of a dismissal. However Moy knew his wife well enough to continue sending her a generous weekly allowance. The money barely saw her through those weeks of unpaid rehearsals. Tex had become quite the spendthrift after arriving in New York. It seemed as if the moment she stepped out on the street in the morning and exhaled, she'd spent a dollar, maybe two. To add to this, she soon found that in order to really mix with the right crowds in theater, she had to be somewhat extravagant. One of her teachers and closest friends who taught her much in that field was the actress Nora Bayes, notorious for her expensive tastes and habit of renting an entire floor of a hotel when she toured.

Tex acquired some new flashy clothes, fake jewelry, and before long, a handsome southern gentleman. She wasn't troubled by the fact that she was still legally married, for in moving from Chicago to New York and casting off her identity as Marie, she had declared her freedom. But Moy didn't see it that way. He still had hopes. Eventually he would realize that she was gone for good.

Tex's first new friend was a stove salesman named Jack Warren. He was actually the beau of another girl in the chorus when she first met him, but Tex didn't mind. She had had some unpleasant encounters with the girl and was more than willing to snatch her man away. And certainly he never complained.

Tex later told Stein that Jack Warren was nobody special. Like many of the "stage-door Johnnies" that were to follow, his place in Tex's memory was minute and vague, and he never appeared in any of her public memoirs. Stein believed that Warren was mostly interested in Tex for her money, though we know she wasn't making very much. If this was true, then Warren was the first of many "younger" men to flow in and out of Tex's life, men who seemed motivated by mercenary intentions behind their professed love. Tex was a sucker for them every time. How could she resist? Her young beaux were handsome and attentive, but most turned out to be scoundrels. Other men Tex chose tended to be the opposite: solid, fatherly types like Moy.

Finally, rehearsal for *The Snowman* ended and the show went on the road. In November of 1907, the show arrived in New York City under the new title, *The Girls of Holland*. The operetta tells the story of a snowman that comes to life and is involved in several mix-ups created around his awakening. Reginald De Koven's latest comic opera was produced by the famous Shubert brothers. Though De Koven had a good, strong reputation in the musical theater world, he could not save the show from the media. *Girls* was panned and declared "as lively as a Dutch windmill."[7] Its run in New York was shortlived.

While *Girls* still ran, however, Tex had her first big break in the business. Sometime during the early part of the show's tour, Tex reported that prima donna Vera Michelena fell ill with laryngitis. In her memoirs, Tex marked the spot in Boston. When the show finally came to New York, it was Tex who played the starring role, not Vera.

> Now if this were a fiction story, I'd have to tell you that I stepped bravely on the stage and sang my role in the grand manner of Galli-Curci. But it isn't that kind of yarn. This is real life, so here's the lowdown.
> I was scared blue. With my knees knocking together, my head whirling and my whole body numb, I burst into song without waiting for the orchestra's intro. The leader was frantic as he drove his musicians to catch up with me. Even at that, when I finished, that friendly, sympathetic audience gave the little girl a hand.
> The antics of Willie Edwin, English comedian in the show, brought me back to earth and bolstered my shattered nerve. And with that first applause ringing in my ears, I prayed that Vera Michelena would stay sick.[8]

None of the clippings or programs on file make note of this substitution. The only document verifying Tex's presence in the show at all is an itemized bill for the show's costumes dated March 8, 1907. (Tex is listed as Miss Guiman.)[9] No one connected with the production remembers the switch, but it makes a good story. It's the same old star-falls-ill-chorine-gets-big-break story, similar to the stock company incident back in Waco. The main difference between Tex and the other typical heroines is that Tex doesn't wait to have the part handed to her, she asks for it. Even though she uses the incident to illustrate her famous good luck, one can begin to see that Texas Guinan is never merely lucky—she goes out and creates that "luck" for herself.

In an interview with *Pictures* magazine in 1926, Tex would talk about her large pile of clipping books and about the first time she saw her name in print. "I got an awful thrill out of the first slight mention of me in print, when I became the lead in Snow Man. I didn't keep that clipping."

Though there is no proof that Tex took over for Michelena, the prima donna did play a role in Tex's life. For the young chorine admired the star, was inspired by her. Tex would continue to have role models as she moved through her theatrical career, but she never forgot Michelena—down to her very costumes. In the last movie she ever made, Tex wore a dress she told Stein was modeled on one Michelena wore in *The Girls of Holland*.

At this point in her memoirs, Tex was notified that her mother had fallen ill; so Tex sent for her. Even though Bessie's presence and the ensuing doctors' bills were taxing on her pocket, Tex liked having her mother with her. From then on, Tex would never be separated from Bessie for long and would even take her on tour. The public loved this display of filial devotion.

Tex had discovered, in the years away from home, that she could trust no friendship to be as secure or as long-lasting as her family ties. She also believed that her family depended on her, needed her. All the while, she had been sending the family money whenever she could, and she wanted to bring them all to New York City. Michael, Bessie, and Tommy would come to live with her in 1915.

After *The Girls of Holland* closed, Tex began working on the vaudeville circuit. In the early years of her career, show business was still largely synonymous with vaudeville, which combined acrobat, juggler, toe dancer, and performing animal acts with the musical numbers and comic skits that starred headliners like Tex. In the U.S. at that time, there were over two thousand vaudeville houses, and New York was dotted with a large percentage of them. In "big time," one might put on a mere two shows daily, but in "small time," one might do as many as three to six. There were either large audiences and good pay or months of interminable road tours back and forth and up and down the United States. Also making their breaks in vaudeville at that time were budding comedians, dancers, and singers like Buster Keaton, Charlie Chaplin, Fannie Brice, Eddie Cantor, W. C. Fields, Mae West, Fred and Adele Astaire, Sophie Tucker, Eva Tanguay, and Anna Held. Some of these, like Mae West, became Tex's lifelong friends.

Vaudeville provided an excellent opportunity for an actor or actress to develop his or her own style. The shows were well attended by audiences varied enough to make flexibility and ingenuity a requirement for success. The prime aim was to "get" the audience as soon as possible. These skills came naturally to Tex, and she used vaudeville to perfect them.

To Tex, however, vaudeville also meant uncertainty. In her memoirs, she wrote that the gap between shows made her anxious, especially after Bessie came to live with her. "When the blues turned to deep indigo," she wrote, "I used to go up to the Cathedral and pray. I never have forgotten the religious training my mother gave me as a kid. At all hours of the night, on the way from the theatre, I would stop to say a prayer." Never self-conscious, when the doors were closed, she prayed outside.[10]

By February 1908, Tex had landed an engagement with the celebrated light-opera and musical comedian Franklin Farnum in the vaudeville show, *Simple Simon Simple*. The show toured throughout the Midwest and back again. This is the first mention of her career in print. Texas "Guina*m*" and Farnum were the only two of the principals in the cast to really catch the critics' eyes. Tex was remembered best for her song, "That's What the Rose Said to Me."

By this time, Tex had outgrown her infatuation for Jack Warren and was flirting with Farnum. Although the two grew to be close friends, nothing romantic developed, and Farnum married actress Alma Rubens shortly after the play closed. Later Tex would costar with Rubens in one of her first silent films.

Farnum was an older, more experienced actor with a good feel for comedy. He had traveled the vaudeville road long enough to have a sense of humor about the unpleasantness of the many one-night stands in isolated towns across the United States. Life on the road was both physically and mentally uncomfortable, and often the local opera house of a town would turn out to be a drafty hall stationed over a jail, an unheated stable, or even the public baths. Tex's memoirs of circus travel could easily have come from this era in her life.

Returning to New York, Tex soon found herself another role, this time as a supporting actress for Broadway's sweetheart, Elsie Janis. Janis, thanks to a pushy mother—sometimes known as the most terrifying mother Broadway had ever known—had been acting on the stage since childhood. At the age of ten, she had mimicked the beauty Anna Held with such precision that some credited her with helping popularize many of Held's signature songs.[11] As Janis grew older, she came to represent the all-American girl, with an acting style filled with freshness and new energy. She often wore a tam-o'-shanter perched rakishly on her head, and was considered so "hoydenish" that the producer Charles Frohman was said to have bought her Charles Dillingham's play, *The Hoyden*, on the title alone. Tex joined Janis in that production in May 1908, a production full of lively tunes and "clean comedy." Playing the role of Rita Santacierci, "Guina*nt*" was proclaimed by Chicago critics to be "handsome, clever, and a decided feature in the reckoning of support."[12] Through these several supporting roles, playing second to a better-known actress or actor, Tex was slowly coming to the public's notice. Soon the critics would even learn how to spell her name.

Texas stepped happily into the role of promising actress. She wore her long, brown hair wrapped up on top of her head, and miles of silks, ribbons, lace, and satin upon her voluptuous figure. There was a tease to her glance that was enhanced by the soft fullness of her face and figure, and although by today's standards she was overweight, she wore the plumpness with grace. Men noticed how her upper lip seemed to thin and slant to one side, as if it resided in a constant state of flirtation. To this, she added a pair of laughing eyes which seemed to announce she was out to have fun.

Tex worked alongside Janis throughout the summer of 1908 and often found herself surrounded by a number of handsome suitors. Here was her Charlotte Walker dream come true in just a matter of a few years! According to Tex, because Janis was much shyer, she was constantly inviting her to step out and have a little fun. Janis's mother, Mrs. Bierbower, who had accompanied her daughter on tour, was not very impressed by the wild Miss Guinan and preferred to keep her daughter away from Tex's influence. Her attitude was not unlike that of Mrs. Gorman back in Waco, who would send her daughter Kathleen ahead to school in the family carriage rather than have her accompanied by that tough Guinan girl.

In Elsie Janis's autobiography, the story is told a bit differently. In her version, she is the one surrounded by many admirers and Tex tags along, "a buxom, rosy-cheeked 'little girl,'" weighing 190 pounds.[13]

Between tours with the many shows that Tex moved in and out of, she maintained an active romance with New York. She enlarged her circle of acquaintances and cultivated a staunch group of friends. These friends, in turn, cultivated her, influenced her tastes, introduced her to new extravagances and to even more people. There were very few, besides her mother, who ever really got close to Tex, however, and one of the privileged was Hannah Boyer.

Hannah Boyer was a black laundress who had won Tex's heart when Tex had first started out as a struggling actress. To Tex, Hannah was a good-hearted aunt of sorts. She was someone whom Tex trusted in a city of strangers, who would feed her, take her into her home if she needed a place to stay, or lend her money. Occasionally, she even clothed her. Tex later told Stein about the time she was preparing to audition for a new job. "Aunt Hannah" wouldn't let her go until she changed her clothes which, in Hannah's opinion, lacked the right amount of class. Instead Hannah "borrowed" an outfit from one of her more successful customers and dressed Tex in it. Tex got the job, and Hannah washed the borrowed outfit again before returning it to its proper owner. Ever after, said Stein, it was Hannah and Hannah only whom Tex would trust with her precious wardrobe.[14] Because clothes were very important to Texas, helping her to create her roles both on and off the stage, Hannah's job was an important one.

Tex's friendship with Hannah was to last the entertainer's lifetime. Tex never forgot those who helped her on her way up, and often, when she took a liking to someone, found a way to keep them close to her.

Tex's newly acquired fans began to grow curious about her unusual first name. In an interview published November 22, 1908, she told reporters of the *New York Telegram* that Texas was her "real name." She explained that her father was the first white settler in Waco, Texas, and that of the four generations of her family that had sprung up in that region, the first born of each bore the name Texas in honor of the state. The "Texas" stories multiplied. Columnist Louis Sobol later dated the name change back to when she was a "broncobuster in a small circus."[15] Others, like her nephew, claimed she had always loved her home state and had taken the name when she came east. Perhaps back in the days when her Denver playmates called her "Flaming Mayme of Gigglewater Gulch," they also dubbed the ex-Wacoan "Tex." When she finally arrived in New York, "Texas" seemed an ideal stage name that linked her to the "Wild West" she treasured.

Tex enjoyed her emergence into print. She loved the attention and quickly learned what to tell the public and what to keep to herself.

Tex next appeared in *The Gibson Girl Review*, a seventeen-minute pictorial musical by Bissing and Sloman. It ran on the vaudeville circuit but was said by *Variety* to be a "real production." At that time, pictorial musicals were the latest fad in vaudeville. The idea was to present "living pictures" in which the actor or actress would pose in a role, then act or sing the scene represented. In *The Gibson Girl Review*, the celebrated Gibson Girl, a turn-of-the-century ideal "girl" invented by artist Charles Dana Gibson, was presented in some of her more characteristic poses—in moods ranging from "deepest sorrow" to "sublimest love." Tex, the "beautiful girl" who had "the endorsement of no less an authority than Charles Dana Gibson himself, as being ideally fitted for the part in face, form, figure, carriage and expression,"[16] played the central role of the Gibson Widow.

One can picture the plump Tex posing for her tableaux with the proper amount of "sorrow" or "love," illuminating her numbers with a spirited soprano. Unfortunately, not everyone found her treatment of the role appropriate. Tex was very much a product of the traveling stock shows she'd grown up watching. She tended to overenunciate and overact to the point of melodrama, and the critics noticed. Sime Silverman, editor of *Variety*, reviewed the show on November 8, 1908, and called it an artistic gem, an ornament to the stage. He suggested, however, that "perhaps if Miss Guinan would relax just a trifle upon her very distinct enunciation for the benefit of her voice, she would more fully justify the special mention on the program." This was the first of several similar reviews. Tex's grassroots training out West and her love and fascination for the melodramatic would continue to influence her interpretation of the roles she played.

By May of the following year, Tex was appearing nightly in an airship suspended about seven feet over the stage. While floating above her audience, she sang "To the End of the world With You," "Pansies Mean Thoughts," and "Shine on Harvest Moon" in her own act as the Lone Star Novelty at Keith and Proctor's Fifth Avenue Theatre. Staged by Jack Mason, the act was Tex's first attempt as a soloist. *Variety* was somewhat more complimentary this time and commented that "someone got orders to build an act around a good soprano voice, and whoever undertook the task did fairly well. . . . Miss Guinan has looks, and dresses well. Her well-trained soprano does the rest." An unnamed famous "theater man" advised the public to "keep your eyes on that girl. She has zip and fizz, and that's what the public wants."[17]

During her engagement as the Lone Star Novelty, Tex was lucky enough to attract the attention of John P. Slocum, one of the foremost producers of musical comedies at that time. In one of Tex's versions of the discovery, she again attributed her success to luck.

"I was appearing at the Fifth Avenue Theatre, the Palace Theatre of its day. Across the street, John P. Slocum, a well-known producer who rarely went to the music halls, was rehearsing a play called *The Gay Musician*, by Julian Edwards. In vain he had been searching for a star of personality for his forthcoming production. By some strange chance Mr. Slocum happened into the Fifth Avenue Theatre of an afternoon. He was not impressed by me, for in the midst of my act he suddenly rose to leave."[18]

Or, as Tex tells it in her *New York Evening Journal* version, Slocum came into the theater assuming the Lone Star Novelty was a cowboy act, as he had a spot in his show for a Wild West number. When he found out Tex was only singing, he reached for his hat and started to leave. Tex turned her flashlight on the insulting man and in the tradition she was later to create as a night-club hostess, she cried out, "If you're going out, bring one back for me!" Slocum sat back in his seat and waited for Tex to take her light off him, but she kept on singing to him and kidding him. "I learned it in the Colorado mining towns," she told *Evening Journal* readers. "Find a grouch and kid him to death. Believe me they love it. If you don't believe me, you ought to see the way it works in a night club!"[19]

In her story, Tex didn't find out who her victim was until the next day, when she received an invitation to lunch. Slocum was well known as the manager of Richard Mansfield and the producer who had developed the career of Tex's former idol, Vera Michelena. Over lunch, Slocum offered Tex the leading role in *The Gay Musician* and a four-year contract.

There is no other record of how Slocum discovered Tex, but he did indeed catch her show and did make her an offer. At first, unable to break her vaudeville contract, Tex refused. Later Slocum came back to her, and the newspapers assumed that "the management [had made] a still more tempting offer, which induced her to cancel her remaining vaudeville contracts and leave at once for Ottawa, Canada, and join the company there. Her success was pronounced instantaneous."[20]

Tex told readers of the *New York Evening Journal* that the original contract with Slocum promised her $500 a week for the first two years and $750 after that. The night her second year ended, Slocum supposedly came to her with a check for $15,000 in addition to her salary. The bonus check amounted to a percentage of the receipts for the last two years. That night Slocum tore up her contract and the two became partners.

Whatever arrangement Slocum and Guinan shared, Slocum was good to her. While he treated the entire cast well, taking them to his Adirondack camp for vacations when he thought they needed a rest and advancing salaries when requested, he bought Tex gifts, clothing, and jewelry. He was clearly infatuated with her.

All through the fall of 1909, and during the next two years, Slocum was to influence his protégé heavily. It was Stein's opinion that Slocum spoiled Tex with so much attention that he helped spawn an egotism that was to remain with her throughout her life. However, Tex was already in a position to hear what he had to say. Twenty-five years had helped her choose this path long before she met Slocum. He was merely a guide.

Slocum was a bit excessive in his star treatment. Not only did he make sure Tex had her own drawing room when the show was on tour but once even booked an entire railroad car for her, (allowing her to travel like the famous Lily Langtry). He also counseled her in how to think like a star. "Don't let anybody get away with the impression that you're not the greatest thing in show business. Talk big, think big—be big. Remember nobody is as important as you—keep thinking that way and you'll be important."[21] Now Tex had often thought such things in the privacy of her room, but to hear them uttered aloud—that was amazing. Slocum seemed to believe—as she did—that one must come from a state of being that is "star," that one must live life as if one already had the trappings of success.

Tex had always wanted to be the greatest, to show them all. She needed to be the best, hold everyone's attention, prove her worth. The character she was creating couldn't show any doubts, needed to appear strongly independent and single-minded. If she had worries, she pushed them inward. The payoffs for the great success she'd soon have were obvious and enticing: money, applause, renown, even numerous boyfriends and the company of other interesting people. Slocum provided a way to get to those prizes, and he worked hard to extinguish any insecurity that Tex might have had. Offstage she was such a great actress that he thought he had succeeded.

Along with his constant encouragement, Slocum often told Tex how much he adored her. She later told Stein that she found all this "very nice," but never really let it go farther than that. "I used to want him to say he loved me—and I'm sure I loved him, but I could never bring myself to say it in that many words. He was a thoughtful darling and gave me the chance of helping my darling mother and Tommy and the rest."[22]

It is striking how often Tex connected her lovers to the welfare of her family, assigning them tasks that normally would be left to a father. It is not surprising then that Slocum often acted the father. He coached Tex, babied her, told her what to do. Tex, in turn, respected what Slocum said and did as he told her. She knew if she followed his instructions she would end up on Broadway.

Thanks to Slocum, Tex finally saw her name up in those big, bright lights of Broadway. ("Was I thrilled? Why, every night before I went into the theatre I would walk up and down the street, gazing almost unbelievingly at that sign with my name spelled out with mazda bulbs.")[23] *The Gay Musician* opened with a tour in Canada starting in Guelph, Ontario, on September 7, 1909. Tex continued to tour the West gathering good reviews until she hit Los Angeles. On November 24, the *Los Angeles Times* reported, "Miss Texas Guinan is in the budding prima donna stage. Her whimsical little egotisms are calling loudly for a strong stage manager to put an end to them. A pretty and vivacious girl, she loves the spotlight too much. She would make better use of her voice if she did not try for so many effects. And finally, she would appear to be more in the play if she would address herself more to the people of the stage and less to the front."

Tex never forgot this review, though she attributed it to her next show, *The Kissing Girl*. She also altered the contents. In her memoirs, she wrote that the drama critic, a Mr. Julian Johnson, had stated that although Miss Guinan was a clever girl, she played to the actors instead of the audience. Tex sent him the following letter:

"Dear Mr. Johnson: I have been getting away with this for years but you would come along and spill the beans and tell my dear public I was fooling them."[24]

The insulted prima donna then informed Slocum that she would not continue playing in the show unless she received an apology from Mr. Johnson. Slocum went to Mr. Johnson to complain on her behalf and was told that although Texas was a clever actress, he would not take back his criticisms. She needed to learn a lesson.

Months later, Tex took a vacation in Los Angeles. At a luncheon, she sat next to a man who turned out to be very charming. Tex was feeling lonely without Slocum by her side telling her how wonderful she was. She was feeling dangerously single. She liked the handsome, solid-looking man by her side and wondered what he had said his name was. Soon the two were such buddies that she found herself telling him the Julian Johnson story.

"I was still sore about it and I told my visitor that if Johnson ever happened to meet me he would be in hard luck. That got another laugh and my young man invited me to dinner.

"Facing me over a table that night my host nearly knocked me out of my chair by telling me he was Julian Johnson.

"It was his turn then to do some kidding."[25]

To complete the fairy-tale nature of this encounter, Tex fell for her critic.

Tex finished out the season with *The Gay Musician* and began touring with *The Kissing Girl* in October 1910. *The Kissing Girl*, like the majority of Tex's vehicles, had a typical musical-comedy plot, which is to say, several plots that twisted and confused. One reviewer attempted to describe it, with little success: "The play is about—well, now let's see—what is it about? . . . Let me see—somebody married quite a nice-looking young person and then a German comedian sang a French boulevard song, and there were electric lights inside the beer steins, and—oh! I give up. Let's forget the plot and let matters proceed with the statement that the show numbers a lot of pretty girls, that most everybody sings well, the costuming is lavish and the settings most splendid."[26] A later description added that Lina (Tex), had gained the title of "kissing girl" because she was to give the winner of an important archery contest the grand prize of a kiss. "The star part," said another review, "that of a young lady who smacks rather promiscuously is played by little Texas Guinan. She dances a little, sings better, and in a sort of happy-go-lucky way injects so much natural good nature into the performance that you are glad when she is on stage and sorry when she is not."[27]

This time, the *Los Angeles Times* wrote of Tex, "Miss Guinan, who made a big hit here last year in the Gay Musician, returns as a star of the first magnitude." Did Tex take Johnson's advice from the previous year's column? Were they already an item? After she finished the season with *The Kissing Girl*, she told Slocum she was "mad about that Julian Johnson." Slocum tried to calm her down. "Are you still worrying about that?" Tex said no, she wasn't mad *at*, but mad *about*—she was in love.[28] When *The Kissing Girl* reached New York, Slocum closed the show and he and Tex parted ways.

Following her heart back across the states, Tex landed on Johnson's doorstep—3103 North Griffin Avenue, Los Angeles. Though he was still working for the *Times*, Johnson had by this time joined the Oliver Morosco Theatrical Enterprises as special press representative and was able to get Tex a job with one of Morosco's stock companies.

Working in stock was less than amusing because Tex was no longer the pampered star. She lived in a rooming house and frequently could not pay the rent. Still, Mr. Johnson was exceptionally romantic. He made Tex feel like a star whenever they were together.

Johnson, like Moy, was a solid, levelheaded, conservative man, someone who could always be counted on. He was a heavyset five-foot-seven and often wore the appropriate serious expression to support this image of security. Like Moy, he was also a newspaperman, and in part responsible for Tex's introduction to the many journalists who later helped establish her name across the country.

Born in Chicago, one year after Tex came into the world, Johnson had earned the title of dramatic critic for the *Los Angeles Times* by the age of twenty-five (1907). When Tex arrived on the West Coast, Johnson had just been invited to join the editorial staff. In a letter to producer Lee Shubert, one of the famous Shubert brothers, Oliver Morosco described Johnson: "He is about the 'livest' guy on the Pacific Coast and [he] runs the biggest and best dramatic page outside of New York. . . . I really believe he is the most valuable single influence to us on the Pacific Coast; he is up to date and desires to grab and exploit every new idea . . ."[29] Later, in a letter to Lee in July 1913, Johnson described himself as plainspoken. Indeed, he comes across in his letters as someone who isn't afraid to say what he thinks, though he is sometimes a bit long-winded. Yet on the subject of Tex, he could be whimsical.

"Hilarious as a Hurricane
Variable as a weather Vane
Bounteously beautiful
Generously good
Erratic as a Chaste Nymph in the wood,
Is Texas.
She goeth where she listeth like the wind."[30]

Johnson loved his pet "Bird" the way she was. He loved her extravagance and frivolity, loved her hurricane nature and flamboyance. He loved her plumpness and big heart. He watched her move with the flashy people he had introduced her to and watched her acquire an addiction to beautiful glittering things like diamonds and furs. In a letter to her father, he wrote, "The Bird has ermine even though she is wanting of a bath towel."[31]

While Julian called her "the Bird," Tex affectionately called him "Bird Seed." She knew, as she reflected in her memoirs, that she had been a demanding young wench in those days. "I can't understand why the old darling put up with me. He should have slapped a hand over my mouth instead of a mortgage over his property."[32]

Julian Johnson. JJ. Tex's involvement with him was the great romance that all heroines were supposed to experience at least once in their story. Tex's relationship with Moynahan was more like a practical arrangement, in the way we hear of it. Her affair with JJ would last more than eight years, long enough for him to make a deep impression on Tex's lifestyle. He introduced her to good-quality literature as well as to all the "fast set" on the West Coast. He was responsible for what Stein termed an era of "good taste" in Tex's life.

Julian enjoyed being Tex's educator. He taught her to appreciate art, poetry, and especially opera, one of his passions. When Tex went on a tour and left JJ behind, she often read a book a day, mostly biographies, classics, and once in a rare while, a modern popular novel. Somewhere inside of her there was a thirst for learning, and yet when asked why she read so avidly, she answered, "because Julian told me so."[33]

And somehow, because Julian told her so, she shook off the scatterbrained approach to money and fans and began to answer her mail, keep a budget, buckle down. Later she would thank the man who had helped her create at least a semblance of business know-how, and her memoirs noted, "Julian Johnson was my idea of a real good scout, a regular guy."[34]

In the *Evening Journal* version of her life, Tex reduced her longest relationship to "Marriage Number Two." Portraying JJ only as a "nice man," she told the public very little about him. They never married, commuted frequently from coast to coast to see each other, and maintained separate residences during the years of their affair. As Tex was a Catholic, divorce was a heavy consideration for her.

In the fall of 1912, Tex returned to New York to join the Shuberts at the Winter Garden in *The Passing Show of 1912*, their version of the Ziegfield Follies. It was an extravaganza of numbers by fabulously costumed, long-legged, beautiful women interspersed with comedy, musical, and acrobatic dance acts. To be a star of such a show was an indication of how far Tex had moved in the musical theater world.

There was a problem prior to the show, however. As Tex told it, before she joined the Shuberts, she took a trip to England with her mother. While there, good eating led to a huge weight gain. When Tex showed up at the theater after the trip—if indeed she had actually gone to England—the brothers Shubert were horrified. She was *fat*. Tex then proceeded to go on one of her soon-to-be-famous crash diets, and rumors had it she lost as much as seventy pounds in two months. She dutifully informed the public of her amazing weight loss and told them she had gotten the formula from the famous stage star Lillian Russell.[35]

Lillian Russell and daughter Dorothy had befriended Tex early in her career and often met her for tea at all the ladies' luncheon hotspots in New York City—places like Sherry's, the Waldorf, and the hangout of the stars, Rector's. Russell encouraged the friendship between Tex and Dorothy and played mother to them both. She was another woman, like Nora Bayes, who had a strong influence on Tex and her tastes. Known as America's greatest beauty at the turn of the century, the burnished-blonde actress was fond of good eating, quite the fashion in the early 1900s, and she taught Tex that plump could be beautiful. Tex however, took her lessons too far and approached "fat" more often than she would have liked. Ever since she had left her rye-bread-and-milk days behind her, Tex had become a fan of good food wherever she went. To her, a fine meal meant success.

Russell began cultivating Tex at a time when the young actress began desiring jewelry and furs. This was long before Tex had the money for them. So she had taken to wearing fake jewelry. In a conversation that Tex never forgot, Russell told her to stop wearing all the paste (fake jewelry). "But I can't afford real diamonds," sighed Tex. Russell replied, "Ah, but some day you will. Until then, my dear, wear nothing."[36]

Tex really began her jewelry mania when she joined *The Passing Show*, for she could finally afford some of the real stuff with her new salary, even if that meant only tie tacks and cufflinks that she couldn't wear. Drawn to glitter, Tex began to collect anything that contained a jewel. This attraction remained with her throughout her life, and later she would not be seen without numerous diamond bracelets, rings, pendants, and earrings. The only "fakes" she wore were the rhinestones on her shoes. Jewels, like good food, came to symbolize success for her.

As *The Passing Show* toured the Midwest and Canada, Tex generated much publicity. In late December 1912, telling amazed reporters and readers of the *New York Review* that "there is more individuality in the thumbprint than in the mere writing of one's name," she initiated the custom of bestowing a thumbprint instead of a signature as an autograph. To do that, she carried a small pad of purple ink wherever she went.

In late June 1913, Tex passed through her old home town, Denver. There she lectured the public on the virtues of horseback riding.

"There is no exercise in this whole world so exhilarating as horseback riding. I was fairly reared on horseback for I came from Texas and spent much time on a ranch. It is great to feel a horse bounding under you, especially out on the great open prairies . . . it is to this early training on horseback that I ascribe my robust health . . . The exercise is good, at any rate, and I would advise all actresses to take it up."[37]

While still in Denver, Tex and some of the other cast members and theater friends went to visit a Mr. W. W. Kirkwood at his Doremus Ranch outside of town. During their visit, Kirkwood showed them his black horse, Satan, a horse nobody could ride. Daredevil Tex, of course, wanted to try him, but Kirkwood refused. Later when Kirkwood went to drive his guests back to the city for their evening performances, his car wouldn't start. How was the prima donna going to get to town in time? She crept off to the stalls, saddled the unrideable Satan and set off. She later repeated a similar stunt in a film called *The Stampede*.

Later when the tour reached Canada, Tex scandalized all of Winnipeg by riding a horse astride instead of sidesaddle, as the Queen of England had decreed. Announcing the story, the headline in the *Detroit Journal* read: "Ride Astride, Says Texas Guinan, If You Would Be Safe And Sane."[38]

Although Tex seemed to have enough energy to star in a show and do these publicity stunts on the side, she was wearing herself out.

In July 1913, Johnson wrote Lee Shubert requesting that Tex be relieved from the show and given a chance to rest. "Her singing and speaking voice have for months been at least 60% below par," he wrote, "not by overwork, but because of too continuous work." He went on to declare that "the girl really can sing Mr. Shubert; she has one of the most beautiful lyric soprano voices I have heard in my life. But probably you do not know this . . . no one does who has heard her voice lately. I want her to improve her enunciation in dialogue . . . to get the *velvet* back into her singing voice and the tremolo *out* of it."[39]

Tex had herself requested to be released, but it wasn't until Julian had received a telegram from her doctor warning that she needed to rest, that continuous strain would be fatal to her voice, that he understood how serious her condition was. He felt in part responsible for her situation, having already noticed her pattern of working to the point of exhaustion. So he wrote to Lee Shubert, "What Miss Guinan should have done last fall, had she been financially able to do so, or had I at that time been able to help her, was to take a long rest and study; but she was not able, I was not, and it was a wonderful thing for her to receive, at your hands, Shirley Kellog's role in the '12 show."[40]

The Shuberts would not release her. JJ offered to finance the search for a substitute. Then, a week after his first letter, Tex's maid sent him a note saying Tex had collapsed twice at home and requested he send a prescription for strychnia stimulant. She claimed an old heart complaint (valvular enlargement) had made an appearance.

On August 3, Tex sent JJ a telegram—"VERY SICK HAD DOCTOR FOUR TIMES TODAY I AM IN BED DOCTOR REFUSES TO LET ME LEAVE CANT PLAY SHOW AT ALL THIS WEEK PLAYED SHOW TONIGHT WITH FEVER 102½ THIS WILL PROVE I AM SICK MY GOD I MISS YOU GIVE MY LIFE TO BE HOME. BABY."[41]

Eventually, the Shuberts let her off.

In his letter, JJ refers to previous episodes of collapse from overwork. Tex worked hard for her applause and did not seem to know her own limits. In the years to follow, Tex would continue to walk a tightrope between exuberance and exhaustion. She never really understood about balance. Part of this was her belief about what it took to get her show across, that getting a show across was all that mattered. In an interview a few years later, during her tour with the show, *Whirl of the World,* she was asked by a reporter how she got through the night. She replied, "I first work up a case of nervous autointoxication. . . . I have a hard job in front of me, and I have got to work myself up to it as a soldier works himself up to a desperate charge, a forlorn hope."[42]

By now Tex had already passed her twenty-ninth birthday and sixth year on the road as an actress. She was well known and well liked, but she felt that she still wasn't making enough money to have everything she wanted. She wondered if she couldn't try and make a little money on the side. While recuperating in Los Angeles, she had the opportunity.

Tex was introduced by some friends to a man named Walter Cunningham, who had read about her amazing weight loss in the *Los Angeles Examiner* earlier that year. Cunningham was at that time conducting a business selling the Marjorie Hamilton Obesity Cure. He had been hoping to meet Tex because he thought he could make a tidy profit from Lillian Russell's formula if the two went into business together and sold the formula as an antifat remedy under Texas's well-known name. Cunningham purchased the formula from her—fifty cents worth of alcohol, ten cents worth of alum, and ten cents worth of iodine— and the use of Texas's name for five hundred dollars down and fifty dollars a week. The incorporation of Texas Guinan, Inc., followed, and ads began appearing in such magazines as *Variety*, illustrated by photos of "God's masterpiece and the most fascinating actress in America"—Tex.

These ads were written in the first person and were calculated to lead the reader to believe that Tex herself was conducting the business and giving each client her personal attention. The reader was offered a free book that Tex had supposedly written, *Rapid Weight Reduction Without Exercise, Diet or Internal Remedies.* "This book has just come off the press," said the ad/Tex, "and is offered free to fat-burdened men and women, as I learned early in life that the only way to know happiness is to give it to others and if by letting the world know of this harmless quick method of reducing weight I can do a great good, then I will feel I have not lived in vain."[43]

After the ads came out, all types of rumors began circulating: Tex had sold the remedy for $50,000 and was planning to retire from the stage! Tex was sailing off to Paris to spend her $50,000! Though she hadn't yet seen a cent from Cunningham, more and more women began buying the weight-reduction remedy, for anything from three to twenty dollars a bottle. Then some started noticing that not only had they failed to lose any weight with the formula, but they had developed rashes and all sorts of other skin irritations as well.

Texas Guinan — Quack, Actress, or Saleswoman?

> Q. On page 11 of the pamphlet alleged to have been written by you, appears this statement: "Then out of chaos came an inspiration. For it was an inspiration. I cannot lay claim to scientific knowledge. I cannot say that I studied books of medicine. I cannot lay claim to superior education in medical science. I just had an inspiration, and womanlike I followed my intuition." Is the treatment which you followed the result of an inspiration?
> A. No. I will tell you how it is. A doctor told me that iodine would cut fat. Then I knew that alum would shrink your flesh. So I thought how to get the stuff on. Then I put in alcohol.
> —TEXAS GUINAN, AFFIDAVIT, U.S. POST OFFICE, JANUARY 14, 1914

At some point Cunningham had changed the formula.

Tex had been too busy running across the country with *The Passing Show* to keep her eye on her "partner." She had been so flattered by his offer to name the entire company and product after her, to advertise her as "God's masterpiece," that she hadn't thought not to trust him. Women everywhere watched Tex, modeled themselves after her. If she recommended the weight-reducing product, her fans would try it. And Tex loved the attention—wasn't that a successful actress's due?

In the years preceding the Cunningham deal, the public had been notoriously hungry for nostrums. Most were harmless mixtures sold by clever quacks adept at claiming to provide an antidote for whatever the current ill might be, and sometimes making a terrific profit from the sales as well. Before Walter Cunningham's involvement with Tex, he had been known as a beauty specialist, a bust developer, a wrinkle eradicator, and most recently the "hero" of a well-publicized "calendar girl" divorce suit. In the past, he had been able to escape the notice of the authorities by repeatedly transferring his offices to a new state and starting his deceptions under another name. This time, however, the American Medical Association had their eye on him, as did the U.S. Post Office.

In September 1913, the AMA began to investigate Texas Guinan, Inc., by sending away for the free booklet that had been advertised. The investigator, a thin, bald-headed man of forty, soon received a volley of letters inviting, rather pleading, with him to buy the formula. The letters were very personal and as the account published on December 17 in the *Chicago Tribune* described them, "These are not mere communications; they are literature."

The letters, written in Tex's voice, were littered with superlatives, promises of regaining the "new and bewildering grace of youth," of Texas's "mad impatience for every fat human being in the universe to get the wonderful benefits of it right away." They were designed to be intimate and persuasive—behind the confidential *you and me*'s, the careful reader might hear the chant of "buy, buy, buy." The company sent five of these missives, offering increasingly better deals, coupons, and finally a bottle for the reduced price of three dollars. The AMA sent for a sample, analyzed its contents, and printed a detailed laboratory report. Comparing the ingredients of other bottles from the same company, they found that each mixture varied. They also found that the contents had no apparent weight-reducing properties.

Then a sixth letter arrived. "Tex" was wondering why her new customer had not ordered a second supply. What would happen if "she" should run out? Tex was worried. "You are now as one who has climbed three-fourths of the way up the Pinnacle of Happiness—do not falter in your steps, do not hesitate, do not lag, do not doubt or fear. . . . The Golden Goal, The Sweet Reward Is In Sight; It Is All Up To You! It Is For You, And You Alone, To Choose! Success Or Failure? Which, My Dear? Yours with Affectionate Anxiety, Texas Guinan."[1] Alas, for this affectionate "Tex"! The AMA had already decided to expose Texas Guinan, Inc., as a fraud and print its findings in its *Journal*.

Tex opened Thanksgiving Eve at the Manhattan Opera House in *Hop O' My Thumb*, a British import, direct from the Drury Lane Theatre in London. The all-star cast included the comedian De Wolf Hopper, known best for his rendition of "Casey at the Bat," and the

British Iris Hawkins. Tex played Zaza the Queen in this "curious hodgepodge of fairy tale, pantomime, ballet, New York jokes—political and otherwise—with here and there a little vaudeville."[2] She had one big number, "For a Girl Has a Living To Make," and *Variety* didn't think much of it. In fact, *Variety* suggested that the song would not be missed if entirely excluded from the show. Yet the rest of the papers in town remarked that Tex had "scored heavily," especially after having "rendered most cleverly a song called "For a Girl Has a Living To Make."[3] The ancient law in theater seemed to read, For every critic's point of view, there is an equal and opposite point of view.

The influence of critics on the theatrical public had only just begun to grow during the years when Tex was rising to stardom. *Variety*, chiefly interested in vaudeville and burlesque during those years, was quite powerful, and managers studied it religiously before hiring a new act. Other papers were not as reliable and were known to favor a show only if the company had previously bought an ad in their publication or if the critics had been bribed beforehand. Even if the criticisms were not always to be trusted, the descriptions of the plots, scenery, and costumes were generally accurate. Tex said personally she didn't care what they said about her, as long as they said something.

While Tex was entertaining audiences as Zaza, reports of the Cunningham scandal began hitting the papers. Though journalists put the blame on Cunningham rather than Tex, (she's the "fat lady" of the combination), she was forced to retire from public view, and that was painful. However, she needed to clear the adjective *quack* from her name.

Tex had so loved the idea of seeing her picture in all those advertisements. When the pamphlet was first printed, she had sent it to JJ for approval, and he had advised that although some of the statements contained in the pamphlet were "very nice," she ought to request that Cunningham omit the "rubbish" and the use of the first person.[4] Unfortunately, Cunningham had not complied. JJ was smart enough to have her release a statement to the Post Office, and presumably that would keep her out of trouble, but the news was still in the paper, and her name was linked with scandal.

Tex, however, was already adept at turning pain to profit. She took the disgrace and turned it to her advantage as advance press work for her next theatrical adventure and garnered some audience sympathy while she was at it. Poor Tex, persecuted by the U.S. Post Office (later echoed by "Poor Tex, hounded by the U.S. federal agents"). She'd never admit it, but the title of "quack" was quite appropriate. Vaudeville had trained her to sell anything, everything, especially herself.

In January 1914, the Post Office concluded its investigations with the declaration that Tex had been part of a "scheme for obtaining money through the mails by means of false and fraudulent pretenses, representations and promises."[5] In spite of her testimony and turning in evidence on Cunningham, the Post Office stopped sending her her mail.

While JJ fought the Post Office for her, he also began directing her in a new vaudeville skit entitled *A Musical Mix-up*.

Eventually, the great weight-loss scandal came to an end. In her memoirs, Tex told a revised account of the story without embarrassment for having been so easily duped, shifting the dates from 1913 to the middle of World War I in order to explain why she hadn't kept a better eye on Cunningham—she'd been overseas. She also used it as an opportunity to poke fun at her earliest tangles with the federal authorities and to refer to her later involvement with dry agents. In twenties lingo, the scandal became just another racket.

> That chemical business gave the Federal Government its first shot at me. All it took was the World War to give me the works. It was in 1916 that I took another trip to Europe with an entertainment mob to sing for the soldiers.
>
> The price of alcohol had been boosted and Cunningham had broken out with the idea of using less alcohol and more alum to keep up our profits. As a result of his helpful idea there was an epidemic of itching among the fat people who were using our reducer. The alum did it.
>
> Well there was a federal investigation. That scared me in those days. Cunningham took the air and when I came back I was introduced to a federal jury and an $80,000 bundle of debts. I proved I had no part in giving all those people the itch, but I had to kick in and settle all the damage suits.
>
> I never saw so many summonses. Every time I ran down the aisle of a theater and kissed a bald-headed man he would stick a summons down the back of my gown. . . . Anyway they cured me of playing with the anti-fat racket.[6]

Neither the scandal nor the war kept Tex from continuing to play the musical-comedy circuit. The medium suited her, and audiences liked her. However, as with all other theatrical entertainers of her day, her popularity depended on the ficklest of fans and threatened to evaporate at the appearance of the next theatrical fad. Tex knew she was not the great operatic star she had set out to be, nor was she a great dramatic actress. However, she knew how to entertain, how to make people laugh. Her critics declared her a good singer and clever actress and noted her enthusiasm and willingness to work hard for her audience's enjoyment. When painter Paul de Langpre, known best for his flower paintings, proclaimed that Tex was the only prima donna with orchid-colored eyes, reporters began raving about the lady with "orchidaceous eyes."[7]

Tex never missed a season. She starred in *The Little Cafe*, Sigmund Romberg's *Whirl of the World*, Romberg's *Maid in America*, and *The Masked Model*. She also costarred in *Honk, Honk Maybe* with the famous vaudevillian William Gibson and even supposedly took a vacation in Europe. She rode horseback when she could, courted her fans, and created new fads. In the *Whirl of the World*, she excited audiences as she ran down a runway through the audience and kissed bald men on their heads. Some found the feature titillating, others merely a burlesque feature grafted upon a "so-called first class show."[8] Tex's own version credited her with the invention of the whole runway routine. One night her audience had not been interested in her song, so she leaped over the footlights to make them listen.

Even as Tex maintained her popularity and roved from role to role, other aspects of her Broadway were changing. When she had first come to New York, New Yorkers liked to relax with an evening of good eating and soft music. They liked large, late dinners after the theater—a bottle or three of wine, a tray of oysters, and other luxuries. They had just begun to enjoy the concept of having a public life, of taking such private pleasures as dining into the large ornate restaurants like Maxim's or Reisenweber's, which had opened their doors at the turn of the century. These were the lobster palaces—named that for their grand decor and the post-theater seafood suppers. But the era of the lobster palaces was coming to an end. Soon even Rector's, where people thronged before and after the theater to catch glimpses of celebrities, would become outdated. No longer was a serene evening of fine food and violins enough. Now New Yorkers were eager for syncopation and dancing—ragtime.

In 1911, a musical upstart named Irving Berlin had written a song called "Alexander's Ragtime Band" and introduced a new kind of beat to the Broadway musical vocabulary. That beat was just an echo of the whole changing rhythm of life in general, of progress. Berlin attributed what he called the speed and snap of jazz to the popularization of the automobile.

The new music, with its easy, danceable beat, invited a dance craze along for the ragtime ride. The craze necessitated larger dance floors, and as the lobster palaces made room for dancers, their purpose and clientele began to change. Every week a new step came out, and everybody wanted to do it. New hairstyles accompanied the swell of dances, along with freer, looser clothing and freer, looser morals. Everything began rushing toward the great shriek of the twenties.

World War I had begun in Europe in 1914. And still, Tex's life continued to be dictated by a heavy road schedule. She changed roles as often as Americans changed their opinions about the war in Europe—from neutrality to anti-German sentiment, from going so far as to reelect President Wilson because "he kept us out of war" to booing his peace policies.

On April 6, 1917, the United States entered the war. Everybody was touched by it, from the young boys who joined the service to the women who left their housework to roll bandages for the Red Cross or to sell Liberty Bonds. If they hadn't been enthusiastic before, people were wooed into patriotism by the entertainment industry, which had been adopted by the government as its wartime right arm.

Tex could not have avoided being part of the entertainment world's war effort. Box-office profits rose after the United States entered the war, only to fall drastically by the second half of 1917, when money saved for theater tickets went into Liberty Bonds. The young men who habitually haunted the theaters were off in the war plants working overtime or at the army bases learning how to fight. By December, the government ordered a blackout and curfew on Broadway.

Though the war had severely crippled the box office, entertainers performed in benefits, raised funds, and spread prowar sentiment nationwide. They sang "Over There," "I'm in the Army Now," "Oh How I Hate To Get Up In The Morning," and "Beautiful K-K-Katy." They told jokes about the army and the girls in France and sang about their mothers and the "U.S. of A." They ended all finales with flag-waving and moving speeches designed to bring patriotic tears to audience eyes.

Tex played her share of benefits, partly because she saw herself as the antidote to despair and saw it as her business to cheer up Americans, and partly because she knew that any act having to do with war would be well attended. Her desire to remain in the spotlight even took her into Red Cross work and though no documentation exists, it is assumed she took her place among the rest of her compatriots who played the army-base circuit.

Later, in her memoirs, Tex would take her patriotism onto the battlefields of Europe and even claim she'd been awarded a medal from the great French General Joffre at the famous battle of Verdun in November 1916. She was at that time peacefully entertaining American audiences in *Honk, Honk Maybe,* and neither the United States nor the French have any record of the medal. In fact, no evidence remains supporting Tex's many stories about her work overseas. This is frustrating because one could easily picture Tex entertaining the tired and hungry troops in French camps and hospitals as well as the German prisoners in jail, as she claimed. It was her style to be involved in any activity aimed at cheering up others. More difficult to imagine, though, is Tex astride a horse at the head of the 145th Infantry for six months—which she said she did—or cooking for whole platoons of troops and driving an ambulance.

The hunt to uncover Tex's war career was as fruitless as the search to prove she had meandered down the Brazos River in a wooden tub as a child. Letters to the French Service Historique, the Ministère de la Défense and the Bureau Central d'Archives Administratives Militaires returned with polite answers of, "never heard of her," "what medal?" Neither the National Archives nor the military personnel records had anything on her or her brothers—who she said had also joined the armed forces.

With her love of publicity, Tex would not have served her country and not acquired good press from it—but not a word exists from that era, not a photo. At the National Archives such wartime performers as Elsie Janis, well known for her camp tours, have files of publicity shots, and Tex even claimed to have gone over with Janis and her mother, but again—not a word exists.

Why did she insist on it? Throughout her life, she would refer to it: "I have often wondered why I can control a crowd so well. When I was in France I could control the emotions of a whole regiment. I would have them swaying to the 'dark laughter' of a Mammy song one minute, and listening intently or sometimes with tears in their eyes to Joyce Kilmer's 'Trees' the next moment."[9] On the stand in court, in answer to the question, "Did you do war service?" she replied, "Yes, for two years, as an entertainer at Bordeaux, Tours and Chateau Thierry. I went over for myself, solely. I was not an entertainer for any particular organization."[10]

During the years of the war, there were short gaps in Tex's road schedule that are unaccounted for. It is possible she made a quick trip over during that time, though more likely that she used that time to entertain at home. In 1933, the *Chicago Illinois Examiner* noted that veterans of the war were planning to honor Tex. "It seems

Quack, Actress, or Saleswoman?

that Tex was one of the most highly appreciated of the many celebrities of the show world who went overseas to help the boys keep up the morale, and the event tomorrow is just to let Tex know the boys haven't forgotten."[11]

The image of "Little Texas Nightingale" suited Tex, and she adopted it. Thus Tex exploited the war as she had exploited any other newsworthy event. Yet she would later declare, in her syndicated column of January 5, 1931, that she was against war.

"It is unnecessary, it is costly, and in the end, nobody knows what he has been fighting for. It seldom, if ever, kills off the right people.

"The history of war is brief as to its origins and consequences: daft, draft, graft. . . .

"Too much of war's patriotism and flourish is left to the men who are still bragging about their war records. A good many 'suckers' just went down town and bought 'Over There' for the phonograph.

"Will someone please shut that record off?"

On the home front, the thirty-one-year-old Tex became more artistically diversified and published a poem in Julian's magazine, *Photoplay*. (By this time, JJ had moved to Chicago where the film magazine had its offices.) The poem, entitled "The Modern Cinderella," marked "the cyclonic Winter Garden star's initial effort in rhyme." It discussed the fate of three sisters, Cinderella, Arabella, and Prunella, who had "made a vow upon the screen to go." The two beautiful sisters scored star roles but soon found that the work spoiled their looks and was hazardous to their health. Cinderella took their place, having no beauty to lose and undisturbed by the dangers of the stunts. In the end, she won the heart of the famous movie prince.

> Her sisters now as ushers are employed.
> The family lives in Lens, and some time since
> She had a son, and called him Cellu Lloyd.[12]

It was no accident that Tex had turned her attention to the film industry. She was well aware that the movie business was becoming more lucrative and more popular than any other branch of show business. She'd heard that an actor not only didn't have to go on the road, but the hours were better. Just do what the director said, and she could take the day off and sit with her feet up under an orange tree. Or visit with her friends. Or have a wild old time in Hollywood, driving fast cars.

In 1917, some time after President Wilson declared the United States was joining the war, Tex was "discovered" by Triangle Studios. In her memoirs, she was singing "Ragtime Cowboy Joe" and playing the cowgirl in Shubert's *World of Pleasure* at the Winter Garden. H. O. Davis, manager of the corporation, was impressed by her lassoing ability, and thought her a genuine western character, especially with that name Texas. After watching her in action, he decided to hire her as a female William S. Hart, Triangle's leading male western star. Tex's first role with Triangle, however, turned out to have nothing to do with the Wild West.

In 1915, the studios of Mack Sennett (comedy), D. W. Griffith (melodrama), and Thomas H. Ince (westerns), had joined forces to form what promised to become a formidable Hollywood triumvirate—Triangle Studios. The money behind the corporation came from Harry and Roy Aitken of Waukesha, Wisconsin. These men believed in spending lots of dollars in order to make the films they dreamed of selling. Stars who had shone brightest during the early days included Gloria Swanson, Douglas Fairbanks, Mabel Normand, Fatty Arbuckle, William S. Hart, and Charlie Chaplin. Unfortunately by the time Tex joined their ranks, the Aitken brothers had involved themselves in some questionable financial deals, and the future of the corporation looked uncertain.

In desperation, in 1917, the Aitken Brothers hired H. O. Davis, known by those in the profession as "Dr." Davis. He began to produce low-budget pictures and sold them at good profits. He hired established stars from vaudeville like Tex in order to improve the quality of the productions and attract their fans. The company's monthly magazine's advice for advertising one of Tex's films said bluntly, "It will pay you to play up Texas Guinan's appearance in this picture, as she has a host of Winter Garden friends all over the country."[13] Davis billed Tex as a newcomer "whose record for brilliant and versatile characterization is said to be enviable."[14] Among the other new stars heading the casts for Davis's pictures were Olive Thomas, Alma Rubens, Roy Stewart, and William Desmond Taylor. In addition, Davis hired Julian Johnson as editor-in-chief and made him responsible for all the final products, a quality-control advisor. (JJ arrived on the set on September 22, after Tex had completed her first picture. One wonders if he was discovered with her help, or she with his.) Hand in hand, Davis and Johnson worked to upgrade the quality of the Triangle features.

By the end of September, New Yorkers read about Texas as she talked her way out of her fourth speeding ticket in Los Angeles. She was completing the shooting of her first major film—she'd played a bit part in *The Stainless Barrier* and did not even appear in the cast list—and was living up to the Hollywood star tradition of fast cars and late nights, regardless of having to be on the set early every morning. That film was *The Fuel of Life,* directed by Walter Edwards, a former character actor from the legitimate stage and one of Ince's directors. Tex played the adventuress/vampire Violet Hilton, who tampered with the affections of Angela De Haven's husband and inadvertently converted the innocent wife to her decadent way of life. For Angela De Haven (Belle Bennett) had known only the good in the world. "She had been the wife of a Wall Street broker, sheltered and protected from all the sordid side of life. She had her motors, her beautiful home, a large circle of friends and a loving and devoted husband."[15] When she discovered her husband had been unfaithful, she started out on "a wild career of homewrecking and heartbreaking, determined to make all men pay for one weak man's infatuation."[16]

Triangle Studios thought the film would attract and intrigue large audiences because the story introduced what they called an "unusual" method of handling divorce. "Angela De Haven found her husband was untrue to her!" exclaimed the advertising. "Did she rush to the divorce court and air her troubles? She did not. What she did do may prove interesting to YOU. At the Liberty Theatre tonight."[17]

If audiences were intrigued by the idea, critics were not. Perhaps the first of H. O. Davis's cutback productions, *The Fuel of Life* came out to mixed reviews. *Variety* said on November 16, 1917, "Whether the fault lies with the story, scenario, or direction, this Triangle is under standard."

"Texas Guinan as the vampire overacts considerably and can't quite shed her musical comedy mannerisms," said one reviewer for *Motion Picture News* on November 24. Indeed, Tex, used to being heard, found herself exaggerating her actions as if her body could speak for her silence. Other reviewers said Tex more than justified her selection for one of the most important supporting roles in the film.[18]

Tex had made an uncertain entrance into the film business. Davis had cast her as the adventuress, but she wanted to get out on a horse. Then supposedly someone made a mistake and cast her for the star role in a western film. People began to remember her first name.

Never Jilt a Woman Who Can Shoot

> *Miss Guinan can handle a gun, roll a cigarette and boss a mob of cowboys all at one fell swoop. To me, the idea of a woman as a western character, no less brave or daring than a man and at the same time portraying her womanly side is indeed a welcome addition to the motion picture art.*
> —WILLIAM SHERILL, MOVING PICTURE WORLD, FEBRUARY 1, 1919

*T*ex played a woman "loved, hated, feared, and from her ways, well-named 'the Tigress.'"[1] Then she went and fell in love with the Gent, a no-good stick-up man with a smooth and handsome exterior. Staking him with her own, hard-earned money, she sent him off to make a "decent" home for her in a "decent" land. Soon she discovered that he had used her savings to set up a gambling hell in a nearby mining camp and had never intended to marry her as he had promised. Instead of shooting him on the spot, she gave him thirty days in which to "make good." Then she went and collected—in full.[2]

Life had become exciting for Tex the silent-film star. Monthly, sometimes weekly, she had a new name and a new challenge. She had instant romance and adventure, could ride a horse and brush up on her gunwork. All this because Triangle Studios had cast her as the Tigress in *The Gun Woman*, directed by the soon-to-be-famous Frank Borzage.

As the Tigress, Tex began to build her reputation as the female counterpart of western star William S. Hart, playing a rough and tough cowgirl not unlike the Tomboy Tex she later created in her memoirs. Tex was one of the first women to enter what had previously been male territory, and throughout the next five years, 1918–1922, she would create a new role for women in film— that of the heroine who was self-reliant in every crisis and could handle a six-shooter like a man. No longer would women be decorative and unable to act. In *The Gun Woman*, Tex was a tough lady who killed the man she loved because he betrayed her. She had feelings like a woman, but shot like a man.

The roles for women in film in those days reflected both the times and the visions of the men who directed them. For the most part, the values of the Victorian age still reigned—thus decent women were pure, passive, and destined for marriage. If not, they were "wicked"—either prostitutes or adventurous vampires out to wreck homes (like Tex in *The Fuel of Life*.) Perhaps filmmakers also felt that there wasn't a market for any other female character, especially a strong woman. They felt audiences wanted to identify with a romantic heroine, fall in love with her, idolize her, or boo a villainness.

But in the context of the Wild West, perhaps a strong character might work. Tex would be a true hero—would ride well, shoot, even rescue other women. But although she'd appear tough and self-reliant, she would still need and depend—as did the happy ending—on the love of a man.

Tex's characters fell between the cracks. They weren't exactly "good," not being pure and all that, and they weren't exactly all bad—bad women were not heroines. In *The Gun Woman*, as the Tigress, a name that implied a growling sex kitten, Tex was a bad woman with a good heart, a "good-bad woman" as she was later named by film critic Lawrence Reid.

Later, as a real-life night-club hostess, she was described as a "bad" woman, affiliated with gangsters and illegal liquor activity, while those who knew her saw her as a generous, God-fearing good soul. A good-bad woman again! The night club replaced the cowboy saloon, and the gangsters became the bad guys.

As a two-gun, good-bad woman, Tex had few competitors, perhaps because she didn't really play a woman's role but a man's. In a later film review, Reid said, "Miss Guinan IS Bill Hart."

The male exterior–female interior conflict sold well. Fans particularly loved to watch the heroine in emotional tight spots where she had to choose between killing the one she loved and casting down her deputy's badge and saying, "I'm not a deputy at all but a girl."[3] Theater owners could exploit that image with catchy phrases: "She was tough, but she was a woman."[4] They also warned, "Never jilt a woman who can shoot."[5]

One of the key elements necessary for the lucrative sale and hence survival of silent films was the "exploitation" of the films by theater owners. Owners were coached by all the trade papers in advertising technique, and for the Guinan films that began to flood the market after *The Gun Woman* took off, exhibitors were counseled to stress that Tex was doing something new. "It is seldom that an actress attempts to assume a man's role," reported *Moving Picture World,* "and it is quite a feat when one can completely hide her identity."[6] Theaters were advised to play up the western idea at the box office and in the lobby. Stunt suggestions for *The Gun Woman* included

"If there is a nearby rifle range offer a month's pass to the woman who makes the best revolver score. . . .

Dress your ticket seller in sombrero and leather jacket for the showing dates. . . .

Over the box office put a large sign, 'check your guns when you buy your tickets.'"[7]

Off the set, Tex handled her own publicity in her own inimitable fashion. She perpetuated the Wild West image with wild antics, from flying in "aeroplanes" to speeding in motorboats and flashy automobiles. She was credited with most of the "inside fun"[8] at the Culver City studios and had friends to tea in a yellow and black dressing room that was the envy of everyone at Triangle. In her spare time, Tex played golf, went to parties, collected antiques, and raised chickens in the backyard of the house she rented on Winona Boulevard. Fans knew from reading the stories in *Photoplay* magazine that she had any number of curious hobbies. "Among these," reported Johnstone Craig, "are lemons, other antiques, swimming, riding, more antiques, the color red, flowers, antiques, anything Galsworthy writes, house parties, motoring, gowns and hats—of which she has at least 50 trunks, Russian authors (particularly Dostoevsky) and finally, antiques."[9]

Tex had one short lapse into a nonwestern role after *The Gun Woman,* and that was in her next and last Triangle film, which was directed by E. Mason Hopper. This film, *The Love Brokers,* was originally titled *Another Foolish Virgin.* In her memoirs, Tex mentioned that she left the corporation after an argument during the filming of a picture called *The Hell Cat.* In 1918, Goldwyn, not Triangle, made a picture with that title starring the actress Geraldine Farrar.

Often, between films, Tex found it necessary to return to New York—to attend dinners in her honor, visit her family, replenish her collection of gowns, or simply recharge her batteries on Broadway. She found it difficult to stay away for long. "Give me New York every time," she told readers of the *New York Evening Journal.* "I couldn't get over my longing for Broadway." This longing earned her the sobriquet of "the world's best little railroad dividend payer."[10]

Tex was back in New York in November 1918, when President Wilson signed the armistice. There she joined the Friars and Lambs amid great celebration as over forty actors marched in a parade on behalf of the United War Work Campaign. In her memoirs, Tex transformed the event into one of the four Liberty Loan campaigns, still using the correct names as well as a few accurate details. Her version saw her astride an elephant, marching alongside one of her former costars, De Wolf Hopper, up and down Broadway and Fifth Avenue.

Tex on an elephant's back? Surely that was an invention! However, the *New York Times* of November 13 supported her story. On that day, the Friars and Lambs paved Fifth Avenue with silver in their march between Thirty-sixth and Thirty-ninth streets. Elephants from Richard's Circus bore banners for the campaign, and there were two full bands marching alongside. Among the actors who took part at the "gambol" that followed were De Wolf Hopper, Raymond Hitchcock, Ed Wynn, Al Jolson, and over forty others.

The many bond drives were not about war for the film industry, but about exposure. Finally, film actors could appear before a live audience and gauge the extent of their popularity. The movies had never commanded the same amount of respect as the legitimate theater, and stage actors were thought the more serious artists. Suddenly, it was clear that movie stars were just as popular if not more so, mainly because their films were mass-produced, widely distributed, and reached large audiences. Thus when film idols Mary Pickford and Douglas Fairbanks stood on the steps of the Forty-second Street library exhorting New Yorkers to donate money to the war efforts, hoards of film fans cheered their efforts and crowded the surrounding streets and sidewalks.

After the armistice was signed, *Variety*'s headlines (on November 22, 1918) counseled entertainers that Americans were developing a "Taste for Entertainment and Happy and Quiet Themes. Public Turning away From War Plays and Pictures. Titles on Current Strife Film Changed. Weary Nation Wants Happiness and Gaiety." No doubt Tex read the headlines over breakfast and noted them for future reference. After she had done her patriotic duty, she returned to Hollywood to the silent westerns production line and didn't step off again until 1922. Though she later claimed that she made from 200 to 312 films during her five years in Hollywood, it has only been possible to find the titles of 36, three of which were "talkies" made later in her career. The trade journals of that day usually mentioned every feature a company was planning and often included titles of pictures that never survived past the idea stage. A company might announce that they were producing 26 two-reel westerns and yet only 13 titles would emerge from their studios. Later Melody Productions cut many of Tex's two-reelers into single reels and added sound.

In February 1919, Tex joined the Frohman Amusement Corporation, a family film enterprise run by William Sherrill and his son Jack. It was Sherrill who really played up the connection between Tex and the famous Bill Hart. He announced to the public that he intended to produce full-length features starring Tex, not merely cheap two-reelers. He leased the Chaplin studios in Los Angeles and launched a strong advertising campaign. The initial ads said boldly, "Texas Guinan To Typify West."

Film critic Lawrence Reid would later say of the films: "The picture themselves carry on the feminine movement as instituted by the star. The West may have its cowboys but it may have its cowgirls too. And Miss Guinan's representation is equally successful as the trousered specie in her ability to take care of herself. There is plenty of rousing action which is dished up in the shape of fast riding and straight shooting, and the usual conflict of decency against villainy provides the dramatic pattern."[11]

In the spring of 1919, under the direction of Cliff Smith, the man who had directed Bill Hart for Ince, Tex made her first feature, entitled *South of Santa Fe*. During the film, she met and fell for her leading man George Cheseboro (often spelled "Chesboro" or "Chesbro"), beginning a flirtation which Stein said eventually cost her Julian Johnson.

Though they had never made a film together before meeting at Frohman, Cheseboro and Tex had worked at Triangle at the same time. Known as the Serial King, he had starred in many early pictures opposite such starlets as Mae Murray, Eva Novak, and Ruth Roland. Some critics described Cheseboro as a combination of leading man and juvenile, and he always played the conventional hero. Opposite Tex, he was often the sheriff/good guy.

Tex had been warned that in real life Cheseboro was no gentleman. He had a reputation as a drinker and in later films, this would be evident. He was also quite a philanderer. But Tex was a fool for love. She was so carried away with her leading man that she decorated the door of her car with the gold initials "G. C." and "T. G." Surprisingly, the affair was not exploited by the press at the time and never appeared in her memoirs.

South of Santa Fe is one of the few silent films Tex made that is still available for viewing. Featured as a physically capable character who could handle any situation as well, if not better, than her male counterparts, she appeared to handle the action scenes with more natural ability than when she had to play at romance.

The film is set at the Bar-K Ranch, "where the men of the Great Open Space Know no Law except their Own Desires and Respect No Thing Except the arm of a Stronger Man."[12] The owner of the ranch, Mrs. Wendell, is married to a good-for-nothing who spends all her hard-earned money gambling and flirting at a particularly shady establishment known as Lopez's bar. He won't help her out with their unruly cowhands, and she can't seem to find a foreman to handle them.

"You can't git a foreman south of Santa Fe that kin handle that gang!"

"I'll get one," she declares, "and make all you coyotes hunt your holes!"

One morning Mrs. Wendell gets a letter. ". . . and they tell me up in Santa Fe you need a foreman who can handle men. I can make men step around like snakes on a hot stone. Say the word and you've hired me. J. Kennedy." Shortly afterward—in the next scene—a stranger rides into "Bar K Country." "The Big Outdoors, which has Bred Such Mighty Men, has also set its Mark in Her Fearless Eyes and Iron Nerve—But Her Heart is Still the Heart of a Woman." Mrs. Wendell as well as cowhands are surprised to learn that J. Kennedy is Jessie, a woman (Tex). The rest of the film portrays how Jessie Kennedy actually gets the men to respect and obey her, and it takes frame-ups, phony bank robberies, and all sorts of intrigues to do so. It seems that the cowhands don't want to work for a "calico foreman." By the end, our heroine also conquers the sheriff. ("Only on Sundays does the Foreman take a Day Off and only after Many of these does she let Herself be a Woman.") The last scene of the film reveals Tex and George Cheseboro (the sheriff) riding off into the sunset.

In quick succession Tex is the She Wolf in a film by that name, a woman whose gun work makes it understood that she is quick at the trigger and will stand no nonsense, in "a better imitation of Bill Hart than a dozen male actors one can name."[13] She is *Some Gal*, fighting cattle rustlers on the Mexican border, then an eastern girl transplanted to the West who learns how to become *A Dangerous Little Devil*, and *Little Miss Deputy*, who has to choose between her duty as deputy and her feelings for a man she is certain is guilty.

These films were an instant success. Trade magazines noted that the surest index to the popularity of any particular class of film was to be found in the independent or states-rights fields, as theaters would only book from an independent exchange if they were certain the film would sell. With states rights, the film rights were sold outright, making these films more of a gamble for the theater owners. Within four days after publication of Frohman's ads about Tex's forthcoming features, more than 60 percent of the U.S. market as well as the entire foreign market had bought rights to her serials.

Part of what made these films a success was Tex's skill on a horse. Tex confessed in an interview in *Photoplay* in August 1919 that she did all her own stunts. In a mock argument with director Cliff Smith, she stamped her foot and said

> "I *won't* let anybody double for me!" . . .
> "Then that horse is plumb apt to break your neck, ma'am," said Mr. Smith politely.
> "If any horse that has only four legs can break my neck," remarked the lady, "it's time it was broke. . . .
> "Outside of a couple of stitches in my right eye, a cracked nose, a game leg and a blister where I hit the saddle, I'm getting along nicely. . . .
> "When I came out here the most daring thing I'd done in a couple of years was to order a meal without looking at the right hand side of the menu. Now they ask me to jump a 150 foot ditch as an appetizer before breakfast."[14]

As good a horsewoman as she was, she was still Mayme Guinan, harum-scarum risk taker. Her film career was studded with mishaps and horse injuries.

While Tex was shooting cattle rustlers and rescuing the good guys, laws were being made that would have a more far-reaching impact on her future than the success or failure of her films. In July 1919, wartime Prohibition went into effect. Congress had proposed to add an eighteenth amendment to the Constitution to forbid the manufacture, sale, and transportation of liquor primarily as a wartime measure to conserve grain. But quickly the "drys" used this to further their cause by equating patriotism with Prohibition. It would only be a matter of time before the adjective *wartime* would be dropped. This was all too obvious to those who noticed that although Prohibition was supposed to be a wartime measure, the amendment was not signed by the President until ten days after the armistice and not put into effect until six months later.

In December 1919, after completing her contract with Sherrill, Tex signed with Bulls-Eye Studios, which was soon taken over by Reelcraft. There she was not only a star, but department head of the unit devoted to the production of her features. This gave her more control over her films and gave her a taste of how she could rise above the role of "just" an actress. Billed as the "Personification of Female Daredeviltry," she began work on another series of twenty-six two-reelers. The films were directed by Jay Hunt and shot on location whenever possible. Within two weeks of the announcement that Reelcraft had begun production on these two-reelers, a large percentage of film exhibitors across the country had already bought the rights to show the films.

Starring opposite TNT Harvey, Tex cranked out films at an average of one a week and became so popular that exhibitors requested her to appear in person where her films were being shown. Though she never became a film star of the magnitude of Gloria Swanson or Mary Pickford, she did what she did well, with little competition and much popularity. In June 1920, Tex took a vacation in New York and made several personal appearances, including one at the Savoy Theater in Newark, New Jersey, where police were called to handle the crowds who had gathered to see her.

The Reelcraft films were not nearly as well made as the Frohman or the Triangle films. Tex herself had become bigger, broader, not as lovely as she had been. She seemed tougher, very masculine, harder. Her jawbone was square and distinctive. Such features as the *Desert Vulture* seemed like parodies, full of grimaces and dumbshow. The plots were thin and the acting thinner. Tex began to prove herself a better saleswoman than actress.

In fact, she sold herself so well that the politicians finally discovered her. Tex had never had much interest in politics. Her attitude was skeptical at best. She said, "A Politician is a fellow who will lay down YOUR life for HIS country. . . . Politics and politicians are always in the public eye, but sometimes they prove to be just a cinder."[15] However in August 1920, she was persuaded to become an official member of the Harding and Coolidge Theatrical League, formed under the leadership of Al Jolson to elect Warren G. Harding president. The committee was a collection of seventy top stars and musical talents of that day, including Ruby De Remer, Zena Keefe, and the young composer Irving Caesar.

On August 24, the Theatrical League departed for Marion, Ohio, Harding's home town. When the group arrived, they were wined and dined. Irving Caesar recalled that Tex sat close by Mrs. Harding and was "well-behaved."[16] In Tex's story, she sat next to Mr. Harding and reminded him of names he'd forgotten as he campaigned through the States. She later used that anecdote to talk about how useful remembering names was to a night-club hostess: "It's just a racket." However, Harding apparently thought so highly of her and her abilities that he gave her a bronze tablet of himself with the inscription, "To Texas Guinan whose friendship is as staunch as the redwood trees of California."[17]

Following Harding's election, Tex toured the South as a member of the Marcus Loew party that was visiting its new theaters under construction. She was one of the first film actresses to make personal appearances (besides those who had worked for the Liberty Loans). Not only would her appearance spark publicity, but it would give her an idea of what the audiences had been feeling about her portrayal of Bill Hart–type characters.

During the tour, Tex was accompanied by another representative for Loew named Nils T. Granlund, known to all as NTG. In his autobiography, NTG described Tex's popularity with the southern crowds, especially with the children. After they had toured through the streets, more than a dozen little ragamuffins followed Tex into the lobby of her hotel. She wanted to invite them all up to her room, but the clerk would not allow it. Tex waved the boys good-bye but not before she'd whispered into the ear of one fellow who happened to be wearing a Western Union cap.

A few minutes later, a Western Union messenger came into the hotel with a telegram for Tex. The clerk sent him up to her room. A few minutes later, another telegram. During the following twenty minutes, Tex received many telegrams, personally delivered by young gentlemen. Though the clerk witnessed their departure up to her room, he didn't see any of the messengers return. Around this time, Tex received a big delivery of ice cream and cake.

Tex later explained to NTG that she had held a party in her room for the boys who had gathered earlier in the lobby. Each time a boy arrived, she'd toss the cap out the window for the next one to catch. (NTG noted that this was not a publicity stunt as one might have expected, as the press had not been invited to witness it.)[18]

Back in Hollywood for Christmas, Tex began an entirely new series with Victor Kremer productions under the direction of actor/director Francis Ford. She had signed a contract that October to make eight westerns a year for states-righters. Tex's alliance with Kremer made a small stir in film circles, for she had become popular enough for several companies to make her "liberal offers." *Moving Picture News* said, "Miss Guinan's career both as a star on the stage and screen has been remarkable. She has a strong personality; her mannerisms are charming and she carries herself in a way that wins her many friends. What accomplishments she has achieved on the legitimate stage have been overshadowed by the success which she has encountered on the screen. She is ranked by some as among the foremost female stars in the industry."[19]

No independent star had ever had the honor of such extensive advertising and exploitation campaigning as Kremer planned for Tex. Their partnership marked a new era in independent production advertising. But it was short-lived. They worked together until May when rumors were circulated that they had split.

Variety told of two separate complaints from censor boards in Pennsylvania and Michigan, which referred to a Kremer film starring Tex that was saturated with "crime." The Pennsylvania board had condemned the film and the Michigan Board of Censors had taken similar action on three of the pictures. The titles of those pictures are not known. All that is known is that Kremer put a stop to all production, though two films, *I Am the Woman* and *The Stampede,* did escape to the public later that year and were hardly full of crime.

The Stampede, released in October, was one of the more important films Tex ever made. Ford was the most sophisticated director she had worked with, and the plot of the film was more complex than that of her usual two-reelers. The dialogue was good, and Ford tried to give a message beyond the usual "Tex is self-reliant and will save the day." He tried to show that the outer trappings of womanhood are sometimes deceptive, and that in general, one should never be deceived by outward appearances. He did this by opposing the character Tex played, who always wore pants, with her cousin Sylvia, a not-so-nice "lady" in dresses. Tex tried to catch a man wearing a dress, but it was her fast thinking and hard horseback riding that would eventually do the trick. Of course, there were also the usual struggles between evil and good, rescue scenes, and a love story.

In the summer before the Kremer films were released, Tex announced that she was forming her own production company and promised the public a series of twelve, two-reel western dramas. Work began on August 10, 1921, under the supervision of J. J. Goldburg, one of the first men in the film industry to employ the then-current methods of states-rights distribution. Goldburg had previously worked for Frohman as sales and exploitation manager before Tex had joined the corporation.

Nobody was surprised when Tex marched off and formed her own company. She was known as a stubborn, levelheaded businesswoman who just about always got her way. Now she would have complete control over her films. But more than that, she had taken a natural step in her film career. As an innovator in the field of selling herself, she'd gone from star to department head, controlling the quality of her pictures. She'd made personal appearances and toured theaters (market research), then become partners with Kremer. It was time to strike out on her own. This would provide training in the business skills she'd use as night-club hostess/entertainer with complete control of her shows.

Tex had big plans for her company and wanted to bring the public something new. It had been the tradition, for example, for most low-budget, independent film companies to use the same actors for every film in a series. Tex decided that instead of the same old stock company, each picture would be cast separately. As her own producer, Tex also bore the expense and responsibility for her own exploitation. Usually the producers of short-length, states-rights subjects let the theaters handle their own publicity. Tex distributed Texas Guinan postage stamps. She sold balloons which featured her on horseback. She even started newspaper contests inviting readers to propose ideas for use in scenarios. As a result, Tex sold the rights to all her films before they were even created.

In the fall of 1921, Tex leased the Fine Arts Studio in Hollywood at 4500 Sunset Boulevard where D. W. Griffith had filmed the monumental *Birth of a Nation*. There, Tex had six stories scheduled for filming: *Texas of the Mounted, Tex Grey, The Soul of Tex, The Claws of Tex, The Girl of the Border,* and *The Code of Tex Storm*. But records list only two as having been completed. The first, *Texas of the Mounted*, was filmed in the San Jacinto Mountains at Camp Keene. Though Tex had a big, six-acre studio, she only used it for interior shots. She preferred the freedom of location for the rest of her scenes. In this film, Tex played both a brother and sister who were twins. As the brother, a member of the Northwest Mounted, Tex was murdered by a vengeful outlaw. As the sister, she donned the dead brother's uniform and went out to "exact full payment for his death."[20] Critics seemed ever fascinated by Tex's recklessly daring riding which "furnished a study in horsemanship that none cannot help but admire" along, of course, "with artistic acting."[21] Again she had attempted the difficult and the new, posing in a dual role. How much closer could she come to the potential conflict of the simultaneous existence of the feminine and masculine within?

The second film, entitled *The Code of the West*, appeared in November 1921. In both films, Tex played opposite a handsome hero, David E. Townsend. Townsend was a British actor from the legitimate stage who had made his name in both England and Australia.

There is much confusion about the Guinan-Townsend relationship. Was this the Townsend that Tex described as her only romantic mistake? The details about who Townsend was and how he came into her life have always been distorted. In fact, in all public record of her life, i.e., newspaper gossip, obituaries, even Stein's manuscript, Townsend or Townley, as he is sometimes called, never appears as an actor. He is a "British financier" and in one case, a captain of the British army who hears Tex sing during the war and comes to find her in New York when the war ends.

In the obituaries, he is Tex's third husband, a millionaire George E. Townley, whom she met aboard ship two months after her "divorce" from JJ in 1920. They were supposedly married in the New York municipal chapel soon after the boat docked, but no such records exist. In 1925, they were "divorced" after a long separation.

According to her memoirs, Tex entered the involvement only because Townsend had lots of money and she was short of cash at the time. She wanted that financial security. She later regretted bartering her fame and glamour for his cash, and her memories of him were anything but kind.

"He was the meanest man I have ever known. I should have taken him like Grant took Richmond. Thank God, I was never his wife. His first one poisoned herself. His second, a Ziegfield Follies beauty, drove her car over an embankment near Monte Carlo. I was the one woman who could take Dave Townsend and leave him where I found him. I was out to take not be taken.

"He taught me one thing, though, that the sweetest things in this life are obtained by the work of one's own hands."[22]

In April of the following year, 1922, Tex began another publicity tour of the Loew circuit in the skit *Spitfire*. (Sources indicate there was also a movie with that title.) The skit was a short western scenario tailored to complement Tex's films that were shown right before the personal appearance. The cast included five cowboys from Tex's company and her pet horse, Waco. At the climax, Tex would leap on Waco's back and save the Post Office from being robbed. "The act," reported *Variety* on July 14, "proved a novelty and went over well." President Harding attended her performance when it passed through Washington, D.C., and afterwards stood up in his box to salute her, declaring that he hoped he could do as good a job as President as Tex did with a horse and a six-gun.

As on her previous tour, Tex seemed interested in attracting children as fans. Perhaps her manager or publicity agent thought it a good publicity idea to show how clean and wholesome her films were. Or perhaps there was a part of her—the tomboy self that loved a good adventure story—that still identified with kids. In Atlanta, she told the *Atlanta Georgian* she made her films for them: "When I was a kid I used to worship the cowboys and everybody in Western pictures. [There were no films back then.] Raised on a ranch in Waco, Texas, is enough to account for that."

In the same article, it was also reported that "Miss Guinan asked that all the children in Atlanta come to the theater to see her. She said she was going to ride a horse on the stage and do lots of things they would like. After the show she said she was going to try to arrange to meet them and have a real heart to heart talk. They must be her pets, for she says so."[23]

Children did adore her. She was infatuating her fans to such an extent that when she left Hollywood on tour, a fifteen-year-old boy named Gilbert Salmon decided to run away from his home in Oakland, California, and follow her. His parents hired the FBI to find him and pointed to Tex as their prime suspect. They thought Tex had sent notes to their home inviting Gilbert to meet with her. She had taken him out in an auto, bought him meals, and in other ways, "induced the youngster to be with her."[24] The Guinan woman was said to have had this youngster with her in Long Beach and also in San Jose, having enticed him from his family by promising to put him in the moving pictures.

For a while FBI records described Tex as a "moral pervert, her activities centering primarily on young boys. She has been in trouble at many different points and has been reported to have been charged with federal violation of the postal act pertaining to fraud." The FBI wanted to curtail this notorious woman's activities, this woman "of more than thirty years of age, having been married and divorced several times."[25]

The federal agents, after exploring the old files on Tex's postal violations decided to interview her. She told them that three months before the investigation, Gilbert Salmon had met her at the theater and told her he was ill-treated by his parents and did not want to go home. He had followed her to other cities and had last been seen by her in Long Beach, California, on August 12, 1922. It was now November.

Interviewed again in December, she said everyday both boys and girls followed the show or ran away from home to ask her for a job. She had advised the Salmon boy to go home to his mother and had even given him enough money to pay his train fare. Eventually, the police were convinced that Tex had no hand in the disappearance and closed the case on her end. However, her attention to children continued to get her into trouble, whether it was merely a matter of incurring large bills for ice cream or requests to bail a choice few out of jail.

In November, Tex returned to New York City after seven months on the road. Her tour had put her back in touch with her audiences and she was eager to return to the stage. She wrote Jake Shubert a letter describing her successful tour and stated she had a proposition if he'd like to capitalize on the great publicity her tour had generated. There is no record of his response. One would like to think she had more than just a stage engagement up her sleeve, that she was actually about to propose some scheme to exploit the rise of the Prohibition-era-inspired cabaret industry. However, there was no indication that she wanted to stop producing films other than the claims of her friend Ben Finney that she'd grown weary of "kissing horses in horse operas." Actually, all she'd said to Shubert was, "I can't make any more pictures for at least six months because I have twelve to be released."[26] However, she was never to make another silent film. By December, she'd found something even better suited to her talents.

Birth of a Hostess

> *A night club hostess—if she is successful—should make people forget they have homes. This proves the old theory that an indiscretion a day will keep depression away.*
> —TEXAS GUINAN, "TEXAS GUINAN SAYS," SEPTEMBER 1930

*I*t was really supposed to be Joe's big night, not Tex's. Tex had been sitting in the audience minding everybody else's business. She had stuck her inquisitive nose into Pearl White's affairs and noted smugly that the actress who had made "Pauline" famous (as in *The Perils of*) had brought the man Tex had matched her up with and married her off to—Wally McCutcheon. Just call her "Cupid" Guinan. Then Tex noticed out of the corner of her eye that Franklin Farnum sat at a nearby table on the verge of boredom. She was just about to shake her many-braceleted wrist at her old vaudeville co-star when she heard her name announced over the microphone. She looked up in surprise, and Joe gave her a smile she could not ignore.

Not that she would have even considered refusing to join him on stage, still it was all so very unexpected. The turned heads and attention felt good. She was glad to be back in New York, where the action was. It was as if a magnet had pulled her back here to be part of the rising shout of the twenties.

The year was 1922. It had been fifteen long years since Tex had first stood on the pavement, suitcase in hand, absorbed in the heartbeat that was Times Square. In all her wanderings since then, she had found nothing to compare to the dance of the lights that animated the Main Stem, the brilliant Squibbs sign or the glimmering advertisement for Fisk Tires above the Capitol Theatre, words that became loud with light when darkness fell. There was no music, except maybe something that Gershwin fellow had written, that could even approach the percussion of high heels, the underscoring of tire sounds, the syncopated rhythms of doors opening and closing and swinging around. Tex might be able to outgrow a young girl's fantasies about the future, but she would never lose her fascination with Broadway. Here was home.

Tex was heading toward forty now, and her bleached blonde hair, a great success with her fans in her final films, was a thin disguise for the time that had crept up on her. Sometimes she worried, but she told herself, "Be gay. It's too expensive to grow old. And have your hair bleached and your face lifted."[1] Although her body was no longer young and firm—the years of constant losing and gaining of weight had left loose skin around her arms and the hint of a double chin—she was still an attractive woman. She had used those forty years to develop into a personality, cultivating a powerful magnetism that drew people to her, made them like her.

Tex's absence from New York had affiliated her with the West Coast "Cinamese" (film people), and she was determined to capitalize on that connection. How could she begin to reaffiliate herself with the New York that had changed so drastically in the first few years of the twenties?

The twenties had done more damage to New York than Tex's absence had. People now dressed and talked in a different language. At first it was mostly the younger generation, the "jellybeans" or "sheiks" and "shebas," who giggled such nonsense as "go cook a radish" and "absotively" or "posilutely." They went out to speakeasies and got blotto, cock-eyed, oiled and ossified, and God knows what else. They lived for the moment and the fun of the moment and cast aside the old morals and fashions for newer, less restrictive ones. Young girls wore makeup, bobbed their hair, and shortened their skirts. Then even their mothers caught on.

Tex saw that she might be required to roll down her stockings and change the style of her dress, but she wasn't sure that at her age, she could afford to discard her corset. She did understand that more women had discovered a new freedom. Tex didn't particularly care if her knees showed below her dresses but felt somehow that flapperdom was for the younger generation. However, she didn't mind adopting a few minor vices. She liked to go out, stay up late, smoke the occasional cigarette, until recently taboo for women. The only thing she had little use for was drinking.

Drinking was on everybody else's mind when Tex got back to the city, for the Eighteenth Amendment had been in effect for enough years to show it was planning to stay for a while. Still, few took it seriously. It was easy enough to get a drink, if you wanted one. You just needed to be careful about where you bought it. Prohibition had served only to reduce the quality, not the quantity of available liquor. Speakeasies had become increasingly more popular, and though they were crude, for the most part, and offered little entertainment beyond the thrill of an illicit drink, they were the rage. People liked them at first because they were new and mysterious. There were passwords, secret cards, locked doors, peepholes. Subterranean locations and tacky decor only enhanced their charm.

By 1922, there were over five thousand speakeasies and so-called night clubs in Manhattan, a thousand of which were located in the upper half of the theater district. Just about every basement had one, and for the first years of the twenties, such informal setups sufficed. But as time went on and drink itself was no longer the only attraction, the quality of entertainment began to grow in importance. The stage was set for the true night club to appear.

Among Tex's large circle of acquaintances were quite a few entertainers who had begun dabbling in the restaurant-turned-speakeasy business. Some played music, others played comedy.

When Tex returned to New York City in 1922, she found her old friend violinist Joe Fejer conducting an orchestra at a small Hungarian restaurant on Forty-fifth Street called Gypsyland. Nils T. Granlund mentioned in his autobiography that though Gypsyland had an elegant menu, no matter what you ordered, you always got goulash.[2] One night NTG claims he brought both Tex and "Fehar" (NTG's spelling), along with several other celebrities, to eat supper at the club. Their presence was such a big hit that the three went into business with the owner, providing star-studded clientele (their many friends) each night. In that way, the restaurant grew very popular and became a hangout for actors, singers, film stars.

In other versions of the story, Tex was already a regular at Gypsyland. She brought her friends to see Fejer almost every night, and as a result, he grew very popular with the theater crowd. His success at Gypsyland soon caught the attention of Emile Gervasini, owner of the Cafe des Beaux Arts, a well-known French restaurant in midtown. In the past, the restaurant had been noted for both its "superb sauces" and "famed filets" as well as its clientele of "well-fed old-timers, many of whom later made history."[3] Its location at 80 West Fortieth Street assured it crowds of theatergoers as well as the protection of the lions who guarded the newest and largest public library in Manhattan. Gervasini thought Fejer would be the perfect headliner to open his brand-new, luxurious Gold Room.

Opening night, Fejer invited all his special friends as his personal guests, including Tex. Tex recalled later that among the other guests that night were Mrs. Morris Gest, Franklin Farnum, Joe Frisco, Sig-

Birth of a Hostess

mund Romberg, Lt. Getz-Rice, the actress Pearl White, and her husband Wally McCutcheon. In addition, Tex dragged along half a dozen of her film friends. Once settled, she noticed the place was packed. Then Joe called her name.

"We had a great time that night at the Gold Room," wrote Tex in her memoirs. "Joe asked me to sing so Sigmund Romberg played his song 'Sweetheart' from 'Maytime' and I got a great big hand when I finished singing it. I dragged Blanche Ring on the stage and she said she would sing if the composer would play her song. Getz-Rice sat down at the piano and played the accompaniment for 'Dear Old Pal of Mine.' The Beaux Arts stayed open that morning until 5:30, and it usually closed at 1 a.m. So you can figure out for yourself whether it was a good party."[4]

Gervasini quickly saw that he had a good thing here, and after some consultation with Fejer, invited Tex to come work for him.

Later, in the retelling of the tale for the book *Luck, Your Silent Partner*, Tex assigned her initial success to luck. She had done that before. However, it was clear to others who knew her, that the luck, if there was any, was in the timing, that it was early in that fabulous decade, the Roaring Twenties, and the climate was right for one such as Texas Guinan to step in and be her gregarious self. "It was not a gesture," declared journalist Colgate Baker of Tex's hostessing. "It was self-expression, a thing she did unconsciously by force of breeding, training, environment and heritage."[5]

Hostessing allowed Tex to be a friendly, talkative arranger of others' destinies; a meddler, a nosy (and noisy) "old" lady; and someone who liked to see others enjoy themselves. She was a mistress of ceremonies par excellence, someone who knew how to read audiences and give them what they wanted.

At first, Tex found her work overwhelming and surprisingly difficult. She might be okay at it on occasion, but to be spontaneous like that every night? She found she needed to start stockpiling good jokes, special events, stars. Fortunately, Tex knew enough people to shout "hello" to as they entered the restaurant. If she didn't remember their names, she remembered where they came from. People liked to be recognized even if they acted embarrassed at first. She shook hands with strangers and was friendly to all. She seated great stars next to nobodies and made sure they talked. Tex was starting something new, playing both the entertainer and the good-natured hostess. The way she saw it, she'd been one of the customers only just last week, so why make a distinction?

Before long, Tex's guests became the entertainment. At first, her only performers were dancers Peggy and Cortez. Soon, however, she initiated the guest-of-honor tradition. Just as Joe had invited her to the stage to sing, Tex now invited a sometimes unsuspecting, but usually forewarned guest to join her. In an attempt to increase the size of the already large clientele, she also featured celebrity nights. The earliest piece of evidence documenting Tex's presence at the Beaux Arts Cafe is an invitation-ticket to a special night celebrating the visit of the actress Pearl White on December 11, 1922.

Early on in Tex's career at the Beaux Arts, Joe Pani, owner of the popular King Cole Room at the Knickerbocker Hotel on 152 West Forty-second Street caught her act with Fejer and invited the two for a stand at his place. It is not clear if Fejer came with Tex. However, in the early spring of 1923 at the King Cole Room, Tex inaugurated a series of motion-picture nights. She used her large list of acquaintances to lure paying guests who wanted to be included among the "Eastern Cinamese." Her first big name of the season was none other than film idol Rudolph Valentino.

Valentino was the "great lover" of the day. Though his life was short—he died at the age of thirty-one after a seven-year screen career—he remains in the minds of the American public as one of the greatest film heroes of all time. Women found the Sheik irresistible—all women, that is, except his wives. When Tex invited him to perform with his most recent wife, Natacha Rambova (art director and costumer for the celebrated Russian actress Nazimova), he had just been suspended from Paramount and was touring the country performing exhibition dancing. As Tex told it, when she began to arrange the evening, Rudy had readily agreed to her terms, unable to resist the publicity the engagement would produce. He insisted, however, that Tex make sure that his first wife, the actress Jean Acker, was not invited. Tex was on gossiping terms with Jean and could hardly snub her without repercussions, but she was well aware of the animosity Jean bore toward her ex-husband, and the way she had of showing it—publicly. Whenever she watched her ex-husband perform with his new wife, she had the nasty habit of hissing. When Tex called Jean and requested her not to come, she promised she would throw a big party in her honor to make up for it.

That night, personalities at the club included President Woodrow Wilson's daughter Margaret, actors John Barrymore and Lowell Sherman, Mrs. W. K. Vanderbilt, and Tex's closest friend Nora Bayes, the actress. As show time approached, customers took their seats in anxious anticipation. Julia Hoyt, society girl-turned-actress, then showed up with a big party and no reservations. As Tex tried to find some seats in the crowded room, she noted an empty table opposite the Valentinos' table of honor. Whoever had reserved it was too late, and Tex told the waiter to seat Miss Hoyt and company there. The waiter told her that the table had been reserved in advance and that one hundred dollars had been paid to make sure no one else took it. Tex was astounded. What kind of fool would pay that kind of money just to reserve a table at her show? "Peggy Hopkins Joyce," replied the waiter. The much-married Follies star was a good friend of Tex's. Why would she go to the trouble of reserving a table and bribing a waiter to hold it when she knew she could always have a seat at Tex's shows?

At that moment Valentino and Rambova entered the club. Tex greeted them and decided to take a quick trip to the powder room in search of Peggy. Sure enough, there she was, accompanied by the strangest-looking redhead, who, with her hair styled in spikes around her head, looked as if she were masquerading as the Statue of Liberty. And the cut of her dress! It was so low the embarrassed eye sought immediate diversion and found it in such an enormous set of pearls that the pearl-conscious Tex gasped with astonishment and envy. Yet Tex had the feeling she knew this woman from somewhere. Peggy introduced her guest as the Countess of Itch.

Tex escorted the two ladies into the dining room and installed them at the table next to Rudy's. As she did so, she happened to glance over at her star to see how he was doing and noticed that he seemed terribly upset. She rushed over to him with a concerned look on her face and he pointed to the Countess of Itch. "That's Jean Acker."

At first Tex was furious. She was furious because she'd fallen for Jean's ruse and furious that Jean had sought to trick her to begin with. She turned to Rudy and suddenly the two burst out laughing.

Meanwhile Rudy's dance with Natacha went off (almost) without a hitch. Jean didn't bother to hiss; she rattled her plates, and attempted to throw them on the floor, but Tex had stationed two busboys by her table, and they seemed to be in the right place at the right time every time the "countess" was tempted to drop anything. After Rudy's dance, Tex took Jean out on the dance floor and introduced her as the Countess of Itch, formerly Mrs. Valentino, who was so thrilled by her ex-husband's new wife's dancing that she could hardly refrain from breaking the china to show her enthusiasm. She then proposed that Jean and Rudy dance for the audience, knowing that Jean was not a very good dancer, and before long the embarrassed Jean had stumbled off into the wings. Tex never forgot the near-disaster of her opening night and never forgave Jean. She also never bothered to throw the party she'd promised her.[6]

Business continued to be good wherever Tex was, and soon the Beaux Arts made a bid to win her back. There, she attracted the attention of the underworld, who instantly saw how valuable she would be to them as a front for their liquor-selling operations.

At that time, the underworld rumrunners were supplying the liquor for all the speakeasies, as well as bankrolling the more popular establishments. They wanted the retail profits as well as the wholesale ones. Larry Fay was one of these men, but he was interested in the speakeasy for other reasons. Once upon a time he had been a simple taxicab driver, earning a paltry twenty-five dollars a week. When the Prohibition game began, he took a rich customer clear to Canada one night and found out about rumrunning. Soon he had rounded up enough cash to buy his own fleet of cabs—through the sale of ten-dollar cases of whiskey at a profit of eight hundred percent. He bought control—with the help of Owney Madden, another underworld personality who had emerged from Sing-Sing earlier in 1923—of the taxistands at both Penn Central and Grand Central. Soon rumrunning and taxi driving were not enough for him. For one thing, they had no class. He wanted now to rub shoulders with the best, to be considered a gentleman. To him, a gentlemanly operation would be a swanky club where the chairs were covered in cloth and the tables filled with diamond-studded clientele. He'd need an orchestra, a master of ceremonies, and maybe an act or two. He wanted to make sure he attracted the right kind of people.

Fay wanted Nils T. Granlund as emcee, and he told him as much. NTG was at that time emcee at the Loew radio station WHN. He also played publicity director for the Loew Theater but was best known for his side game as talent scout for Florenz Ziegfield, Earl Carroll, and other men who featured beautiful bodies. He considered himself an expert on the available showgirls in town—and he was—since he had gotten most of them their jobs.

When Fay approached him, NTG knew it would not be easy to say no to this horse-faced man. Then he thought of Tex. He and Tex had worked together before. In fact, their paths had often crossed. They were alike in a crucial respect—both knew just about everybody in the business. NTG also knew of her great success at the Beaux Arts and was sure Fay would never turn her down once he met her. So he steered Fay to the Beaux Arts, and as the story runs, Fay was so overwhelmed by the high-class setting of the club, by Tex and her apparent mastery of the audience and the art of emceeing, that he went for her immediately. In NTG's autobiography, however, he takes more than his share of the credit and tells how he created a show of girls to back up Tex and how he put her in the Beaux Arts to make her more marketable. Either way, NTG and Tex teamed up to create a show that was later featured in Fay's club.⁷

Some sources say that it was not just the desire to be more respectable that prompted Fay to seek a night club and join forces with Texas Guinan but rather that he did it to please a "dame." That dame was Irene Delroy. As far as Fay was concerned, NTG could set up a show of girls for him, but all that mattered was that Delroy be among them. The El Fey Club would be her showcase.

Thus the El Fey Club was born, on May 1, 1924, and, declared Ben Finney, who proceeded to spend almost every night there after the club opened, "I still do not subscribe to the general belief that Fay called his club El Fey because he could not spell his own name. He had signed too many bail bonds not to know how to do that."⁸ The club quickly became, in spite of its owner, what Finney affectionately named the "granddaddy of the all night speakeasies."⁹ It was easily the hottest spot in town, and everybody made sure they were seen there. "You had to go there," said Finney, "damned near every night. You got used to it, and you'd feel strange if you weren't at the El Fey."¹⁰

The El Fey Club stood at 105 West Forty-fifth Street with its back to the Sixth Avenue Automat and a shoulder to a barbershop. Fay's good-luck swastika, embossed on a downstair's window, was the only clue to the identity of an otherwise unremarkable building. Customers walked up to the second floor to a long, rectangular room the size, as Tex described it, of an ordinary theater stage. It seated almost eighty people, but held "about as many as the Yale Bowl." In fact, vowed Tex, "The two places are somewhat similar."¹¹

"One entered it," recalled NTG, "by a narrow stairway and a yard-square landing on the second floor. Here was the entrance door and the inevitable peephole. The stairway continued to the floor above where we built a lounge and a dressing room for the girls."¹²

The doorway was manned by Sam Thorpe, and as doorman, he had the important job of screening prospective customers. Ben Finney recalled that downstairs from the club was a hangout for "all the guys looking for a drink—detectives, cops and everybody—they'd drop in downstairs for a drink. . . . And of course the booze was kept in the house next door, which Fay had bought for that purpose. So that the liquor wouldn't be 'in' the El Fey. It was brought through a hole cut in the wall, and then from the basement went up in an elevator where it was bottled upstairs."¹³

Drinks were an enticement, but the food was nothing much to remember. Nobody came there to eat, anyway. The main club profits came from the drinks and the cover charge, which varied. When the club first opened, guests paid two dollars a head. The cover charge had puzzled guests for years. Some thought it was charged to pay for laundering expenses, tablecloths, napkins, etc. Others thought it was needed to cover the expenses of running an illegal operation that risked constant raids and closedowns.

Most of the guests ordered "champagne," which was merely cider spiked with alcohol—at twenty-five dollars a bottle. Others drank whiskey that cost only ten dollars a case and was watered down and sold at one dollar a throw, which meant, calculated NTG, that they made one hundred dollars a quart.[14]

The El Fey Club quickly became known as Tex's place, thanks to her wit and charm, and Fay didn't care, as long as Irene still worked for him. However, Delroy quit the club shortly after it opened. Columnist Jack Lait said years later that he thought Tex developed her most famous greeting in Fay's honor:

> As each show went on, Larry would stand in the extreme rear, where it was dark and where he—always in plain blue serge suit, white silk shirt and black windsor tie—was inconspicuous. As Texas would mount her chair (that was how she worked) she would look across the room at him. And, thinking of the lease, her pay, the flop of his romantic objective, she would cast a glance right over the heads of the audience and call out—to him— "Hello, Sucker!"
>
> Through some phenomenal human quirk, every other sucker thought it was addressed to him. And, as strangely, every man liked it.[15]

Tex's "Hello, Sucker!" inspired other theories about its origin. She was accused of stealing it from circus slang and the notorious Barnum, from cowboy argot, or from her good friend Wilson Mizner. An old Colorado miner swore she first heard it in Cripple Creek from a barber named Walter Tug Lee, who used the expression to greet one of Tex's crestfallen suitors. Whomever she got it from, Tex took the expression and made it her own. Its value lay in the fact that she had the showman's sense to use it.

"In this day and age—in New York particularly—originality doesn't mean a thing," wrote Richard Milne of the *Boston Post*. "It's the man who first gets the line over in public—using the stage, magazines or newspapers—who takes in the cash and credit. Columnists rob obscure vaudevillians of gags, and then accuse other columnists of stealing from them.

Birth of a Hostess

"But what difference does it make who sprang the idea first? Broadway doesn't care. The world doesn't care. It's part and parcel of Texas Guinan's act. She made it famous. It made her famous."[16]

Tex had a unique way with the simple expression. There were times when she just seemed to sing out, almost laugh out, "Hello, Suckers!" It was a happy, warm greeting from one pal to another. A display of affection for humankind and all its foibles. It was also an acknowledgement of Tex's own weaknesses. She used to say that she was the biggest sucker of them all.

"'Hello sucker' is my night club salutation to one and all. I mean it to say 'Hello, pal, aren't we all alike after all?'"[17]

As time went on and the club grew more and more popular, Tex found the new lifestyle difficult to adjust to. She became a night owl, sleeping days and breakfasting at 11:00 in the evening. She hung dark curtains in her bedroom to keep the daylight out. Some days she wanted to stay up until the afternoon, instead of going to bed at dawn. But she found she paid for it later on that night, or even the next day. Still she didn't think such living could harm her. She declared that she entered the night-club profession because she had insomnia. She became addicted to coffee and cigarettes. After a while, her friend Walter Winchell noticed that "you couldn't put one [cigarette] between your lips and light it without Tex taking it."[18] Still she steered clear of the liquor. That was an amazing feat in those days, but it was crucial for the successful hostess.

Tex became known for her "indefatigable industry" and good humor. Everyone thought they knew her intimately, but in fact, says Finney, "practically nobody saw her except in the El Fey. She never went around, at least not often. I don't think she ever went out except to go to the El Fey or wherever she was working. She wasn't what you'd call a round-the-town girl at all."[19]

What people knew about Tex came mostly from third-hand sources. All kinds of stories surrounded her, about whom she spent her time with and what she did after hours. And she had the press to perpetuate the fiction.

Every night Walter Winchell, Heywood Broun, Mark Hellinger, Ed Sullivan—rookie and seasoned reporters alike—came and sat in the back of the club to see who was with whom and what kinds of tidbits they could garner from Guinan after hours. Her club was said to be a news source as essential as the courthouse or the jail. It was said by some that no scandal became official unless it came from Tex's doors.[20] Several newspapers hired tables and kept at least one staff person there nightly.

Tex was kind to all the "boys," felt she was part of their circle. They, in turn, liked her because she was quick-witted and literate as well as generous, kind, and an excellent gossip. Even the literary chaps like Ring Lardner and Damon Runyon enjoyed having her around. Also, Tex recognized the power the press had, a power which had increased in the 1920s. Besides, former romantic involvements with members of their clan had left a permanent soft spot in her heart.

It was Winchell and Hellinger, though, whom she now adored above all the others. Tex treated them as if they were her brothers, invited them to the private sanctuary of her home, introduced her friends to them, wrote them letters, and sent gifts. When Winchell's beloved daughter Gloria was six years old, Tex sent her a box filled to the brim with toys. "We didn't have to buy our children a doll or toy for years," recalled Winchell.[21]

Some said the press made Guinan what she was. The press declared that she made them what they were.

In his autobiography, Winchell credited Tex with the invention of the modern gossip column—that is, the one for which he was best known. After a long night of entertaining, Tex liked to relax for an hour or two playing poker and chatting with the boys. Winchell often escorted Tex back to her Greenwich Village apartment as early as "7:00 in the yawning."

> But between 5:00 and tata time, Tex drank as many cups of java as she smoked cigarettes. And she kept up a running commentary about the people who jammed her night club.
> "Oh, Brutha!" she said one 6:00 A.M., "could I tell you one!"
> "Frinstance?"
> "Mrs. Vanderbilt is going to have twins!"
> "Who?"
> "Mrs. Vanderbilt! One of the most famous society ladies in the world!"
> "Oh!" My world then was populated with show folks. "Vanderbilt? So wot?"
> "I just gave you a heckuva scoop," said Tex. "Why don't you make a note of it for the column, you fool!"
> "How does anyone know," I asked, "if a woman is going to have twins?"
> "Doctors can tell. They listen for two heart beats. Don't you read the papers?"
> The next column included that item. Weeks later, Mrs. Vanderbilt had twinfants.[22]

Birth of a Hostess

Tex knew that beyond the superficial games of gossip and publicity, the press could do someone a good turn as well as a bad one. She once told Winchell about a nice young man named Sherman Billingsley, who had recently opened a new restaurant and was struggling to keep it alive with his personal funds. She urged him to stop by and take a look at the place. Winchell visited the Stork Club and put in a good word for it.[23]

As for Mark Hellinger, Tex liked best to drop him short notes at odd hours of the day. At one time, she noticed that Winchell had mentioned Hellinger's preoccupation with serious matters in his column. In response Tex wrote, "My sweets, why will you insist on taking life seriously—in a hundred years we will all be gone or in some stuffy book. . . . I don't know what you are looking for, but I find as I told you Saturday, give me plenty of laughs and you can take all the rest."[24]

The El Fey Club, a hotbed for news and excitement. Even if the shows were the same every night, the audiences never were, nor the spontaneous entertainment. One night a man with a slow midwestern drawl came in and cheerfully began dispensing fifty-dollar bills to all the dancers. He bought everyone in the house a drink and made no fuss when he got the bill. Thrilled by this rare phenomenon, Tex decided her guest needed a proper introduction. Leading the dandy to the center of the dance floor, at this time the size of a small white envelope, she signaled for a distinguished drum roll and said,

"'Folks, here's a live one, a buyer, a good guy, a sport of the old school, encourage him.'

"There was applause and cries of:

"'Who is he?'

"'What's your name,' asked Tex.

"'Nix on the name,' said the unknown.

"'What's your racket, then?' queried the hostess.

"'I'm a big man in dairy produce,' he muttered.

"'That's applesauce to this mob. I'll send you in right,' and Tex shouted,

"'He's a big butter and egg man.'"[25]

Night after night, the big spender came in and ran up large bills. Everyone soon knew him as the big butter-and-egg man, and the expression quickly spread throughout New York. George S. Kaufman immortalized it by making it the title of a Broadway play about a rich midwestern sucker so free with his money that some smart Easterners take him for a ride.

In other, audience-inspired incidents, uninvited amateur entertainers clamored for attention. Tap dancer Ruby Keeler recalled that Tex had a knack for finding the audience ham. "There'd always be some extrovert in the club who could do a special trick like going down on his back with a glass of water on his head or something. She'd always let them do their little stunt, which was fun. And if there was someone loud—we used to call them Broadway Als. They'd probably spend money, probably have a pretty girl with them and want to impress them."[26]

Sometimes audience members would stage their own sideshow dramas. Once a woman caught her man entering the club with another lady—her replacement. How could she make her rival jealous? She looked at her hostess and noticed the rows of sparkling diamond bracelets covering the lower half of her arm. They were as much Tex's trademark as "Hello, Sucker!" was. Catching Tex's attention with a loud shout, the woman told her she'd buy any one of those bracelets off her arm, just name her price. Tex said $25,000 and without flinching the woman counted twenty-five $1,000 bills before an astonished Tex. No one ever found out if her ruse did the trick.[27]

Although the club atmosphere depended on the unofficial entertainment, the official club show featured Miss Texas Guinan and her famous troupe of "little girls," the "lil guurrls" who had inspired another of Tex's famous phrases: "Give the little girl a big hand." (Later, this would be bastardized by the press in numerous fashions, including "Give the little girl a big handcuff.") Many of these "children" came from the Ziegfield chorus lines when their evening performance was over; they were long legged and full busted, perfectly shaped with radiant smiles.

Tex liked the arrangement because although she enjoyed being the center of attention, she found it quite taxing to be constantly witty. With a troupe of eight or ten pretty girls to take the customers' attention, Tex could rest up between acts and catch up on jokes. The young girls, ages ranging from thirteen to sixteen, became the children she'd never had. So she took charge of their education. She taught them right from wrong in the world of show business, gave them such memorable advice as, "Remember he may be all the world to his mother, but he is just a cover charge to you,"[28] and instructed them not to point unless they were ordering French pastry.[29]

In order to protect the dancers from the unsavory side of the nightclub business, Tex forbade them to mingle with the guests. Some brought their mothers along nightly. Few were even aware that liquor was being served in the club. Doris Vinton, former Follies star and retired national president of the Ziegfield Club, recalled that when she worked there, "Ruby [Keeler] and I never heard a cuss word, a dirty word, never saw a fight. They told us later that Larry Fay was a gangster. Why he was the nicest man! I never saw anything that I wouldn't want a child of mine to witness. You could have come out of a convent and gone there and worked."[30]

Tex did her best to make sure her girls had the opportunity to be "seen" by producers and potential husbands. Though she was sincerely out to make their careers, she also had mercenary intentions. She wanted the credit for launching them.

In training her girls, Tex set them up with the biggest of dreams. She played Slocum with them and fed them star thoughts. They were the greatest—they were Guinan girls. "Ziegfield's girls are glorified; George White's girls are scandalized; Earl Carroll's girls are immortalized; Texas Guinan's girls are idolized."[31]

Tex had the habit of predicting glorious futures on her visits to the girls' dressing room, with a gesture of diamonds here, and a puff of a cigarette there. "We'd all end up married to millionaires," recalled former dancer June Carroll, "who'd load us down with furs and hang so many jewels on us it would take a special train to pull us along. And motor cars! Oh three apiece at least. Why, we were the sunrise he was waiting for."[32]

The most substantial part of these dreams was the woman who wove them. The girls felt, recalled Keeler, that Texas was their one security in an uncertain life. When they performed, each looked to her for support. "It was frightening out there on that little floor," Keeler said. "But she just stood out there and kept everything going on around us."[33]

The dancers knew that Tex would always be there to take care of them and their families. Most of these girls came from families who didn't have much—and whose parents would never go to a club like Tex's as a paying customer. Many were religious and worked to support their families. Some wanted a career or were simply star-struck and liked to see and meet the many celebrities who frequented the club. Others, like Claire Luce, wanted more than anything to become *sophisticated*.

Among the girls, there were actually a few talents who eventually made it big. Though each was assigned her own specialty act, few could survive without the rest of the group as backup. One who could stand alone was Ruby Keeler. She was also Tex's favorite.

Keeler began work at Tex's in much the same fashion as the rest of the girls. Through NTG. She was all of thirteen when, already a performer at another club, she was invited to tag along with several other dancers from her show and NTG—"Granny," as they called him—to catch the act at the El Fey. Before she knew it, she was working there. She later starred in such musicals as *42nd Street* and for a time was married to Al Jolson.

Other girls came in different ways. Claire Luce, who later danced in the Folies Bergère in Paris and gave a command performance for the king and queen of Spain, was discovered by Larry Fay. He saw her at another night club and developed a slight crush. One night he approached her and asked, "How would you like to dance in a club of mine?" "Well it was a job," recalled Luce, "and a job is a job. He offered me a really wonderful salary."[34] It wasn't until months later at a party that she found out he was a gangster. "I didn't even know what a gangster was. My friend said, a gangster is someone who puts water in baby's milk."[35] Not long after that, Fay began sending her flowers and dolls, which she sent back. Soon after she quit the club.

Not only had Fay been an unwelcome admirer, but Luce found the night-club life hard work. "It was exciting, of course, meeting everyone who came into the place. By the end of the three- or four-in-the-morning performances, instead of crawling off home to bed, Tex would take us in her car (limo) and drive us out to Long Island for fresh air before we went to bed. It was a good idea, actually. Then I had a dancing lesson at ten A.M. Then a matinee."[36]

It was a hard life for the moonlighting would-be, could-be stars, and Tex would do her best to give them opportunities most other struggling actresses and dancers could only hope for. NTG also helped get the performers out and seen in other places. "Often on a Sunday night that we didn't play," recalled Doris Vinton, "we would go and appear at supper clubs up in Westchester, out on Long Island. They'd come and take us in private cars and we'd get fifty or seventy-five dollars. There were three regular salaries for the girls at the El Fey—$85, $100, $125. Or they'd take us to the Winter Garden."[37]

Once in a while, a girl from a wealthier background would join the club. For debutantes and "subdebutantes," recalled Mrs. Damon Runyon, then Patrice Gridière, it was very fashionable to have a brief flirtation with the theater. These girls had no need to earn a living and had little investment in staying with the show. Patrice, for instance, only worked at the El Fey for six months.

In addition to the girls, there were a number of comedians and dancers like Walter O'Keefe, Lou Holtz, and Georgie Raft—who was billed as the fastest Charleston dancer in New York.

The club, the acts, Tex, booze, famous customers—NTG summed up the El Fey operation and significance in the 1920s in a succinct two sentences. He said, "In this second story bandbox, financed by a bootlegger and spiced by the rollicking personality of Texas Guinan, was born that incredible period of American life immortalized by Damon Runyon as the era of wonderful nonsense. It was a bacchanalian feast, a Roman orgy, a politician's clambake, all rolled into one."[38]

Later the *Daily Mirror* confirmed that "associates and competitors alike agreed that Tex changed the post-war cabaret into the modern Broadway night club."[39]

As she played the friendly hostess, Tex continuously calculated who would spend and how much. ("Lesson No. 1 in Professor Guinan's sucker psychology course is charge, charge and then charge some more. Of course, you've got to make 'em like it.")[40] She became good at seducing the wealthier customers to spend and as they got more and more cozy, would invite them to bring their chairs to the front. As the night progressed, the dance floor would shrink in proportion to the number of big spenders. Tex never seemed to notice. One night she told Ben Finney, one of her favorite regulars, that he was looking flabby. In his autobiography *Feet First*, Finney described how Tex encouraged him to step out on the floor to dance.

"'Where?' I [Finney] asked, 'upstairs or in the kitchen?'

"'On the floor, darling. The dance floor. There is room for at least eight couples out there and only two are dancing.'

"The dance floor, which shrank as more tables were brought in for fresh customers, was at that moment approximately the size of a manhole cover.

"'How,' I asked, 'could eight couples possibly dance in that space?'

"'Piggyback, darling, piggyback.'"[41]

Tex's clubs were always crowded; that was part of their charm. Her theory was to get a small place and pack 'em in, no matter who they were. From the nurses of the local hospital to Prince Edward of Wales. The prince happened to be at her club the very night the Prohibition agents decided to stage a small raid. Perhaps they had known he would be there and were eager for big publicity. However when the alert was given, Tex rushed him to the kitchen. She dressed him as a chef and handed him a carton of eggs, a frying pan, and a spatula, and told him to fry eggs until she returned. Then she put his escort, none other than Lord Mountbatten, behind the kettle drum and told him to play musician for a while. After all, she reasoned, anyone can beat time to a song.

When things quieted down and the disappointed raiders had left, Tex, who had forgotten all about the prince, heard a voice from the kitchen. "Texas, for Heaven's sake, do something about these eggs!" Tex rushed in and there stood a stack of fried eggs two inches high.

Tex told several versions of this story years later. Sometimes the person frying the eggs was not even Prince Eddie.[42]

Around the time of this raid, March 1925, it was rumored that the club was heading for a shutdown. The newly appointed U.S. attorney in New York, Emory R. Buckner, announced that he would close any cafe or club caught selling liquor. Of course, that was what the law was supposed to have been doing all those five years of Prohibition. Despite Buckner's announcement, Fay thought he was safe because of his "connections."

Prohibition had paved the way for corruption by necessitating strong friendships between the underworld and the politicians. For Larry Fay, as for anyone else wanting to open a night club, a good relationship with the political organization known as Tammany Hall was essential. Fay was especially friendly with James J. "Jimmy" Hines, one of the most powerful men in Tammany, and the underworld's best contact. Their friendship allowed Fay a wide choice of "sympathetic" New York judges and public officials.

Unfortunately, the day Fay came to court a federal judge with no connections to Fay's connections had charge of his case. By April 30, the club wore the inevitable padlock that was soon to be associated with Texas Guinan and her establishments. Tex took the show to the Hippodrome while searching for a new building and featured the regular songs from the El Fey in the stage revue. These included "If Ma Ferguson's Good Enough For Texas, Texas Is Good Enough For Me," "Buckner, You Have Padlocked My Heart," and "Hard-Hearted Hannah," made famous by Alice Boulden, one of the girls. Then the merriment continued at the Texas Guinan Club at 117 West Forty-eighth Street until it, too, was decorated with a padlock on August 13. Tex returned to the site of the old El Fey and opened with Fay under the new name, Del Fey Club.

Tex's attitude toward the padlockings was practical — she simply wouldn't take a padlock for an answer. She continued to supply entertainment while her bosses served booze. However, it looked to the authorities as if she were deliberately flouting the law. Though she was not the money behind the operation, she was the most visible aspect. And the papers made her look as if she were proud of the number of padlocks she was acquiring. If she liked them, it was because they brought her publicity; in truth, she found club-hopping tiresome.

Tex began to think that it would be helpful if the next place she worked in was not backed by rumrunners. She didn't like Fay's friends, for one thing, especially when they brought their guns into the club, and she had begun to have a series of arguments with Fay.

However she was smart enough not to upset him. They had made lots of money together—some said as much as $700,000 in the ten months the El Fey had been open—and they needed each other. Though later she would see that it was not quite possible or at least not nearly as profitable to run an establishment without the aid of the underworld, she foresaw a split with Mr. Fay. First, however, the two were suckered into another partnership when they fell for the myth of the Miami boom. Rumors had said real estate down there was selling like hotcakes, and money was flying around town just begging to be spent. The way Tex saw it, working down in Florida in the winter would be like making money on vacation. Unfortunately the boom went bust, and Tex soon found herself back in New York City, not totally broke, in time to open the 300 Club on New Year's Eve.

Where the Bread-and-Butter Men Roam

> *Home is a great place—after all the other places have closed.*
> —TEXAS GUINAN, "TEXAS GUINAN SAYS," DECEMBER 1, 1931

When dawn came, and Tex's "day" was over, she always felt a mixture of relief and sadness. Dawn meant sleep, brought death to the night club, and the weary Tex saw that she courted this odd death each night, holding the day at bay until she and her customers were exhausted by fun and games. Tex was so attracted to this image that she chose the entrance of dawn in Oscar Wilde's poem, "The Harlot House," to be her epitaph:

>   And down the long and silent street
>   The dawn with silver sandaled feet,
> crept like a frightened girl.[1]

When Tex left the club each dawn, sometimes she would drive out to Long Island with some of the girls for some fresh air, or drop in on her friends at the ungodly hour of 7:00. More often, though, she headed home.

Arriving at 17 West Eighth Street, Tex would climb the stairs to her sanctuary, unfasten all the locks and pass through the burglar-proof iron gate. Perhaps her parrot would cry out, "It's about time you got home." It might then proceed to run through its repertoire of "Scram, you bum"; "Hello, sucker!"; "Aw go to hell"; "Leave me alone."[2] Or the parrot might be sleeping and allow the four yellow canaries to sing a welcome instead. Then her Pekingese might poke its snout in the door and nuzzle her ankles, reminding Tex it was time for his walk.

Every morning, Tex walked the dog up and down Eighth Street.

As she did so, she was frequently observed by a young woman, Franny Schwab, who was dressing for work. Franny often watched Tex in her finery wearily walking her dog while the rest of the neighborhood brewed coffee and shook the sleep out of their heads. How old she looks, Franny would think. How overdressed. Daylight doesn't suit her.[3]

Tex herself preferred darkness to daylight, especially at the end of a long night at the club. It was time for bed! So she kept her home dimly lit. This made the place seem somewhat mysterious, seductive, conducive to sleep. Like her clubs, her apartment was meant to be a world without time, removed from reality. The muted lights helped create this illusion, along with candles and incense. Tex had a preference for the exotic (perhaps because she believed she'd been an ancient Oriental soul once), and she loved textures, fabrics, cushions. These added to the effect. She also particularly loved the furnishings that had come from the Far East, like the Satsuma Buddha that perched upon a cushion on top of a cabinet. Visitors would enter and immediately feel sleepy or prepare their palms for a reading.

Most of these select, by-invitation-only visitors were entertained in the dining room, where they could watch the water playing from the fountain in the center of a large walnut table. Here, they might have coffee from any of several silver tea services that cluttered Tex's two large buffets. This was the only room where anything seemed to match.

Sometimes, though, a lucky guest would be permitted to pass through Tex's bedroom to get to the living room and there be greeted by a full-length painting of Tommy, Tex's mom, and Tex. Everywhere there were small photos and paintings, many of Tex in her various roles, and quite a few pictures of famous friends like Nora Bayes, John Barrymore, Mary Pickford. They looked out upon the contents of the apartment from the safety of their frames, and if they could have talked, they might have commented on the variety of items, from the player piano to the leopard skin rug; from the multitude of clocks, lamps, and draperies to the massive oak synagogue chair. Everywhere was a memory crystallized in an object. Here was the silver-plated miniature clock that President Woodrow Wilson himself had given her, inscribed "The Only Tex." Here was the troupe of ebony elephants bestowed by the glorious Indian prince who had declared nights on the plateaus of Tibet were second only to nightlife in New York. Then there were the piles of books—Galsworthys, Dostoyevskys, the Bible, an overstuffed bookcase with signed copies from Thornton Wilder, Carl Van Vechten, and Sinclair Lewis, among others.

Tex's home was her great "vice," her vanity. Everywhere she looked, she was reminded of herself—in mirrors, photos, paintings, objects that told stories. Tex loved things because she knew she couldn't keep people. Friends were friends until something came up. But she could keep *things*. Things meant success, permanence. Things were memories, the past. Perhaps her instinct to accumulate had begun back in Tex's Victorian childhood, and as she was trained back then, she continued to keep the clutter immaculate, sometimes rising in the middle of the night to tidy and dust. It seemed no one was neat enough for Miss Texas Guinan—she left notes for her maids wondering, "Am I working for you?" and habitually cleaned up after them.[4]

Tex enjoyed the actual act of acquiring objects and took pleasure in expeditions to the customs house to see what had drifted in unclaimed from Europe. She also liked to wander through antique stores and odd hole-in-the-wall shops in lower Manhattan. Add to that the game of kleptomania, and the apartment became a storage place for useless stolen items: odd bottles, butter dishes, hotel towels, pewter mugs—not to mention that the place had been a makeshift hotel when her family first came to New York, so that there was a couch, phone, bellpull, and radio in every room.

Tex's bedroom was the smallest room in the house. The single window was usually covered with cloth to keep the daylight out when she slept. From the window, though, Tex could see the court below and tend her windowsill garden.

In a corner of the room lay Tex's treasured jewelry box, where each dawn she placed the bracelets, one by one, the earrings, the necklaces, the rings. Favorite items included the gold, black, and green enamel vanity case studded with diamonds that "Eddie" Windsor, Prince of Wales, had given her. It was inscribed "Listen, Miss Tex," signed "E," for Eddie. And there was Lillian Russell's diamond-studded, gold vanity case, a gift from the Czar Nicholas. There were cameo rings, emerald brooches, pearl bracelets, diamonds, and more diamonds.

Every dawn, after a ritual "dejeweling," Tex would slip into the peach silk pajamas that Hannah had laid out for her, climb into her canopied bed, and slide into sleep.

Most nights around eleven, in the year 1926, Tex would polish off a quick breakfast of oranges and ice cream or melon and chicken, and rising from the caress of her canopied bed, trot off to take care of "business." Business included peeking in on various clubs, the fights, or her kid brother Tommy's operation the Texas-Tommy

Club on Fifty-first Street. Then before one could say "Hello, suckers!" Tex was perched on top of two chairs placed back to back on the tiny dance floor at 151 West Fifty-fourth Street, surrounded by the chatter of customers and the sound of the little red kleeterklappers that she herself had distributed amongst the crowd. The transition between waking up in her quiet apartment and instigating an atmosphere of noise and animation in the rose, green, and yellow room of the 300 Club was surprisingly smooth. Tex had decorated the club to match the mood of her home, mixing comfort and the exotic, creating a dark, soft, intimate place for friends and strangers to meet and mingle. Walls and ceiling were covered with pleated cloth, and folds dripped down from the ceiling to create a tent effect, not unlike the canopy over her bed at home. Figures of parrots climbed up and down the walls, some said because Tex herself had an old pet parrot and liked to be reminded of him. More likely, the parrots wove in and out of the patterned wallscape in order to cast a spell, to seduce the wandering eye into another land, another way of thinking and feeling. Chinese lanterns hung from above the parrots on the walls and cast a soft light upon the room. If customers were to spend an entire evening here, the lighting must be perfect, the furnishings comfortable. The surroundings must encourage them to stay.

On this particular night, the thirty-some-odd tables were filled with the customary assortment of rich businessmen, bankers, and basketball heroes. There was the film star Tom Mix, Lady Diana Manners, the Stork Club's own Sherman Billingsley, playboy Harry Thaw, and Follies star Peggy Hopkins Joyce, not to mention Mayor Jimmy Walker—but of course, one oughtn't mention Mayor Walker.

A young fellow named Lou Rigler spent many an evening at the 300 Club watching with fascination. "The people who sat at her tables—amazing!" he exclaimed sixty years later. "My eyes were popping—the things that I was seeing! Here people were paying a $5 cover charge—men of affairs, men that had made their mark, men who were 40, 50, 55—and here I was sitting witnessing all these sights."[5]

Perched on her chairs in the middle of the floor, Tex began to distribute more clappers to the newly arrived. She tapped a bald man on the head with one, when it seemed he wasn't paying attention, and she laughed with her whole body when he turned to her in surprise. Exhorting the customers to have a good time, she watched the new arrivals enter and called them by their first names. She threw out more noisemakers and noticed that her guests seemed grateful for the silly recognition and intimacy the tossed noisemaker implied. That was power, to be able to control a smile—or feelings—with a wooden toy.

"Three cheers for Prohibition!" she shouted. The small portion of the audience who weren't regulars looked puzzled. "Without Prohibition where the hell would I be?" Someone shouted back, "Nowhere!" "That's right!" she guffawed.[6] She lit a cigarette, thought better of it, took a frantic three puffs, and gave it to a passing waiter. She gathered up her energy once again and bellowed even more loudly. "Who's the greatest little flapper in the whole wide world?"

"Ann Pennington!"

Tex shook her head.

"Clara Bow!"

Tex's cupid lips formed a "no."

"You, Tex!"

A brilliant flash of a smile and still a "no." Tex reached between her breasts and pulled out the American flag and waved it.[7] The joke was many nights old, but it stirred the crowd into laughter and more shouting. Tex's voice was full of the gravel that came from so many nights of shouting. To keep the audience's attention, she had to use her voice beyond its normal strength. To assist it, she usually pulled out an old police whistle and topped the noise with a shrill blast. The blast grabbed the audience's attention long enough for her to introduce the next act. She climbed off her throne and went to sit by Walter Winchell, who was chewing on the end of a pencil at a far table.

From the back of the club, Tex had a good view of the crowd's energy. They were having a grand time. They'd had a grand time last night, too, and the night before. How long would it be before the padlock-happy agents decided to blow their whistle on the 300 Club? Though the New Year's opening had promised that 1926 would be a good year for the night-club business, raids were still a threat, and working in clubs, a dangerous business. Tex had finally disengaged herself from Larry Fay, but it hadn't been easy. Though the two were talking again, it had taken months and costly bodyguards for Tex before Fay had given up his antagonism and let her move on. Now they were gift-exchanging friends, and Tex saw to it that she maintained a careful relationship with her highly inflammable former partner. Her new partners, Owney Madden, Frenchy De Mange, Nick Blair, Feets Edson, and her brother Tommy were also friends, but they were still involved in unsavory operations, and they were even more dangerous, when crossed, than Fay. And rum-running *was* illegal.

Where the Bread-and-Butter Men Roam 113

But what was actually "illegal" in the twenties? Prohibition had, in many ways, made crime "legit," and gangsters the new elite. Liquor profits bought respectability, and people came to value those who supplied them with booze, grew to depend on them. So did the police and the agents who received their cut, and the health inspectors who received *their* cut—not to mention Tammany Hall and miscellaneous connected businesses.

Thus the night-club industry was built on the deliberate flouting of the law—by the night-club owners, entertainers, clientele, and even by the lawmakers themselves. It seemed contradictory—weren't laws supposed to protect and serve the people? How could Tex feel badly about breaking the law if that was how she made her living? Hadn't she just made a joke to that effect?

Tex's underworld partners certainly knew how to make money. They had paid $8,000 for the club and made more than that on the opening night alone. Usually, they kept a low profile and instead of sitting around the club, preferred to play poker upstairs on the rolltop desk.[8] Tex was content, as long as they kept their friends with the guns out of the club and as long as the customers continued to come and she got her 50 percent of the profits. Tex was paid $2,500 a week for her 50 percent, and the other $2,500 was split between the five other partners who hoped the club would continue making $5,000 a week.

The operation seemed fairly safe. The liquor, hidden in a potato sack, was left in a dead-end alley behind the building —about five hundred dollars' worth at a time. Only the waiters and bartender Harry Harder had access to the alley. Since most of the customers brought their own, liquor was a small item at the club, anyway, at least compared to the cover charge. If the club took in three or four thousand dollars a night, only 10 percent of that would be for whiskey. At least that's what Harder calculated, and he was the one in charge of the liquor concession. When someone wanted a bottle, he took them out in a hall—to prove, if necessary, that the transaction had not taken place in the club itself—and the customer paid cash. That let the club out of trouble, supposedly. The going price was twenty dollars a quart for rye or scotch, and twenty-five dollars for champagne, which was nothing but alcohol, and Frenchy made it over in New Jersey.[9]

Besides liquor, the waiters and even Harder had their own little rackets to increase their take-home pay. Because the headwaiter and doorman were so powerful in the customer's eyes, they could bamboozle timid newcomers for all kinds of extra fees. If, say, a fellow forgot to tip doorman Sam Thorpe—only a fool or college boy would be that ignorant—Sam would stall them. When they finally got in, they might complain to Harder that they had had trouble getting in, and he might say that was because they didn't have a club card. Of course, there was no such thing as a club card, but Tex could hear him saying, "Yes and I'd be glad to issue you one for each member of your party for the small fee of $10 apiece."[10]

Other ruses included the time-honored, ringside-table racket. Nothing like watching the boys get tipped extra to move a table up front, only to accept more money to place other tables in front of that one. So the poor sucker who had had the ringside seat at the start often found himself fleeced again to move up. One night a fellow paid three times to be a ringsider. Harder, the headwaiter, and Albert Berryman, the manager, later split the tip three ways.[11]

Well, it was a racket. And the place was such a success, one supposed the suckers didn't really care. They paid to get taken for a ride, seemed to revel in it! There was never an end to the inflow of customers. Why, when Helen Morgan or Jimmy Durante turned their customers out of doors at 4:00 A.M., everybody headed to the 300 Club.

The girls had finished their number. Tex returned to the front of the club and shouted, "Come on, let's get hot! And let's give that little girl a great big hand!" She signaled the band to play some dance music, and the dance floor filled quickly.

God bless those musicians. Though there were only seven in the band, they were seven stalwart players who drank tea instead of whiskey and made faces at the bitter taste just to show the customers they weren't getting the good stuff, no sir. Hey, now was a good time to put in a pitch for the boys. The floor was full of fox-trotters who looked as if they were enjoying themselves tremendously, enough at least to pay a little extra for it. Tex signaled Tony Giannini, the trumpet-playing bandleader, and he signaled the boys to stop. Before the audience could argue, Tex was saying, ". . . and the union won't let me pay these mugs a proper wage—they can hardly make ends meet—little kids at home starving—rent overdue—so let's pass the hat and help them out." The audience, as always, obliged.[12]

Tex was feeling generous tonight. Earlier in the evening, a couple of young kids had stopped by after a school dance. The boys couldn't have been out of their teens. When they saw their bill, Tex saw their faces. Materializing by their table, she smiled and said, "I'll match you for it." Of course, the kids won and went home without paying a dime. One of the girls in the party, Elizabeth Lawton, recalled the incident and years later said it was "a rather endearing story about a rather tough lady, isn't it?"[13]

Tex had a weakness for people in tight spots, but her sympathy did not extend to the sucker who could afford her prices—and she let them know that point blank. Heywood Broun said, "She was an extremely honest and candid person. The prices for mineral water and ginger ale were fantastic and the kitchen was generally a gag, but she was always the first to admit as much. Texas never sneaked up on the spenders who came into her place."[14] She also kept her eyes on her friends who could not afford to act like suckers, like Broun.

Broun had once been foolish enough, probably thanks to the young lady he'd brought with him, to order a bottle of champagne. Tex had come over to his table to tell him not to be silly. "You know we're charging $30 a quart for champagne and you know it isn't champagne. Tell your young lady to take gin and like it."[15]

As if to make up for Tex's friends without money, countless thousands slipped through the soft fingers of many a customer. Take the time Harry Thaw cashed a check at the club for $1,000. Within an hour, damned if he didn't have a cent of it left. Clean evaporated from his pocket. Bewildered, he asked Tex to look and see if he'd really written that check to begin with.[16]

Then there was the time another big spender complained that it cost him $1,000 just to fix a cigarette lighter at the club. Of course, Tex had had nothing to do with the fact that he'd spilled some of the lighter fluid on an expensive fur coat, which proceeded to catch fire when a neighboring cigarette accidentally brushed against it. A quick-thinking waiter doused the small blaze with water and ruined the coat—which cost the spender that $1,000 to replace.[17]

Another story circulated about how blasé the waiters had become over the large amounts of money spent at Tex's clubs in a single night. A waiter once overheard some Romeo tell his honey, "I feel terrible. I lost $337,000 on the market today." The waiter was later quoted as saying, "These drunks will cry over any little thing."[18]

Besides spenders, the club seemed to attract a lot of highbrows, too. Everybody, it seems, liked to play. Why one night the previous week a waiter found the most fascinating design sketched onto one of the tablecloths. He went over to Tex and the boys, who were sitting and yakking after the customers had all gone home, and he asked what it was all about. It wasn't until they'd nabbed an architect friend that they found it was the Pythogorean theorem all worked out—in detail.[19] Whatever that meant. Tex was suitably impressed.

To start the show again, Tex shouted "Cohen" and listened for an answering "Cohen." That was the signal to lower the lights. Scouting the audience to make sure all were noise-equipped and ready, she moved to a ringside table to sit by Peggy Hopkins Joyce. The girls began the next act with their notorious "Cherries" number, and Peggy asked Tex where Rudy (Valentino) was tonight. Rumor had it that he was ill. After his suspension from Paramount, he'd been in the club practically every night. All the girls—and even Georgie Raft—had been impressed by "the Sheik." In fact as a joke, Nick Blair and Feets Edson had once told Georgie they'd throw $100 bills at him as he danced, just to see if he could impress Mr. Valentino. Of course, Rudy hadn't paid any attention, though he did pay notice the time Tex had bamboozled an East Indian fakir, Rahmin Bey, to appear at the club. His gag was that he could pierce his arm and he wouldn't bleed. Well Rudy, not to be outdone, had taken his jacket off, rolled up his sleeve and pierced! Alas, he bled.[20] Two months later, Valentino would die of a perforated ulcer. His funeral that August would attract the most splendid turnout for a nontheatrical event she had ever seen, and newspapers would quote her as having said "What publicity!" In fact, the funeral *was* largely a stunt to boost the receipts at the box office and pay off Rudy's debts. Tex took proper advantage of the situation and made all her girls attend the funeral in full regalia. It was part of their education, she explained.

Tex looked up and saw that Georgie was doing his famous fast Charleston. The show was hurrying toward the last number. Then the girls would emerge from backstage with baskets of cardboard snowballs to toss at the audience. Everybody knew the finale as well as the chorus number and the audience-response lines to the song about the onions. One of the shapelier girls began her instructive song and dance number, pointing first at her eyes to tell the audience she had two eyes, then at her ears, to tell the audience she had two ears—and so on down her anatomy. The refrain for waiters and audience ran, "and she knows her onions." Tex knew that the song—the whole scene—would not translate beyond the room, that anywhere else, even on paper as a description, it would fall flat. But here at the club, it was a roaring finale. "AND SHE KNOWS HER ONIONS."[21] The crowd continued to chant. Suddenly, snowballs fell everywhere—some lodged in Chinese lanterns, others inside the piano. Tex shouted encouragement to the chaos and one heard "lil guurrls," "a big hand," "onions," and "Cohen!" The dancers evaporated even as the confetti-covered, snowball-throwing customers continued their civilized brawl, and their absence was not noticed. Even though the music had changed, and Tex had begun visiting from table to table, the audience was still wrapped up in the fight. "Yes Sir, That's My Baby" eased the customers into the next phase of the night—into drinking more, spending more, dancing a token two-step. If a newcomer entertained the thought of leaving, or imagined the evening's fun was over, he or she would find quickly that the excitement never stopped—unless there was a raid. Then things grew even more hectic and all were treated to an additional show down at the jailhouse.

Tex's knowledge of federal Prohibition agents and their disguises had not been enough to keep the 300 Club from accumulating its share of summonses and raids. The laws of Prohibition were changing rapidly, and the government sought to buckle down on those like Tex who kept eluding them. By 1926, the agents were playing the roles of "loose-moraled millionaires," and the government footed the bill.[22] The *New York Times* bragged on their behalf, that "so thoroughly did these polished prohibition agents worm their way into the good graces of Broadwayites, according to a statement made at Mr. Buckner's office that Texas Guinan, on their second visit to the 300 Club, threw a kiss to them and asked them why they were leaving the place so early." That was after the December raid, when the "drys" had sought to cash in on holiday liquor. The new weapon they were using against the proprietors of night clubs was the serving of personal injunctions. Get one of those, and if caught serving liquor even on the next day, you would face a possible prison sentence for contempt of court.

The first time the government sought to snag the 300 Club was in early February 1926, shortly after it had opened. Using the excuse that the club was violating fire codes by housing two hundred bodies in a space designed to hold seventy-five, Police Commissioner G. V. McLaughlin tried to shut the place down. Counsel for Texas, however, said that in order to remove the supposed fire hazard, Tex would be glad to build a new exit. The summons was dismissed.

The next time the government looked for a better excuse. Members of the New York Police Department were given permission to go into night clubs like the 300 and spend as much as they needed in order to become known as big spenders. Once they became trusted customers, they could spring a raid, easily acquiring the necessary evidence by simply ordering some booze. At 3:00 A.M. on July 4, 1926, detectives in evening clothes seized two bottles of gin, one of rye, and one of scotch. They had mingled with the four hundred guests celebrating the return of the golfer Bobby Jones, who had just won the British Open golf championship. Among the crowd were two U. S. senators. Although the evidence grabbed seemed damaging enough, the 300 Club continued to operate. To think the government could close a club on the strength of a few bottles of whiskey! One employee tried to explain that the club didn't even need to sell liquor, for they got at least $6.00 from every person who sat down at their tables—in cover charges and for soft drinks like ginger ale at $1.50 a glass.

The government knew that people watched Tex, followed her antics in the local papers. Scarcely a day went by when she didn't appear in someone's column. If they could prove that she was a public nuisance, people would sit up and take notice that liquor was illegal. They might even accept her arrest as proof that Prohibition was here to stay. In addition, the government had so many church groups, temperance groups, and ladies auxiliary clubs breathing down its neck that it needed to take a stand. The truth was, people like Tex kept the government agents in business.

In *Vanity Fair*'s "Impossible Interview Number 14," the Queen of the Night Clubs met the Queen of Temperance, Ella Boole, head of the Women's Christian Temperance Union (WCTU), in a mock conversation where she admitted she was in full favor of Prohibition—only the "gay," or amusing side of it.

"Listen, Dearie, let's get this straight," was the way they imagined Tex would chat, in a tone of hushed confidences. "We're both honest, hard-working girls. And what do we live by? Prohibition. I earn my living running night clubs, you make yours running the WCTU. You edify your customers—I amuse mine. They both love it. But just suppose that the Eighteenth Amendment were finally repealed—"

ELLA: Perish the thought!
TEXAS: . . . we'd both be out of a job.[23]

In January 1927, New York began to enforce a new curfew law of 3:00 A.M. Of course 3:00 A.M. was the time when Tex's club really got hot, and she continued to stay open until 5:00 in spite of the warning. Subsequently, she was arrested. She appeared in court and as usual paid bail and walked out. There were rumors of her opening a new club, but the 300 Club was still going full blast at the time of the final raid on February 16, 1927.

Texas's bartender at the time, Harry Harder, thought the club was asked to close because of the public school down the street. Every day the kids would see women in evening clothes and men in high hats leaving the club as they were arriving for class.

In the end, the club was closed, not by irate parents, but by James Walter Longcope, a wealthy college boy turned Prohibition agent. Having been fleeced in more than one night club to the tune of $7,000, Longcope had a long-standing vendetta with the clubs of New York. By taking his revenge on Tex, he thought he'd get back at them all. He was a very useful weapon for the government, and he did their dirty work for them. However, a year later, Longcope would be arrested for extortion while posing as an agent at an Italian restaurant in Greenwich Village.

Customers present at the 300 Club on that night in February almost missed the show. Raids, in their minds, were big, noisy affairs, with cops running around blowing whistles and hacking furniture with axes. Several clubs had, in fact, experienced such violent activity, but none of Tex's establishments ever had. Raids at her clubs were always "civilized" duels of wit, and she never put up much of a struggle. She simply signaled the band to play the 1924 top hit, "The Prisoner's Song," and followed the agents out. On this particular evening, one of the guests walked calmly up to where Tex was sitting, on the back of two chairs directing the show, and informed her that she was under arrest. That was the whole raid. Rising to the occasion, Tex replied, "What again? I hope I can ride in a taxi."[24] Tex continued to make light of the situation and would once again turn the arrest into an opportunity, even though she'd spend a night in jail. She left the club yet again to the tune of "The Prisoner's Song" and the cheers of her customers.

The customers decided, in the fashion of the twenties, that if they were not to have a show, in the form of a messy raid or otherwise, then they would have to create one themselves. While someone spread the news of the raid to some of the other clubs, the rest of the guests threw on their wraps, jumped into cabs, and headed—singing all the way—to the West Forty-seventh Street police station. Soon there was a tremendous traffic jam by the station. Denizens of the neighborhood stuck their heads out their windows and watched the 300 Club patrons emerge from the many cabs and start singing "The Prisoner's Song." Their next number turned out to be, "The Prisoner's Song." And the next. Those of the window audience who despaired of ever recapturing their night's slumber found themselves seduced into joining in, while more cars arrived with more fur-coated night-club clientele in search of some late-night fun.

Meanwhile, inside the station, Tex was coyly telling the lieutenant that her age was thirty-six (she was forty-three). As she gave her address, she was informed that she and her cohorts were accused of violating a court order—that rotten old personal injunction from last December—the penalty for which, if she were convicted, would be a jail sentence.

"How sweet," replied Tex. "What a thrill! Texas Guinan going to jail."[25] This was her cue to sing. She sang "The Prisoner's Song," or so said the *New York Post* the next day. Reportedly, the lieutenant tactfully had her removed to the adjoining room which was supposedly soundproof. An hour later, Tex was transferred to the West Thirtieth Street station.

It was by now 2:00 A.M. Tex emerged from the station nine hours later, after paying the $1,000 bail and treating the station's workers and the more steadfast followers (who had loitered around the station all night) to a luscious breakfast ordered straight from the Waldorf. After some caviar and orange juice, she looked quite disappointed when her attorney arrived to rescue her. She turned to a police officer on her way out and simpered, "They're not going to make me go home, are they?"[26] She then sang a new version of "The Prisoner's Song," insisting that she loved jail. "Why go to Palm Beach for a rest when you can stay in town, rent free?"[27]

Tex had once again turned an unpleasant situation to her advantage. She had her picture in the paper and the sympathy of all New York. She was now the veteran of six raids and four padlock decrees, acquired in the space of only three years, yet she had never been long out of business and never personally suffered either fine or imprisonment until now. It was whispered around town and even printed in the *New York Times* on February 19, 1927, that the secret of her success was that she was always "an innocent, if not victimized employee." Okay, maybe Tex wasn't all that innocent, but she had enough to worry about without thinking about the booze as well. She was an entertainer first and foremost.

While the press carried the intimate details of Tex's jail stay and the padlock proceedings, the *New York Graphic* offered the first full-length version of Tex's autobiography. It was entitled, "How I Became Queen of the Night Clubs" and was written in collaboration with Ruth Ridenour. It is a close cousin to the *New York Evening Journal*'s version that emerged in 1929.

Although the club was told it would be receiving a six-month padlock, Tex went to work the evening she was released from jail. Unsurprisingly, business had increased in proportion to the padlock publicity. To add to the excitement, the evangelist Aimee Semple McPherson decided to visit the club. She was in town on a twenty-two–city tour in an attempt to recover from a recent scandal related to her mysterious disappearance/"kidnapping" the previous spring. Though West-Coasters had had their fill of Aimee, the East Coast was still interested in her.

Like Tex, Aimee was a charismatic personality who lived in the spotlight and thrived on publicity. She had a husky, vibrant "contralto of the midway,"[28] a voice she milked to its dramatic utmost and which aided her in her salesmanship of her Foursquare Gospel. Though Aimee sold religion, her revival meetings were a theatrical event, geared toward giving the folks a good time. So it was not a surprise that film stars Gloria Swanson and Adolphe Menjou stated that if there were two women who could exchange places in life, those two would be Texas and Aimee.

Aimee was in town, as the *New York Times* put it, "to purge [the] city." On this particular February evening's tour of the city's clubs, she stopped in at Fifty-fourth Street. Some thought she'd chosen the club to cash in on some of Tex's latest publicity, yet she played the shy visitor, fumbling to preserve her anonymity. When she walked in, Tex's brother Tommy noticed her immediately and jumped out of his seat to grab her hand. One of her escorts waved him back and tried to explain that Miss McPherson was traveling incognito. Incognito, my foot, thought Tommy, knowing his sister's eagerness to make the most out of the visit. He signaled her over his shoulder, and Tex left the floor and rushed to Aimee's side. A henchman of the *Post* saw the whole thing. The two clasped hands and Tex, with an air of "I, too, have suffered; I, too, have known publicity," sought to draw Aimee to a table "where everybody can see you, dear."

"No, no," protested the evangelist. "This is very nice, back here." As she protested, Aimee took a look around the club. Unrecognized by the crowd, she could observe them and plan more what she would say, for she knew she would eventually rise and grab the spotlight—just as Tex knew she would. There was a young girl in the center of the miniscule dance floor at this time, in the midst of a Broadway version of a Hawaiian maiden doing the hula. That decided her. Aimee rose and said to her escort, "I would like to talk to them." He in turn informed Tex.

"Oh will she? Say I'd love her to speak. You know, all the front-page guys land in here, sooner or later—" Immediately, Tex was up on her feet, shouting for silence, shooing the Hawaiian act off the floor. Then she yelled the news that "a great little girl from the Golden West, a wonderful, brave woman, is going to say a few words."

Aimee stepped forward. "Stop before it is too late," she pleaded, transforming the tiny dance floor into her pulpit. "Behind all these beautiful clothes," continued the evangelist, clothed in an expensive gown of her own, "behind these good times, in the midst of your lovely buildings and shops and pleasures, there is another life. There is something on the other side. 'What shall it profit a man, if he shall gain the whole world, and lose his own soul?' With all your getting and playing and good times, don't forget you have a Lord. Take Him into your hearts!"[29]

After a short silence, the audience responded with loud applause. They cheered and rattled their red wooden noisemakers. Saxophones backed them up. Waiters clapped enthusiastically. Tex sat on a table puffing a cigarette with excitement. She shouted to the crowd to give the little lady from the West a great big hand. Everyone present was used to obeying Tex's commands, and the noise level increased. Then Aimee invited all present to attend her sermon at the Chapel of Glad Tidings, and Tex jumped up to encourage all the guests to go. She pulled the cigarette from between her red lips and shouted that she intended to go herself and bring her girls. Tex's voice became evangelical and all were awed by the similarity of the two women.

Without outwardly belittling Aimee, Tex had made her into another night-club act and increased the evangelist's palatability for the customers by adding her own personal enthusiasm. She was not adverse to sharing her spotlight with another female personality because she knew that despite their similarities, the two reigned in different worlds.

Tex was fascinated by Aimee and her brand of show biz. She appreciated the craft that went into Aimee's act and the fact that she was such a successful saleswoman. Aimee, too, was someone who had created her persona, who had exploited the times and the peoples' needs. In fact, Tex was strongly attracted to the idea that one could combine religion and showmanship. She filed that away for the future.

The following day, the Queen of the Night Clubs did attend the meeting of the so-called Queen of Heaven and sat directly under the pulpit with one of her dancers, Laura Wilkenson. Tex made sure the press noticed her, noticed what she was wearing, and afterward shook hands with Aimee. In later years, relating the story to various friends and reporters, Tex added this anecdote: Aimee had asked if Tex knew any hymns, thinking she would not, and after Tex had squeezed in a wisecrack about all the "hims" she knew, she burst forth with a classical hymn and greatly surprised the congregation.[30]

With a padlock on the 300 Club and another club about to open, Tex thought she might take a quick trip to Havana. However, lingering charges of contempt kept her around till the end of February. By early March, rumors began circulating that Tex had used the quiet weeks of vacation to have her face lifted. Her father denied the reports and said his daughter was outside Atlantic City, New Jersey, visiting friends. Of course, no one believed him, especially when Tex reappeared looking much younger and many pounds thinner. Tex said she had simply taken a "rest cure," and that anyone who wanted to look her over could come to her new club on Forty-eighth Street—in the exact same spot where the Texas Guinan Club once stood—when she opened on St. Patrick's Day.

The new club was smaller, more brightly lit, more playful. It was decorated with colorful caricatures of New York celebrities like Paul Whiteman, drawn by an artist named Wynn Holcolmb, who would later claim that he had never been paid for his work. Red, yellow, and blue balloons danced on the many strings suspended from one side of the room to the other.

A mere two weeks after the club had kicked off, Tex signed a contract with Duo Art Corporation to do a show for the Shuberts entitled *Padlocks of 1927*. Her salary was rumored at $5,000 a week, and she was planning to continue to work her club as well.

While Tex rehearsed, she made the acquaintance of a newcomer in town, Belle Livingstone. Tex had heard a little about the former "Girl with the Poetic Legs," now in her early fifties, and knew Belle had just opened a club and might eventually challenge her own title as Queen of the Midnight Revelry. A little competition never hurt anybody, but Tex wanted to meet this woman and look her over. She'd also heard that Livingstone only charged an initial membership fee of $200, after which everything was on the house. That was no way to run a business. Belle needed some counseling. Tex made a date with her to attend St. Patrick's Cathedral on Easter Sunday and lunch at the Ritz afterward. Let the public see them together.

Tex proceeded to impress the newcomer, as Livingstone later wrote in her autobiography, by her showmanship at the cathedral, by her timing and attitude toward the publicity that was accorded her the instant she stepped out of her Rolls. Tex was greeted by name by the police who were on hand at the cathedral to control the Easter crowds. Cameras clicked in machine-gun style the moment she alighted, but Tex seemed not to notice them. When she reached the door, she simply nodded to a man Belle later discovered was her press agent, who was on hand merely to tell the press what she was wearing. Belle noticed that even the magnificent display at the church could not detract from Tex's effect on the other Easter celebrants as she swept down the aisle "beribboned and beflowered."[31]

After the mass, the two walked in the Easter parade and eventually found themselves at a quiet table at the Ritz. Now it was time for business.

> "What's the big idea, Belle?" and [Tex] leaned across the table. "Two hundred dollars a sucker and everything on the house! You're not making a dime out of that place of yours . . . you ought to incorporate and grab off some dough."
>
> "You don't understand, Tex," I [Belle] answered. "I want to live as I did in Europe, and this is the only way I can do it. A bank balance means less to me than having a salon again."
>
> "My God! Oil the wheels of profit with that speech!" [Tex] cried.
>
> "You see, I take pleasure in surrounding myself with people who can talk as well as drink," I went on. "Look at my magic list of patrons."
>
> "Magic is the right word." Tex held to her point. "Now you see 'em, now you don't."[32]

Belle appreciated Tex's practicality but never followed her advice. She prided herself on her sophisticated clientele and used to say that while Tex had the masses, she attracted the classes. Her style was to commandeer a Park Avenue residence and furnish it lavishly with costly ornaments and well-dressed clients. She called these clubs "salons," which afforded the press the opportunity to add an extra *o* to the second syllable of the word. Tex liked to stop by Belle's clubs fairly frequently to compare business and inspect the customers. "My God," she once said to Belle, "look at all those big shots. It's just like the court balls you read about."[33]

In the months following their Easter luncheon, the two women became close friends. They played up the game of competition and kept careful eyes on each other's profits, besides exchanging ideas and pranks. One is never sure how deep this friendship actually went. There was certainly a bit of professional jealousy mixed in with their playfulness. Tex would frequently call Belle to compare the evening's receipts. No matter how high a sum Tex quoted, Belle said she always topped her claim by two or three thousand dollars. Belle wrote in her autobiography how much she loved the "Irish mind of Texas, with its frolicsome unpredictable wit, and I wanted to show the world we had a united front."[34] As far as she was concerned, "Texas and I were two women who passed vigorously rather than happily through Prohibition. Although temporary figures, we were clearly visible. The world is prone to say glibly that there is no one who cannot be replaced. But Texas's throne still remains draped in crepe, and I must confess I don't see anyone on my dais either."[35] And Tex said once in her syndicated column, "Texas Guinan Says," "Like myself Belle has two faces, one for her salon and one for street wear. But both of them are kind and interesting."[36]

Belle told a story of a typical night of mischief when the two were out to a dinner party at the residence of cartoonist Clare Briggs. Among the other guests was the writer Ring Lardner. Clare and Ring had been drinking at the Lamb's Club beforehand and had arrived slightly tipsy. Ring soon settled down in a big, comfortable chair and promptly fell asleep. Watching him dozing, Tex had an idea. She was at that time the talk of all Broadway because she had an entertainer at her club named Nerida who did a dance with a nine-foot python. She sent the chauffeur to her club to pick up Nerida and pal and bring them to the party. While Ring snored, Tex placed the python gently around his neck like a necklace. Whether it was Tex's perfume, the laughter of the guests, or the proximity of reptilian skin on his neck, Lardner woke up. Feeling the unusual weight, the damp, the cold of the snake on his neck, he looked at it, started, and then smiled, palely. Clare asked him if he'd like a drink.

He glanced down at the snake once more and thought perhaps he oughtn't. Belle recalled,

> Very gingerly he touched the torpid gelid neckpiece, looked at us, and tried to smile again. I said he'd better have a glass of champagne.
>   He gave us a searching glance, as if to ascertain whether we saw, and then said weakly: "I think I'd better have just a cup of coffee."
>   The English butler who was serving the coffee needed all his early training in self-restraint as he leaned over Ring to ask how many sugars, please.
>   Finally George Buckley [another guest], being like all men a friend to men, stepped up and took the horrible "dream" from

around Ring's neck. When Ring saw the snake was real, he drained a highball in relief and laughed as hard as anyone present at what was perhaps the meanest practical joke ever pulled.[37]

Padlocks of 1927 opened on July 5, 1927. Critics agreed that like her clubs, the show was all Tex. "All eyewitnesses agree on the wave of deep gloom which sweeps over the club on 48th Street when its hostess leaves the scene," said *New York World*. "Her show collapses with the same flat finality in those intervals when she is not on the stage."[38]

Bushnell Diamond of the *Denver Post* tried to explain this phenomenon. "Miss Guinan hovers over the saturnalia like a benevolent vulture. She is an astonishing woman. Without good looks, youth, voice, charm or style, she manages to keep the show going at blood heat temperature by some dogged technic of personal will power. Even when she is unwittingly comic, she holds her audience in a kind of steel net of compulsion."[39]

Tex's show was pretty much the club act transferred to the stage, complete with the playful tossing of snowballs at celebrities and the unknown alike. It was declared, "a jocose, raucous, high-spirited hurly burly. It is vulgar in that it panders to all the cliches and banalities of its type of entertainment. It is loud, noisy, unimaginative, unbeautiful and lacking in any sort of distinction. But some of it is good fun."[40]

All summer Broadwayites turned out for the show and "shouted themselves hoarse with delight at being permitted to play."[41] By September 23, however, *Padlocks* was ready to close. Rumor had it that this was due to lack of funds. Indeed, the management owed Tex $26,000. But Tex denied the story and said she merely needed a vacation before opening a new club for the Shuberts that October. The new club, the Century Club, would be located in the basement of the Century Theatre on the corner of Sixty-second and Century Park West. The building that housed the club still stands there today and is now an apartment house.

The run of *Padlocks* did more than introduce non–club goers to Tex and her gang, it increased her huge following. Her admirers included an eighteen-year-old Aubrey Hastings who attended *Padlocks* several times before he had the courage to stand with the stage-door Johnnies in Shubert Alley. He was hoping to attract the attention of someone, anyone, who could introduce him to the fascinating Texas Guinan. Finally he convinced Pat Codyre, one of the performers, to take him into the dressing room to meet Tex. He was so thrilled by the experience that he attended the show at least ten times more, often mingling with the intermission crowd to catch the second act. When his father heard about his evening expeditions, he was furious and chased him around his Washington Square apartment with a stout stick in hand. In spite of his father's opposition, the boy continued his attachment to the glamour of the show. Years later, Hastings could still picture that wondrous night during the finale when Tex, shouting good night as she rode down the aisle on a cast member's shoulders, leaned over and kissed him. He followed her to the Century Club when she opened there and became a regular.[42]

Though settling in the Century Theatre's basement kept her club within the theater world, Tex took a risk by opening so far uptown. In order to insure good business, she reintroduced the guest-of-honor night for Thursdays, "when the stars of the stage and screen put on their own impromptu show."[43]

Advertising for the club described a brand-new show, *Broadway Carnival Nights*, a three-ring circus and the Kentucky Derby all rolled into one, with Tex as the ringmaster. The club was decorated like a circus, complete with calliope, games, and a small tank of trout where patrons could fish for dinner. Before the club opened on October 7, 1927, a small advertising broadside by Lew Ney, *Satire Day Night*, appeared proclaiming the club's success in advance. "It has proved to be New York's greatest sensation!!! Come be a REVELLER!" Among those invited were "Big Suckers," "Young Sockers," and "Old Soakers."[44]

Tex's past experiences and love for the circus had in part been responsible for the decor and theme of the club, but her clubs were all notorious as three-ring amusements, and the explicit suggestion that life at her clubs was to be pure play and clowning was redundant.

Credit for the entire operation was given this time to Al Kerwin, who was said to be the sole manager of the new club. Kerwin was one of Tex's many "personal managers." That meant he was her lover as well. He had first made an appearance back when Tex was running the 300 Club. Most outsiders had a rather low opinion of him. Lou Rigler said, "Tex had a fellow, Al Kerwin, a bum—a ne'er-do-well and people used to ask, 'What do you want with this fellow?' I think he was slightly younger, too, and who knows, she probably gave him money, I don't know."[45] Everyone who knew Tex, including her parents, thought she was making a fool of herself. But Kerwin remained by her side for several years, during a time when she repeatedly told reporters she was too busy for love. Here was her declared attitude toward romance:

He: Come into the garden.
She: What do you want?
He: Look at the stars.
She: Guess who was in last night.
He: Look yonder at the moon.
She: We did $1,800.
He: Do you really care for me? . . .
She: That was pretty good for a Monday.
He: Hold my hand.
She: Give me a pencil.
He: Smell the dew-drenched flowers.
She: How much is six times $1,800?
He: Darling you must be mine forever!
She: Oh Hell! I forgot to order some new clappers. . . .
He: Kiss me, my love.
She: Heavens I need some coffee!
He: Tell me you love me.
She: What a life! I gotta appear in court tomorrow and bail out another bunch of waiters.

By the end of the second act, the love interest was carried out exhausted.[46]

As far as the public knew, Tex had no time for love. Tales of three marriages should have been enough to keep them satisfied. But although people knew little about her men, many drew the same conclusions. It was assumed that Kerwin, like many others, lived off the entertainer, doing odd jobs around the clubs to make his pay seem "legit." He was after her for her money, and that was all. Sooner or later, he'd probably go for one of her girls and blow it, maybe marry one of them. Or maybe she'd tire of him. It was, of course, convenient to have a handsome escort for the Friday-night fights at the Garden on Eighth Avenue and Fiftieth Street, but such escorts were replaceable.

At this stage, Tex's success attracted a large number of fortune hunters. Though such involvements kept her feeling young, they never lasted.

The new Century Club was off to a great start. Then a month later, on November 22, Tex's license—rather the Texas Restaurant Corporation's license—was revoked. Tex had broken the curfew laws, for one thing. She appealed to the court and declared the curfew laws unconstitutional, but she lost her case and the club on

December 18. Not to be undone, Tex found herself another space and a way out of obeying the curfew law. She learned, via one of her many lawyers, that if she affiliated herself with a hotel having more than fifty rooms, or some kind of club, association, or society, she could operate as late as she desired. After some searching, she discovered the basement of the Acropolis Hotel owned by John Johnnidis and Nick Prounis.

The Salon Royale opened on New Year's Eve and remained at 310 West Fifty-eighth Street through the month of June 1928—exactly six months. The club featured such acts as Tommy Lyman and his band, and Tex's "gang of twenty." Guinan was at the peak of her career. Helen Morgan, her only real competition in the night-club world aside from Belle Livingstone, could not begin to claim the crowds Tex was drawing.

Morgan, at age twenty-seven, had made her name on the musical stage as Julie in Jerome Kern's *Showboat*. She had been moonlighting in the night-club business for only a short time and was most recently hostess at the Summer Home. She was best known for the way she sat on a piano and sang her traditional songs, "My Bill" and "Can't Help Loving That Man" and "Why Was I Born." These seemed especially designed for the sentimental audience, and everybody loved her—except the Feds. In fact, somehow the young torch singer had attracted the angry attention of the Prohibition administrator, Major Campbell, and was often the victim of the most violent raids of the era. Agents would ax much of the club's furnishings and confiscate whatever remained. They were unnecessarily brutal, as if out to satisfy someone's personal vendetta. Morgan's biographer, Gilbert Maxwell, believed this was so.

In 1928, Texas and Helen shared similar headlines and headaches, all of which could be traced to one source: Mabel Walker Willebrandt. It seemed that the Assistant Attorney General of the United States—that was Mabel—had them on her "get" list. She was after the entire city of New York, and La Guinan and La Morgan appeared to represent the entire night-club industry.

It was Willebrandt, immortalized by New York's Governor Al Smith as "the Prohibition Portia," who had developed the successful new breed of dry agents dressed to pose as big spenders. Tex's memoirs sarcastically introduced her as a skinny little girl who lived across the street when Tex was a child in Waco. Actually, Willebrandt had been born in Woodsdale, Kansas, in 1889. By her mid-twenties, she was an attorney in Los Angeles and public defender for women in trouble. She was assigned to the post of Assistant Attorney General of the United States in charge of Prohibition enforcement, tax prosecution, and federal prisons under the Harding administration in 1921. She had her share of scandals after Harding's death but continued to execute her anti–night-club activities through the mid-twenties.

In her personal life, Willebrandt was strictly self-disciplined. Though she had formerly held a tolerant attitude toward liquor, and had even taken an occasional drink in the privacy of her own home, once Prohibition became law, she sacrificed her personal pleasures. She was the kind of government employee who was always the first at the office in the morning and the last to leave. She had the habit of taking an ice-cold bath each morning and walking the two miles to work each day. Her stoic qualities brought her into sharp contrast with the women she hunted. Morgan's biographer, Gilbert Maxwell, even theorized that Willebrandt was actually jealous of Morgan, in a bitter, old-maid way, and wanted personally to destroy her. Willebrandt was perhaps more afraid of attacking Tex because of the underworld men who backed her. Morgan was more fragile and would not stand the stress. She would eventually crack.[47]

On the evening of June 28, 1928, the evening that New York Governor Al Smith was nominated to run for President opposite the Republican candidate Herbert Hoover, more than 160 federal agents descended upon fifteen New York night clubs in a well-planned and well-timed attack. Included in the raids were Texas Guinan's Salon Royale, Helen Morgan's Summer Home, the Silver Slipper, and the Beaux Arts Cafe, among others. It looked as if Mabel meant business, and all of Broadway shuddered. If someone didn't take a stand, the entire night-club industry would be in danger. Pleasure would evaporate from the neon-lit streets of the city.

Tex and Helen hadn't even been at their clubs on the night of the raid, but after turning themselves in and watching the majority of their companions plead guilty, Tex knew that she had better do something drastic. Maintaining a public nuisance? A lady who brought joy to countless hundreds every night between the hours of 11:00 P.M. and 6:00 A.M.? She certainly was *not* guilty. And she meant to prove it.

On Trial

I have been credited with much and charged with plenty . . .
Whenever they have a new law they try it out on me.
—TEXAS GUINAN, "TEXAS GUINAN SAYS," SEPTEMBER (?), 1931

April 9, 1929

"Miss Guinan's particular function," Prosecutor Morrison was saying, "was to make whoopee. She made everybody feel at home in a jovial way. There was entertainment, the silliest of songs and jokes and the thumbing of noses at the law. These exhibitions of whoopee were going on while the guests of the establishment were getting thoroughly in the spirit of the occasion, thanks to the liquor they had obtained."[1]

Norman J. Morrison, Special Assistant U.S. Attorney and government representative in the case against Texas Guinan was, as the *New York Sun* described him, a ponderous, slightly bald citizen of humorless mien. As he paced back and forth in front of the courtroom, hands clasped tightly behind his back, head erect, listeners began to translate his statements in terms of the nuisance charges. His description of Tex's job seemed accurate enough, only an undertone of sarcasm—no, derision—kept sneaking into his voice. This "thumbing the nose at the law" business, too, made her sound like a bad little girl.

One couldn't help noting how Morrison had linked booze with Tex's "function." One might even be led to believe that Tex was to stand trial simply because she had attracted customers to a place that coincidentally sold liquor—though, in reality, customers could get a drink anywhere and came primarily to see her. Thousands of entertainers did what Tex did each evening all over the country. If that were the sole criterion for arrest, then the entire night-club industry was guilty—or in serious trouble.

A good portion of the courtroom crowd had come to the trial just to catch a glimpse of the famous Queen of the Night Clubs, not caring about the outcome. They wanted to be entertained and knew that wherever La Guinan went, fun followed. They awaited her answer to Morrison hoping for wisecracks they could repeat to their friends.

Others had more than curiosity at stake. These were various entertainers, waiters, people involved in the night-club scene. They were counting on Tex to outsmart the law and save the industry. Surely she would counter Morrison's nasty opening remarks with an observation of her own.

But there were no snappy comebacks. Tex's attorney waived his opportunity to talk, and his line of defense remained a mystery.

The first witness for the government was Agent James L. White, one of Willebrandt's star henchmen. He was a tall, dark man with a thin face, who directed all his remarks at the jury. As he began to testify, Tex drew her chair closer to the counsel table, reached for a pencil from a multicolored silken bag and began to take notes. Several times, she leaned over to her lawyer and whispered comments and questions in his ear. Other times, she sent notes to the press table.

White testified that he had made twelve visits to the Salon Royale between February 2 and April 29, 1928. On his first visit, accompanied by his wife, he had managed to purchase a quart of champagne and two half pints of whiskey for thirty-five dollars. Tex herself, he claimed, had been present when the liquor had been served. Morrison wondered if White had consumed any of the liquor, i.e., was it really liquor, and White replied that he had. He always drank part of the whiskey he bought and kept the remainder as evidence. Was White familiar by experience with the taste, color, and smell of liquor? Several spectators snickered.

White continued to describe his other visits to the club. On one occasion, he mentioned that he had become friendly enough with Miss Guinan to offer her a drink as she passed by his table. She had thanked him and said she did not drink. Tex, over at the counsel table, leaned her chin on her palm and smiled at the witness, revealing about $10,000 worth of diamond bracelets.

On a later visit, White said he invited Arthur Gordoni, emcee at Helen Morgan's club, to join him as his guest at the Salon Royale.

"I knew that Gordoni liked a certain kind of wine and I asked if she had it. She called to Nick, one of the proprietors, and spoke to him. She then turned to me and said, 'No, we have only white wine and champagne and that's all gone.'"

The prosecutor made sure the jury noted the *we*. Later that same night, the witness said he heard Tex tell Gordoni that she wouldn't go on "anybody's floor for less than $2,000 a week," and that she was fifty-fifty with John (meaning John Johnnides, one of the owners). All these tidbits were supposedly building blocks in the government's case against Guinan to prove that she had a hand in the business end of the club and was not just an entertainer. After further questioning, the court called a recess for lunch.

To all, from the twelve middle-aged men who comprised the jury to the Broadwayites, theater people, bankers, and even the court stenographer, Tex seemed quite subdued during her first morning in court, merely listening and noting. However, when she left the courtroom and passed by Agent White, a man she had once thought a swell guy, she glared and snarled, "You're the biggest liar I ever heard." Did it sound like something a spurned woman might say? Some might have thought so. The agent merely smiled and walked on. Tex seemed sour. However by 2:00 P.M., as she headed back for court, she was in a better mood. When asked what she'd eaten for lunch she told reporters, "I'm on a diet, getting ready for prison food. For if White keeps on, I'm as good as in now."[2]

Back in the courtroom, Morrison completed his questioning by asking the witness to identify a small slip of paper that soon became known as the government's exhibit one. The paper bore Tex's name, address, and phone number, and White claimed Tex had given it to him early on the morning of March 14, after "she had invited him to her home." Tex's lawyer examined the paper and noted that the address and phone number were written in different handwriting.

Tex's lawyer, Max Lopin, considered White's testimony so far. The agent had been trying to pin full criminal responsibility on Tex by emphasizing the role that her popularity had played in the drawing of customers to the club. He also sought to emphasize that liquor had been sold and consumed by such patrons on the club premises in her presence and with her knowledge and that she had been fifty-fifty with the owners. Further, she had used the word *we* in directing club activities, indicating some form of partnership. Lopin was ready to ask a few questions and either clear up these accusations, or muddle them a little, if he could.

Tex had not had an easy time finding a lawyer, let alone one with a good reputation, to defend her in what her old friend and longtime attorney Walter B. Solinger had thought was a losing battle. In fact, most people thought she was an absolute fool for pleading not guilty to a charge the world knew she was guilty of. Still she'd tried everyone, from Clarence Darrow, who unfortunately was about to set off on vacation when she called, to Solinger himself. Finally it was Maxwell E. Lopin, a young greenhorn from Virginia, whom she had chosen. Though he had never handled a major case in court, he had come highly recommended. Lopin wrote, years later,

> When the case was brought to me by Miss Guinan and her then personal attorney, Walter Solinger, I felt highly flattered and excited. But Walter seemed somewhat apprehensive as to my ability to defend her in so important a matter. I was quite young, [29] and had relatively little trial experience. He suggested to Tex, with due apologies to me, that perhaps "we" (we included me) should consult with Max Steuer, the then eminent and leading trial lawyer at the Bar.
>
> I was so astonished at this turn of events that I was unable to offer any comment, although I believe that I did feign agreement.
>
> For reasons unknown, Mr. Steuer, at the conference that Walter had arranged, turned to Texas, and said: "I think you will do well to have Mr. Lopin defend you." Texas promptly answered, "That is the way I feel."

Why did Tex choose Lopin over all others? She didn't have much choice. Besides, he was young and malleable, and she could run the trial pretty much as she pleased.

Since the raid, Tex had had her face lifted, gone to Hollywood to make a film about a murder in a night club, been a walk-on for another film, held a few séances, and studied up for her trial. She'd kept her fingers in the club scene and was currently mistress of the four-month-old Club Intime. After waiting a year, she had finally made it to court.

After lunch, Lopin began to cross-examine Agent White, who refused to admit that the phone number on exhibit one had been written in different handwriting than the address. He claimed that Tex had given him the paper upon inviting him to visit her and not, as Lopin suggested, when White's wife asked Tex for an autograph.

"Think I'm a sap," demanded Tex under her breath. "Think I'd give a guy my phone number in front of his wife?" After further questioning, White admitted that the paper had been handed to him *and* his wife after he had invited Tex to join the two of them one night to "paint the town red." The jury examined the paper, and Lopin continued his questioning.

"You told her you were in business in Denver?"

"Yes. I said I was either in the insurance or broom-corn business."

"But you were in neither, were you?"

"No."
"So you lied to her, didn't you?"
"Yes, sir."

White looked very uncomfortable. Lopin asked him to describe his visits to the club in further detail. Soon White found himself stating directly that he liked Tex as well as the show, that the show was a "proper" show and one he would not mind bringing his wife to see. Then Lopin questioned him about the liquor he said he had bought at the club. It was soon clear that Tex had had nothing to do with his purchase. White looked confused. He couldn't seem to keep his figures straight after that.

"Now Texas Guinan had nothing to do with your purchase of liquor, did she?"
"No, sir."
"Your bill for liquor, cover charges and food came to about $60 on your first visit?"
"If I remember right, the bill was about $50."
"On direct examination you testified you had spent only $35."
"Yes sir."
"Why didn't you tell the jury about the additional money you had spent?"
"The question was not asked me."
"Now you paid the check that night?"
"Yes sir."
"And the money was supplied by the government?"
"It was."

After further questioning, the court learned that the club was open to any and all guests and that most of these people brought their own liquor if they meant to drink. In fact, White was not quite sure if the liquor he had seen on other people's tables was "house" liquor or brought by the patrons themselves. Lopin was moving very quickly now, and White wasn't quite sure where he was heading. He went straight from the mention of liquor to the fact that White had seen people drinking, in essence, had witnessed the violation of the Prohibition law, and done nothing about it. White had not been instructed to report these violations to his superiors.

"You were acting under instructions?"
"Yes sir."
"And you were instructed to get evidence against Texas Guinan, weren't you?"
After a moment's hesitation, "Yes sir."
"They wanted to 'get' her, didn't they?"
"Yes, sir."

As White's testimony became a description of his nights at the club, the defense saw that he could be used to create atmosphere. He described some of the show numbers and peopled the club with well-known figures—from actor Richard Bennett and big-game hunters Mr. and Mrs. Martin Johnson to Priscilla Dean, movie actress. Morrison objected to the mention of names, but Lopin insisted that he needed to demonstrate that the Salon Royale, where the defendant had worked, was a "decent" place, patronized for its excellent entertainment, and "not a 'liquor joint' as had been intimated."

Night-club patrons filled the gallery: heavily-mascara'd women; serious, three-piece-suited, middle-aged men; and raccoon-coated jellybeans fresh out of college. Friends and enemies hung on every word, watched the judge, observed the jury. A good many eyes watched only Tex and her reactions, noticed when she jumped at unforeseen noises, dabbed her nose with smelling salts, took notes. They studied what she was wearing, as if they could learn her defense from the clothes she had chosen. Tex felt their gaze, and tried her best to concentrate her "orchidaceous" eyes on the judge and witnesses. When later accused of focusing too much on the jury, she replied sweetly, "They're not at all hard to look at." Her friends the reporters busily recorded the entire scene, concocting clever wisecracks for the evening edition.

On the stand, White attempted to explain why it had taken him twelve entire visits to the club to tie up the evidence against Guinan. When asked if it had been absolutely necessary to attend the club so often, he answered, after a slight hesitation, that it was not. In fact, after Lopin asked whether or not the twelve visits meant he had enjoyed the club, White stated that indeed he had not enjoyed the club.

"You didn't enjoy the club?"

"You enjoy it for about two visits, and after that it becomes very monotonous."

"But nevertheless you continued going back?"

"Yes, sir."

Texas looked up at the witness with disbelief and amusement. These twelve painful visits, lasting sometimes as long as six hours, had cost the government no less than $360. It looked as if White had enjoyed the club at the government's expense and was lying when he said he had found the show a bore. He had already confessed that he had been trying to make a criminal of Tex even though it was clear the show, and not liquor, was the main attraction of the club. In addition, he had not hesitated to bring his wife along and in fact, said he would have recommended the show to anyone.

As White stepped down from the dock, Tex turned and whispered, "He thought he was a sheik. He asked me why he didn't make a hit with the girls. I told him, because he didn't change his hair oil every thousand miles."

Agent Beazell, another of Willebrandt's "four horsemen," was the next to take the stand. His testimony was similar to that of Agent White's, though he made it clear that the liquor purchases had not involved Tex. He also mentioned that after seeing the show a few times it had become "boresome and tiresome, the same thing over again." Yet he had made a total of eight visits "in the line of duty," all at the government's expense. His testimony did not sit particularly well with the jury. Then the judge decided to adjourn for the day, leaving this last, unpleasant impression to sit overnight in the minds of the jury members.

Meanwhile, Tex seemed lighter than when she'd entered the courtroom that morning. As she slipped on her black velvet wrap and matching cap, she posed for the cameras and said, "Say, is it against the law to be an entertainer? They ought to bring Will Rogers down here."

The tenth of April dawned too early. Tex was unused to waking with the rest of New York and felt a bit queasy. Though she'd taken a liberal dose of sleeping tablets, she'd had a miserable night. On went the eyelashes, the mascara, the makeup to paint the face of affability and honesty.

Tex, escorted by friends through the crowd that waited outside the federal building, waltzed majestically into the already packed courtroom. On the way, she passed an anxious Agent Beazell, but he hardly noticed her. He was pacing up and down the corridor with notes in hand, talking to himself and occasionally wiping his brow. He had little training in public appearances—unlike Tex who, upon entering the courtroom, proceeded to glide gracefully to her chair and enthrone herself with apparent nonchalance amidst the rustling of curious spectators who had risen from their seats to see her enter.

On this day, Tex was dressed rather simply in a champagne silk afternoon frock accompanied by the same black velvet coat with matching hat. In order to preserve the image of a teetotaling-good-time-entertainer-and-that's-all, she had left her more exciting jewelry at home. Though she seemed calm, later that morning she jumped several inches from her chair at the sound of distant thunder.

Beazell was completing his testimony of the preceding day with another uncomfortable piece of evidence. It seemed that the only liquor seized in the final raid of June 28—his last visit to the club—had come from his table. Even though he insisted that the whiskey had been bought at the club, spectators couldn't help being embarrassed for him.

Agent Mitchell was the next to inherit the stand, and he looked no better than Beazell. He described how Agent White had introduced him to "the famous Texas Guinan."

"I said to her, 'What are you famous for?' She said, 'Why I'm Mary Pickford.'" There was the sound of what Lopin thought might be a series of popping explosions, which was Texas laughing. Everyone else in the court joined her, except the judge and Mitchell. Judge Thomas, after all, had his position to look after, and Mitchell couldn't see anything funny about it. By the time he had been cross-examined, he had successfully contradicted himself several times. Unlike his predecessors, he did confess that he had enjoyed himself at the club and that he had made three of his four visits by his own choosing, and not on assignment.

The next government witness was Mortimer K. Leister, the accountant for the Salon Royale. He had been with the club since its inception on April 5, 1927, and had been present a year later when Tex's contract had been signed. That contract was introduced by Mr. Morrison without objection by Lopin because Lopin knew it would read well. In fact, it sounded as if it had been written by Tex's lawyers to be read in court.

The contract specified that Tex would receive $1,000 a week drawing account and a choice between 50 percent of the cover charges or 50 percent of the corporation net profits. It stipulated that Salon Royale, Inc., would be known as the employer, and Texas Guinan as the employee, employed specifically as hostess and entertainer, to be featured as "star entertainer" with her name preceding that of her employer. It also said that "it shall be understood that the employee is not a partner or a stockholder." As far as Lopin could see, the contract worked for, not against his client. However, the government used the one ambiguity in the contract as a foothold—if Tex could take 50 percent of the corporation profits "from whatever source" (as written in the contract), then mightn't that include the proceeds from the sale of liquor?

The court and press were most fascinated to learn that Tex's earnings between March 1 and July 1 of 1928 had amounted to $28,500. Tex sent a note to the press table—"And don't those figures make a lot of people sore!"

After Lopin requested that the case be dismissed and Tex acquitted—a request he knew was expected but would not be sustained—he prepared to give his defense. He was ready, after weeks of planning and organizing, but was Tex? He knew that their salvation lay in the hands of the jury. Their strategy was not aimed at clearing Tex as much as creating resentment in the minds of the jurors, resentment about the persecution that attended the development of the case and the pettiness with which it was prosecuted. He and Tex had decided that she would take the witness stand in her own defense as her only witness. She would make a good witness and would not be overly vulnerable to cross-examination. "Besides," reasoned Lopin, "she had no criminal record, her reputation was good, she had a remarkable personality and she was an extremely convincing talker. People liked her and in all likelihood, so would the jury."

Lopin also knew that the jury was trying him as well as Tex. He wasn't half as practiced as she was in the art of persuasion and good-natured affability. Could he win them over?

The last witness for the government was Arthur Gordoni, former emcee of the Helen Morgan Club (as well as former husband of Tex's friend, actress Nora Bayes), presently a stockbrocker. Everything Agent White had said in his testimony, Gordoni contradicted. He said he had been present when White had talked to Tex and that he had never heard her say the alleged "I'm 50–50 with John." Nor had he ever told Agent White that he preferred a certain brand of red wine. Further, he said it was the habit of night-club employees to call their places "our" place, or "my" club.

The government compared Gordoni and Guinan as emcees. Why, for instance, didn't Gordoni demand the same kind of contract that Tex had had? "Because I wasn't big enough to demand it." That's right, Tex's grin seemed to say. It was soon clear to the government that Gordoni's testimony would be far from helpful. Tex took the stand.

Tex swore to tell the whole truth and nothing but. She looked out at the crowd in the courtroom as she spoke, and the room grew silent. Change the lighting, put more smiles and tables out there, and the place could certainly resemble any one of her clubs. Though she'd been studying up for the trial, Tex was encountering a small case of stage fright. She reached for her smelling salts, caressed her favorite diamond, and looked up at the judge with a smile one might describe as approaching timid—indicating her readiness to testify. This would be her toughest role yet.

In fact, it all seemed so solemn and quiet in that courtroom that at first, she answered the questions in a soft tone that sounded all wrong to her audience. They were used to hearing her shout. If only she could relax. To begin with, she was requested to tell the audience—the jury—her life story. She turned to the gentlemen of the jury and proceeded to tell them that she had been an actress for twenty years and had made 312 motion pictures. Once she got started, her testimony flowed quite easily. If she could continue to weave in and out of the petty objections of that Mr. Morrison, she could give lots more information; information that would point out her generosity, her responsible and respectable character, information about her work overseas during the war and the fact that she lived with and supported her mother and father. That would get them. The telling of her own life story had always pleased her, and she began to warm up. The faces out there were for the most part familiar ones; they knew her tale. But the jury did not. These were twelve middle-aged men who had never had the opportunity to catch her act. Twelve suckers, tried and true, given the chance. If all went well, perhaps she'd invite them back to her club, get the girls to muss their hair a bit.

They did look rather stern, though. She guessed they were trying to hide their curiosity and interest behind the poker face of duty. Would it be out of place to wake them with a "Hello, Sucker!"? She would have liked to.

Lopin asked her to describe what her duties at the Salon Royale had been.

"*Well*, the people came in whom I knew. *So*, as people came in I always said 'Hello.' I greeted them and we had a lot of fun, and then it got so that other people who were there would greet them *too*.

"Even the *orchestra* would greet them. I used to get there about 12:00, and I used to always have a lot of fun before we started. That was usually after one.

"*First*, we would bring out my little piano to the center of the floor, and I'd sit up on top of it and sing four or five songs. Then I'd push the *piano off*—it was only a little piano. Then the show would start with a number.

"*All* of the kids would come out. Everybody knows the little girls, and for those who didn't I would introduce each one of them, like Ruby Keeler, Kitty O'Reilly and others.

"Then there'd be more numbers. Some of the guests like *Joe Frisco* and *Grace Hayes* would all get together and sing songs. Then there would be dancing.

"There was always *something* doing *every minute*. My duties were to see that everybody had a *good time* and that everything came *off*."

Tex was quite dramatic in her emphasis on certain details, but it seemed as if she couldn't underline enough for the jurors, who seemed eager to hear everything she had to say.

"What kind of people came to the club?"

"The very best people came to the club, night in and night out...."

"Did you ever sell, or authorize the sale of liquor at the Salon Royale, or for that matter at any other place?"

"I have never sold or authorized the sale of liquor to anybody in my entire life."

"Do you drink liquor?"

"I have never had a drink of liquor in my life."

"Did you know that liquor was being sold at the club?"

"I did not."

"Did you ever see liquor there?"

"I saw what looked like liquor. Of course I couldn't swear it was liquor because I have never tasted liquor."

Asked about that conversation with Mr. White on March 14, 1928, Miss Guinan said: "He came in about four o'clock in the morning and he asked me to hold up the show for a little while as Arthur Gordoni was coming over from the Helen Morgan Club as his guest. Then he said that Gordoni was very fond of red wine and asked if there was any at the club. I said to him, 'I think you've made a mistake. Do you think this is a spaghetti place?'"

"Did you say to Mr. White, as he had testified, 'I don't know whether we have that,' referring to a wine?"

"Never."

"Did Nick say at that time to Mr. White and you, as he has testified, 'All we have is white wine'"?

"He did not."

"When, and if, you used the expression 'we,' did you use it in an ownership sense or as that of an employee?"

"Only as an employee."

"Did you say to Mr. White that you were going to sign a contract with one of the girls in your show?"

"No. I have never signed a contract with any of the people that have worked for me."

"Did you at any time tell Mr. Gordoni that you were fifty-fifty with John Johnnides?"

"I did not."

Lopin asked Mr. Morrison for the slip of paper bearing the name of Miss Guinan, her address, and telephone number. Strangely enough, exhibit one had been mislaid. Tex leaned toward Judge Thomas and asked, "Is that the slip of paper where Mr. White said I invited him to my house?" The judge nodded gravely and the defendant smiled broadly and dabbed her lips with her handkerchief. The judge suggested Lopin proceed without the exhibit. He asked Tex if she had given the slip to Mr. White, and she replied that she had given it not to Mr. but to *Mrs.* White, who had requested her autograph. She wrote her address but was careful not to give her phone number.

"Did you ever ask Mr. White to your home?"

"I never asked White to my home in my life. I told the maid I was not in when he called me. He used to invite me out and send me flowers.

"He sent me orchids four or five times and then asked me why I didn't wear them. I told him that I had hay fever. Once he asked me to go to Ben Reilly's with him and his wife some Sunday and bring some of the girls along. But I said my girls always had Sundays off. I did not go out with them as my mother became ill."

"The agents testified that they saw a number of drunken persons at the club during their visits there."

"Well, *they* were there."

The defendant smiled as she made this last statement. Lopin was pleased with his client. She was talking directly, succinctly, and "as clearly as though she were making a movietone." Everyone in the courtroom followed every word she said and noted how skillfully she had dismantled two of the government charges, specifically, the use of the possessive *we* and the fifty-fifty split with the owners of the club. Lopin then let Morrison cross-examine.

Morrison considered himself quite clever. He knew that Tex adored talking, and he was planning to let her wandering tongue get her into trouble. He told her she could talk as much as she wished and did not need to confine herself to yes and no answers. Tex smiled. She knew what he was after.

Morrison first attacked Tex's contract. He wanted to know what the entire courtroom, the whole world, seemed to take for granted—whether Tex had made a lot of money out of the club. She replied that she had made a lot of money in practically every club she'd been in. Then why, asked Morrison, wasn't she satisfied with the plan of receiving 50 percent from the cover charges? Because there were so many other concessions, she replied. The coatroom concession alone, she estimated, was worth $1,200 a year.

"You were simply mercenary, weren't you?"

"I always have been, a little bit." Tex smiled, then added, "As a matter of fact, I'm not mercenary. When I went to California to make a picture, I turned over all my earnings to my agent—I didn't know how much they were." She looked over in Kerwin's direction.

"You had reached the point where you had determined it would be better to take one-half of the net profits than one half of the cover charges?"

"There was more money."

"And you reached out and got it?"

"Wouldn't you?"

Morrison pressed on. He wanted to know how much more money Tex made when she changed her contract. She said she would be happy to get the checks and show him. The prosecutor hesitated, and a member of the jury sat up and looked at her with new interest.

Morrison decided, after more questions, that he would prove Tex was truly only interested in making money, whatever she had to do to get it.

"Now of course you, not being mercenary, had no interest in increasing the amount of business the club did?"

"I have always wanted to see the club do well. The most vulnerable spot in all of us is our vanity, and naturally the club was the main attraction. I wanted to see that club the best in the city."

"Following that plan you were trying to get the patrons to come back and be at home?"

"They always came back. The people that came to the Salon Royale were that way. They came to see me at the Beaux Arts and the 300 Club. I always used to go to the door and shake hands with them, and when they didn't come back, I used to phone them and ask why they didn't come back—people I am fond of."

"You did that to boost the receipts of the club?"

"I did not. I like people to come in, people like Mr. Heywood Broun, Mark Hellinger, Mr. Walter Winchell. They came every night to the club. Mr. Wesley Turner comes every night to the club. Mr. Paul Boyd never misses a night practically since I opened."

"They are not patrons, they don't spend money there?"

"They are not suckers; I mean they are nice people."

"You sort of took care of them because they are advantageous from a publicity viewpoint?"

"No, they are the same as anybody else."

"They are friends?"

"Very, very good friends of mine."

"You made it a point to take care of men who were good spenders?"

"No, I have a reputation for being nice. The boys come down from college, Mr. Ullman's son and Mr. Buster Edison. Lots of times they would come in and say, 'Texas, we have no money tonight,' and I would say, 'There are probably no tables anyway,' and they would sit on the floor."

"Where?"

"In the Salon Royale, or on top of the piano with me, and then I used to say to Nick and John, 'These kids haven't any money,' and Nick would say, 'That's all right.' And, there have been many many people come to the club whom I made it a particular point to be nice to because I knew they didn't have any money."

"You didn't expect John or Nick to hand them, give them a *drink* without being paid for it, did you?"

"Mr. Johnnidis is the kind of fellow who would let them *eat* all they wanted if they didn't have any money," said Tex alertly.

"That is all done in the spirit of good will?"

Still on a roll, Tex replied, "Not particularly. Lots of times, like nurses of the Park West Hospital, I often phoned them and would say, 'Why not make up a little party and come down to the club, be our guests.' They had taken care of my mother when she was a patient there."

By this time, the witness appeared to be thoroughly enjoying the procedure. She even addressed Mr. Morrison as "my dear" in the next answer.

Mr. Morrison asked about the sale of liquor at the Salon Royale.

"My dear," said Tex, leaning toward the prosecutor. "I have a reputation. I don't lie. I told them I wanted nothing to do with liquor. When I signed the contract, I specifically stated that."

Court was adjourned. Tex went home and read the papers, which focused on the details of her contracts and the amount of money she made. Lopin went home and studied his notes.

The next day, Tex appeared in an attire which reflected a greater sense of confidence in the outcome of the trial. She wore a black, iridescent, close-fitting helmet, a black satin ensemble and a silver fox fur-piece. She also permitted herself a few pearl necklaces, platinum bracelets, and a smattering of diamonds. She looked much more herself. In fact, she seemed quite optimistic. Arriving at court, she was gratified to learn that the courtroom and federal building were overloaded once again and that court attendants could not recall another trial that had attracted so many people.

Tex entered the courtroom promptly at 10:30. "I want to be on time before I'm given time," she quipped. She was in good form. Only several minutes into the cross-examination, she began wisecracking, to the delight of the spectators. Frequently, her sallies caused judge, jury, and the prosecutor to laugh with the audience. Morrison was still on that second contract.

"You told him what you wanted in the contract, didn't you?"

"Mr. Solinger drew the contract, I did not dictate it."

"Did Mr. Solinger draw it out of a clear blue sky?"

"No. I think he drew it in his office."

The audience roared. Judge Thomas pounded his desk and declared, "I want to say, Marshal, if there is any more laughing here, I will clear the courtroom and put the spectators outside. This is a trial and not a show and if there is any more amusement furnished you will all have to go out. Obey this order, Marshal."

Tex continued to toy with her answers, but suddenly Morrison began to cut her off. He didn't want those long-winded explanations that made him look the fool. However, he couldn't avoid her wit. She caught him up time and time again. He would ask her about liquor, and she would reply she didn't drink it, didn't know if a drink were liquor or water.

"You didn't think it was tea, did you?" sneered Morrison.

"I don't know—I don't drink tea either, I drink coffee." The courtroom tittered. The judge looked exasperated, though Tex suspected he was secretly enjoying the show. Morrison wanted to know if she'd seen drunken people at the Salon Royale, and she answered she'd seen a few. Of course, she'd also seen drunks at football games, dances, theaters.

Lopin was watching the cross-examination with delight and anxiety. Tex was certainly holding her own. She stayed calm and made few gestures. She seemed relaxed and at home on the stand, resting her elbow on her knee as she turned to face Morrison. She made little effort to tame her smile and good humor, and the flash of wit and diamonds kept her testimony on par with a night-club performance. However, the next series of questions, and the answers Tex was going to have to give, had Lopin more than worried.

"Do you mean to say you didn't know liquor was being sold there?"

Tex looked startled, horrified, even virtuous. "My dear. I said when I went there to work—I said now listen, I don't want any trouble. I'll have nothing to do with liquor—nothing, nothing at all."

"You mean to say you didn't know liquor was being sold there?"

"I—certainly—did—not."

Hours passed. More questions on the club, the girls, Tex's monthly check, her relationship with the Prohibition agents. Tex wanted to emphasize that people came there for fun. Morrison wanted her to say it was for the liquor and that she only wanted them there for the money she made. After Lopin has asked a few more questions, Morrison did a re–cross-examination and asked Tex to define the word "sucker."

"When you do something you want to kick yourself about the next day, then you're a sucker. Sucker is a word like pal. It's just fun, kind of a gag. Everybody's been a sucker sometime or other. They are all over. I'm one of the biggest in the world."

"But," queried Morrison, "at the Salon Royale you separated the sheep from the goats?"

"I'll say we did. And some lambs got sheared, too."

Lopin saw that Tex was not explaining the definition of sucker in a way that was useful to the defense. He had her clarify so that the jury would know she called folks "sucker" in the spirit of fun and never because she taking advantage of them. Then he rested his case. As did Morrison for the United States government.

As both lawyers stepped down, Tex's facial expression seemed to say, Hey, is that all? She seemed to want to stay where she was, tell a few jokes, encourage everybody to have a good time. Fortunately, the court called a short recess, and she had to retire from the dock.

After the recess, Lopin walked up before the judge and addressed the jury with his final statement. He stressed the contradictions in the testimonies given and the ridiculous measures that the government had taken to make a criminal out of Tex. He attempted to discredit the government agents and stress that they had spent everyone's hard-earned tax dollars. He used the evidence of the trial to show, in contrast, that Tex was an honest and respectable employee of the respectable Salon Royale. Addressing the terms of the indictment, he said,

"You may wonder why I have not mentioned liquor. Well, the indictment does not actually charge Miss Guinan with the sale of liquor. She is simply charged with 'aiding and abetting' in the maintenance of a common nuisance at the Salon Royale where it is alleged liquor was sold. The charge is extremely broad, and is designed to bring Miss Guinan within the circle of the proprietors who have pleaded guilty. In this connection Mr. Morrison contends that if Miss Guinan had not been the main attraction bringing all of these people to the club, the owners could not have maintained the nuisance; but since she had, she is equally criminally responsible.

"This, I insist is absurd, since the club was in operation a full year before Miss Guinan commenced working there. If the alleged nuisance existed then, why didn't the government do something about it? What were they waiting for—a 'Texas Guinan,' to make newspaper headlines?"

Later—the summation was long and broken by a lunch break—Lopin continued to point out that the government had failed to prove that any part of the defendant's earnings were based on liquor sales.

"What is required is proof positive, not circumstantial proof on the part of the government, without per-adventure of *any* doubt whatever. In this, the government has wholly failed. . . .

"The court will charge you that the defendant is presumed to be innocent throughout the trial until proven guilty. Her guilt must be conclusively established by the Government, and if there is any doubt whatsoever in your minds as to her guilt, be it ever so little, you must acquit her.

"A verdict of guilty would most certainly justify the detestable methods employed in this case against Miss Guinan, the false protestations of friendship by the prohibition agents and the unnecessary expenditures of the taxpayers' monies by these informers. I am confident that you gentlemen will not let this happen.

"I sincerely ask for your kind consideration and fair judgment in this matter, and I trust you will find the defendant, Texas Guinan, innocent of this evil and unfounded charge. Please accept my utmost thanks for your indulgence."

The court sat back as Morrison rose before the judge and jury. His approach was quite different from that of the youthful, almost impetuous Lopin. He began by praising the Caesar all knew he intended to bury. He called her the Great Tex, with a flash of southern chivalry. As Arthur "Bugs" Baer said the next day in his column in the *New York American,* "Morrison was unusually gentle for a U.S. Attorney. His whole attitude seemed to indicate that the government didn't want a conviction, but would be satisfied with a suicide. . . . At times he wept gently. Like the walrus just before he ate the oyster."

Morrison's summation was succinct and went directly to the point.

"There are only three things for you to consider," he said to the jurors after several moments of defaming the contract—"a fine piece of paper prepared in advance"—and Tex's defense so far:

"1. Was liquor sold at the Salon Royale?

"2. Did Miss Guinan know that liquor was being sold?

"3. Did she aid and abet in the sale of liquor?"

He concluded, after a discussion of Tex's involvement with liquor at the club, "Bear in mind that she testified that she thrice told her old friend John Johnnides that she 'didn't want any liquor trouble' when she signed the contract. That proves she knew they were selling liquor."

Morrison continued, "A verdict of not guilty, Gentlemen of the Jury, would be framed and hung in her night club as a license to go on doing this sort of thing. Let us show Texas Guinan by your verdict that her license from the U.S. Government has been revoked. We ask her conviction."

Before the jury, Tex, Lopin, or anyone else had time to digest the final remarks, Judge Edwin C. Thomas rose to give his charge to the jury. Though much of what he said was standard, in this trial his words seemed to support the prosecution's final urgings to the jury and was not as favorable for the defendant:

"You must decide what the facts are, what the truth is," he began. "First, you must decide whether the Salon Royale was a common nuisance. If so, did Miss Guinan help maintain it as such? A common nuisance, under the National Prohibition Act, is any place where liquor is stored, sold or bartered."

"If you find the Salon Royale was a place where liquor was recurrently sold, I direct that you find it a common nuisance."

"It is not necessary for the government to prove Miss Guinan was the proprietor of the Salon Royale. If you find she aided, abetted or assisted the proprietors in maintaining this nuisance by contributing time, money or services then it is your duty to return a verdict of guilty against her."

At that moment the judge paused, and a patrol wagon clanged by on its way to the police station. Tex looked rather startled and laughed nervously, never taking her eyes off the judge and the reactions of the jury.

"If she aided in the sale of liquor," explained the judge, "it is not necessary that she shall have personally sold it, but it is sufficient if in helping in the operation of the club she had knowledge of its sale."

The judge explained that the contract used as the government's exhibit two had been used merely to establish the fact that Tex had a substantial financial interest in the club. "If you believe that she is as innocent as she says she is, and that she did not know liquor was being sold there, then you must acquit her." He encouraged the jurors to go beyond the evidence and to draw upon their knowledge of human nature and the motives controlling human conduct. That was the best thing the judge said all day. The rest of the charge, short and ominous, in consonance with the language of the prosecutor Mr. Morrison, left Lopin and his client stunned and apprehensive. While the jury deliberated, the court shifted and friends pushed their way over to the counsel table to surround Tex.

Everyone wanted to encourage her, to touch her. Ordinarily, Tex would have appreciated the homage, but this was one time in her life when she wished she did not have to sustain the mask of affability. She got up from the table with Kitty O'Reilly, one of her girls, and walked up and down the courtroom aisle. She stopped talking. When photographers tried to snap her photo, she turned away.

Meanwhile, Lopin remained in the courtroom chatting with friends, among whom loitered a few reporters. Everyone felt that the judge's charge had been unusually severe and wondered whether or not the U.S. government had been pressuring him.

Movie and book agents were rumored to be at large in the courtroom, just waiting for the outcome to offer Tex "a million dollar contract." One newspaper had already offered her $25,000 for a daily letter from prison and another tabloid had doubled the offer.

Outside, friends, reporters, and fans were waiting. It was as if the verdict were Tex herself, late in getting to the club.

Finally, after what both Lopin and Guinan had found to be the longest hour and four minutes in their lives, a court attendant announced that the jury was returning. As the men filed in, Tex and Lopin scrutinized their faces for some indication of the verdict. Tex sat on the edge of her seat, biting her lips, and made no effort to hide her nervousness.

"Mr. Foreman, have you agreed upon a verdict?"

The foreman rose. Tex held her breath. Maxwell Lopin tried to look nonchalant. One chorus girl stifled a scream. The court hummed with an expectant silence. The judge lifted his eyebrows.

"Not guilty."

Homecoming

> *A great many 'suckers' just keep on chasing the dawn. If they only waited twenty-four hours, the dawn would come back to them. Because they fail to understand that part of life, that's why I call them 'suckers.'*
> —TEXAS GUINAN, "TEXAS GUINAN SAYS," SEPTEMBER 12, 1931

> *Well, folks, your little angel has flown over those prison walls!*
> —TEXAS GUINAN, "TEXAS GUINAN SAYS," APRIL 12, 1929

*T*ex had just finished kissing everyone in the club.

"I played two benefits today, that's right, two benefits. Just before I came here I stopped off to do a little number at the Ritz. That was nothing. The other benefit was down at the Federal building. The D.A. said he expected me to stage a three-ring circus at my trial. Well I delivered the goods." Strains of a familiar vaudeville tune filled the air as Tex sang "This is My Lucky Day."[1]

"I am so glad to be back here with all you folks—yes, even you, Sam, and you, Leo! So let's celebrate. I want you all to have a good time.

"Listen, tonight you can have anything you want, anything—you paid the cover, didn't you? And if you don't see what you want on your table and your neighbor's got it, well don't be shy, reach over to the next table and grab it.

"And tell those waiters to move back and sit right down. This is everybody's party.

"Say folks, that judge did everything but hand me the keys to the jail and tell me the street address."

"Were you scared, Tex?"

"Who me? Nah, I knew they wouldn't convict me, though the judge's charge was tougher than my cover charge. I told my lawyer in the beginning, Max, you're a sucker to worry. Twelve men wouldn't take a woman who has no record and who has been living the life I have, making merriment for everybody in the world, and send her to jail. No sir.[2]

"The day is not far off when this grand old country of ours will be allowed to live as it sees fit without being told what it has to do. Folks, I want you to meet the man who made all this happy occasion possible tonight. I want you to meet the man who won our case. I mean Max Lopin."[3] The spotlight swung over in the direction Tex had been pointing and lit upon the round features of Maxwell E. Lopin's boyish face. He hurried to join her on the floor, weaving in and out of tables, bodies, suitcases.

Lopin had already prepared his speech beforehand. His formal tone stood out in strong contrast to Tex's informal banter. "I am extremely happy to join with you in this victory celebration. I have very little to say as I've been making speeches for several days. Texas won her own case by her straightforward testimony and quick thinking on the witness stand. She proved a wonderful witness—I anticipated that she would—I'm pleased to say that I was quite fortunate in playing a part in Miss Guinan's complete vindication."[4]

Tex shouted, "They all told me hire Max Steuer, but I knew this little fellow was a 'hell' of a good lawyer. He proved it."[5] She gave Lopin a maternal hug and sent him blushing out of the spotlight. A waiter brought Tex a pile of telegrams. She rearranged herself on top of the piano and glanced at the top telegram.

"Okay folks, now the fun begins! This one's from Congress—say that's a place I've never been! Let's see what our congressman La Guardia has to say. 'Let us all give this little gal a big hand.' Hey, haven't I heard that one before?" The audience responded in laughter and applause. She opened another.

"Hey, this one's from Zit's!" (Harry Zittell was the publisher of *Zit's Theatrical Weekly*.) "He says, 'It's a just verdict. Just as I expected. I decided the result on a scientific basis. How could twelve men hold you when one never could.'"

More friends were arriving. The already-crowded Club Intime became "plus et plus *intime*." No one stretched for fear of causing injury, not to a neighbor, but to the neighbor's neighbor.

"Listen fellows, gals, is everybody happy? Everybody comfortable, there enough room? The men can sit in the chairs and take what you brought with you, boys, on your laps.

"Hey!" shouted Texas, spurred by the late arrival of Heywood Broun, "Here's one of the suckers I told 'em about at my trial."[6] Broun smiled sheepishly and found himself a seat. His friends and rival columnists were already there—had been at the Club Intime since the victory festivities had begun. Although Tex sounded in high spirits, Broun didn't think it likely that Tex would be able to stay awake much longer. The trial had been more than just the "strain on her lipstick" that journalists had reported, and she had not slept in fifty-six hours.

Tex's intention was to get the club happy, give her thanks to all, and disappear at the first opportunity. Some sucker was up at the piano, now, crooning his own composition, "If you can't get what you want, take what you can get." Certainly he was no Irving Berlin, but the crowd liked him. Then another fellow began doing bird imitations.

A while later, Tex signaled her chauffeur and headed for the Village. Somehow she made it up the stairs to her apartment. Hannah Boyer was there to greet her at the door with a hug. Dear, faithful Hannah, after all these years taking care of her as if she were her own daughter: complaining about the phone bills and her crazy habits, the incense she burned and the people she collected—never mind the furniture she accumulated—and yet, staying with her.

It was so good to be home. Her eyes caressed the overstuffed rooms, the walls crowded with hangings and photos, with great affection. It was hers, and no one could padlock it or take it away.

Tex shuddered to think what jail might have been like. After she had hugged the jury, she had fed the press such advice as, "Don't let your soul warp. Don't be a crab. My God, have a good time and enjoy life! Have fun! And say—on Mabel Willebrandt, you must give Mabel my love. An' tell her this is the home of the brave and the land of the free and that I represent the FREE."[7] From her cheery disposition, the papers concluded that she had never been afraid of going to jail. Some even thought she'd wanted to try it out for a while. "Bugs" Baer quoted her as saying, "I would like to go to the jailhouse for about six months, I have a few freckles I would like to get rid of." The *Daily News* even reported that in the midst of her victory elation, she lost her smile, saddened at the thought of not being in jail. "Sad? Say, listen, do you know, children, that a newspaper offered me $25,000 if I would write the story of my life in jail? Then after that another paper heard of it and offered to double the price. And now! My God—I lose $50,000 because I'm not in jail."[8]

When Tex awoke on April 12, the newspapers were still full of the trial. She sat with the papers and her breakfast tray in bed. Reading the news was like seeing the reviews after an opening, and this time she'd done well with most of her critics. During the next few days, papers all over the country would discuss what *Variety* called "the Mickey Finn handed to the government by Texas Guinan" and what the *Daily News* called "one of the richest vaudeville shows that has been put on locally for some time." The *Sunday News* editorial on April 14 elaborated on the paper's feelings about the acquittal and their sentiments matched that of most New Yorkers:

> Largely out of admiration for one who helps to make New York famous, and without giving a hand big, little or middle-sized to the night club racket as a whole, we're glad Miss Guinan got off.
> A conviction would have been a victory for the Washington dry crowd which has baited and insulted New York City ever since the dry era began. Her acquittal in the face of all the evidence is a cheerfully hardboiled answer, in the New York manner, to those tactics.
> It is more than that, if the dry snoopers don't change their present habits. Miss Guinan is the wealthiest defendant in a liquor case who will ever get to an actual jury trial in this city.
> It's the little fellow, as a rule, whom the dry agents so bravely haul into their nets. How any jury can have the face to convict a penny-ante bootlegger after Miss Guinan's acquittal we can't see.
> The case becomes, then, a sort of insurance policy for local victims of dry agents' zeal against the savagery of the Jones law. The little girl wasn't tried in vain.

Tex felt important. She began to see the role her trial had played in terms of the bigger picture of New York. She had become some kind of heroine—which actually didn't make sense, seeing that she *was* guilty. Perhaps she was a heroine because she represented the right to do as one pleased, the spirit against unfair laws. That's how her friends and fans saw her.

Not only were New Yorkers up in arms, but so were other taxpayers who had read about the cost of gathering the evidence, estimated at $65,000.

As for the woman who had instigated the whole affair, Mabel Willebrandt, not one word issued from her office on how she felt about the outcome of the trial. She didn't even react when the *New York Evening Post* of April 12 printed Tex's poem to her:

> Now Mrs. Mabel Willebrandt lives down in Washington
> If she doesn't stop her kidding and spoiling peoples' fun,

I, for one, will stand right out and make a little bet,
That Miss Liberty soon will be the girl men forget.
I was carried down to court accused of selling liquor,
I got a hand upon the stand that made the lawyers snicker.
Judge Thomas said, "Tex you sell booze,"
I said, please don't be silly;
I swear to you my cellar's filled
with chocolate and vanilly.

Willebrandt did, however, resign from her post a month after the "not guilty" verdict and made a curious change in career. She became counsel for Fruit Industries, Inc., an association of California wine-grape growers.

Tex had not only received much press from the trial, but many job offers as well. Right after the trial, when Tex had stopped off at home to change before heading to the Ritz to do a benefit, Arthur Lyons of Lyons and Lyons booking agency had been waiting for her. He said to Lopin, "She will get $10,000 a week and she opens at the Fox Theater in Brooklyn next Monday. It will be a revue act, with twenty-six people. That includes sixteen girls and a jazz band. She should break a few box office records. Of course, Miss Guinan won't get all the money but she is guaranteed $5,000 for her share."[9]

The proposition included playing all the Fox houses in the metropolitan area with the additional possibility of hitting the road. Tex would play both in the theater and in her current club. Meanwhile Lyons said William Fox also wanted to make a "talkie" based on the trial. The script would be full of "Guinanisms" and the action would take place down at the federal building.

Tex received many more flattering offers. In the final installment of her memoirs (May 25, 1929), she added that she'd even been offered $200,000 in contracts by European syndicates. She'd turned them all down because she wanted to stay in her beloved New York.

"I've reached the point where I hate to leave Broadway, my friends and the people who helped me to chisel money and fame out of the white light belt. I'd be homesick now if I left Broadway for more than a month, so here I am and here I stay. Here's to Broadway."

While Tex sat reading her letters of congratulations, New York Police Commissioner Grover Whalen was speaking at a meeting of the Church Layman's Committee of the Greater Federation of Churches at the Hotel Pennsylvania. He spoke of Tex's acquittal and called the trial a "disgusting piece of publicity."

"It was an affront to law and order," he continued. "You and I both know that she was guilty of the charges made against her."

Then Whalen added, "This question of a night club hostess is a very serious one. It is becoming close to something else long since driven out of this community, and the young girls who read of this case will be led on by the publicity given her 'heroinism.'"[10]

The "something else" he spoke of was prostitution. Listeners could easily make the connection between the trial, Tex, and that statement for themselves. When Tex heard of Whalen's speech, she was furious. Imagine inferring that her "little girls" were not—WELL. Tex called one of her friendly tabloid reporters and delivered a long tirade. The reporter, in turn, phoned Lopin to see if he would start suit against the commissioner. Lopin was still basking in the glory of the victory and was not thrilled about jeopardizing his recent success and newly attained reputation. He knew Tex had a big mouth, but he'd been hoping she'd keep it shut till he looked into Whalen's charges. Lopin told the reporter with a calmness he certainly did not feel that first, he intended to get a full report of the speech, and if the statements were true, he would give Whalen a chance to retract. If not, they'd sue.

Then Lopin called Tex and told her to say nothing until they found out more. Unfortunately, as Lopin later described it, Tex had gone off like Old Faithful and erupted just before he called. The next morning (Saturday, April 13) the *New York Journal* carried a front-page story with three-quarter-inch headlines: RETRACT OR BE SUED— TEX WARNS WHALEN.

Tex and Lopin soon had a full-fledged war on their hands. In her explosion, Tex had flippantly touched some of Whalen's sore spots. She teased him about being jealous that she'd knocked him off the front pages and asked why he was making all those speeches instead of solving the Rothstein murder case. And she foolishly made some snide remarks about the way he dressed.

Suddenly, there was police activity at the Club Intime, which had been running for four months with little trouble. But Tex hadn't been the only voice to speak out against Whalen. Hellinger wrote in his April 15 column, "Grover Whalen is credited with saying that Texas Guinan is guilty even though the jury said she was not. I understand now why the commissioner isn't paying much attention to the Rothstein case.

"If Texas Guinan is guilty after having been found not guilty, then the man who murdered Rothstein is innocent because he has had no trial at all."[11]

Whalen ignored all criticism and continued to persecute the "girl" who, as *Variety* said, earned her living in *one* night club on Broadway amidst *400,000* speakeasies and joints in the United States.

First, it was a matter of that tiresome old curfew law. Whalen said that every legal means would be used to make sure that clubs closed at 3:00 A.M. Tex thought she was safe because hotels of more than fifty rooms were supposedly exempt from the curfew. Tex's club was located in the basement of the Hotel Harding, a hotel that had its own dining room where music and entertainment were permitted, and it had more than the required fifty rooms. She announced she was not legally obliged to heed the curfew law. However, on April 16, detectives invaded the club just as the late-supper show was about to begin. They asked the manager if he had a license to operate a cabaret. The manager, suspecting trouble, sidestepped the question and said he didn't quite know. He didn't offer to hunt for one, either. In response, they handed him a summons to appear in court.

Meanwhile, the guests, who had just settled in for the evening after paying a very high cover charge, were reassured that there would be no trouble and the show would continue. The orchestra began with the first few notes and several couples moved out onto the floor. As they did so, the detectives asked the manager if he had a license to operate a dance hall. Again, the manager was unable to produce a permit. As he fumbled for an excuse to go back and get some help, the detectives turned to the guests and announced that they were terribly sorry, but dancing would have to cease.

At that point, several of the guests decided it was time to leave. They'd rather read about the evening's events in the morning papers. Others found the police excitement worth the cost of the cover charge. One of the detectives told the remaining guests that they might still enjoy their midnight supper to the music of the orchestra.

A few more bars of syncopation and one of the detectives recalled that if an establishment played music while customers dined, it was, according to the legal definition, a cabaret, and since the club could not show a license, music would be another violation. Another detective joined the officers in the dining room and showed them a bottle of whiskey that he claimed he had found in the kitchen. The man arrested the waiters found at the scene of the "crime"—in the kitchen at the time—and charged them with illegal possession of liquor. This raid, unlike others, reeked of personal vendetta. It had been carefully staged.

The remaining employees of the club were herded by the detectives into the kitchen and those connected with food asked to show their health-department permits. Those unable to produce such documents were given summonses for the violation of the sanitation code. By this time, all the customers had left and a policeman was stationed at the door to see that the club stayed empty.[12]

Tex heard the details of the raid over the phone, for she had been (conveniently?) absent from the club that night. The next morning she was waiting at Lopin's Fortieth Street office when he arrived. She wanted a lawsuit against Whalen and the police department, but Lopin calmly told reporters they were only seeking an injunction, a warning. Since the club was paralyzed by the presence of the policeman at the door, Lopin wanted first to get to the bottom of all the sudden police activity. A few days later, Lopin came before the New York Supreme Court requesting an order restraining the police from further interference. He was refused and on April 20, a short week and some after Tex had won her trial, the Club Intime was evicted from the Hotel Harding.

Tex had little time to mourn the four-month-old club where New Year's cover charges had started at twenty dollars. The same day that she was evicted, Lopin issued a statement to the press that Tex would make no move to fight the verdict because she planned to go into vaudeville for ten weeks with her troupe, at a salary of $7,500 a week.

Tex's new Warner Brothers Vitaphone, *Queen of the Night Clubs,* was showing at the movie theaters in town—"good advance ballyhoo" for her personal appearances. In all the excitement, she'd forgotten about the film, which she had made between her arrest in 1928 and the recent trial. Her contract for the film had come about via a practical joke. As Hellinger's biographer Jim Bishop tells the story, Tex had boasted to her reporter friends that various studios had offered to feature her in a talking movie short. The boys were convinced that she had made the whole story up, so Wallace Sullivan of the *Morning Telegraph* sent her a telegram offering her $60,000 for her and her troupe. Tex ran about waving the telegram and screaming, "Didn't I tell you? Didn't I tell you? Nobody would believe me but here it is!"

"Hellinger and Sullivan went home unable to decide whether the telegram had been a good or bad joke," wrote Bishop. "But Texas Guinan thought it was real and in the a.m. called Warner Brothers' New York office and taunted them with her new offer. They agreed that she was too good a bet to lose to another studio, and signed her up for $75,000"![13]

The *New York Times* described the film as a "somewhat entertaining thriller, with a murder or so, frowning plotters, silly hoofer and none-too gifted young woman who nevertheless, appears to be worth her weight in gold as an entertainer in a night club." Tex played herself—Tex "Malone," along with a cast that included Eddie Foy, Jr., Lila Lee, Jack Norworth, John Davidson, and George Raft. It was directed by Bryan Foy. Unfortunately, no print survives.

To increase the effect of the publicity generated by the trial and movie, Tex's personal memoir, "My Life—AND HOW!" was published in the *New York Evening Journal,* beginning April 29. "And, when her story is finished, you may have a new mind picture of the night club hostess, who, according to a jury, spends her life showing people a good time and is not a public nuisance."

The column was perfectly timed. When it ended, and her readers were caught up to her present, it was just in time to advertise Tex's latest summer night club on Long Island. This was the Show Place on Merrick Road in Valley Stream. Since nobody stayed in the city in the summer, Tex was able to run the club from early June until Labor Day. Although the Show Place was very much in the tradition of the city night clubs, it provided a new challenge for Tex. It was more spacious than the small rooms she had been used to playing in and violated her old formula of crowding many in a tiny space. But the large, cool rooms were better geared to that summery, relaxed approach to fun. If guests were going to actually bother to leave the city and drive all the way out there, the club must be comfortable, the atmosphere cool.

Long Island was new territory, and Tex felt like a pioneer. She took rooms at the Nassau Hotel in Long Beach, installed the family at Tudor Towers, close by the shore, and settled in for a summer of visiting and fun. Her sister Pearl was coming for the summer with darling Paddy, her dear nephew whom she'd never met. It promised to be a summer without police problems and city chaos.

For "Paddy"—Patrick G. Smith—meeting his famous aunt at long last was very exciting and a bit overwhelming. His mother had told him stories ever since he was old enough to listen, and he had dozens of her pictures in his room. Tex liked to send pictures and postcards instead of letters. She inscribed them with such messages as "To little Pat, with all my love from your Aunt Texas who thinks you are marvelous" and "To Pat, the Darling of them all" and "To my little nephew—Paddy—who I love very much."[14] She did seem to love him very much for someone who had never met him. More often than not, she wrote her sentences clear off the card so you could never be quite sure what the message had been. Just "lots of love" from "Auntie Tex."

Patrick had once found a photo of Tex inscribed New York Winter

Garden, 1917—the very year he had been born!—on which Tex had written, "To one good sister from a bad sister." What did she mean? Was Tex a bad woman? How could anybody who sent him a miniature Victor recording machine be bad?

Patrick was staying with his grandparents at Tudor Towers right by the ocean at Long Beach, and the boy didn't know them too well, either. Bessie was a tall, stern-looking woman. He called her "Gran." She and Mike were awfully good to their only grandson and spoiled him rotten, just as they had spoiled their youngest son, Tommy. However, the grandson could also see how the family, in turn, spoiled Bessie—no, just protected her. They didn't want anything to worry her. He always heard Pearl and Tex saying, Well, we won't tell Mama about that. As if she were a little girl.

But Patrick knew his grandmother wasn't stupid. He'd heard that when his mother and Tex had been little girls, Bessie had ruled the home with an iron hand and that when they'd wanted anything they'd run to Mike instead. Grandfather was much more easygoing. Pat watched him play with all those "big business deals" in his spare time. None of these deals ever really gelled, recalled Patrick years later, but Mike certainly had a great time putting them together.[15]

The rest of the Guinan brood, Patrick's uncles Tommy and William, didn't make much of an impression on the boy. Willy seemed like a stick-in-the-mud and Tommy—even though handsome and charming—came across as totally unreliable. Patrick had been told that Tommy was in the restaurant business. All he knew was that Tommy and Tex were very close and that they did a lot of work together. Pearl and Tex seemed close, too, even though the two were so different. Pearl liked to be associated with Tex and her world, even though night clubbing wasn't her personal style. She idolized her sister and respectfully referred to her as "Texas," never Tex.

There were big cars and many different people taking them here and there. Patrick even had a bodyguard, though no one ever called him that. Feets Edson looked after him because Tex was afraid someone might try and kidnap her darling Paddy, the son she had never had. Once Feets and Owney Madden and a few other softhearted gangsters took Patrick to Coney Island. They took him on all the rides and at one point even lost sight of him, temporarily. Some bodyguards!

Patrick could have anything he wanted from Aunt Tex, but if he had asked her for some time alone, he might not have gotten his wish. Because the problem with Tex, he recalled over fifty years later, was that "she always had someone around her, business associates or something. We were never alone with her. There was something doing every minute. When the party was over and the people gone, she had to get some sleep. Then she'd wake up in time to go out again."[16]

But even though she was busy, when Patrick saw her, his aunt was always in the greatest humor. She seemed so happy when surrounded by family.

Patrick sometimes wondered about her friends. Certainly she seemed popular. However, he and his mother suspected that many of these folks were just hanging around "to see what they could get." For Patrick could see that his aunt was generous to a fault. Maybe that was why she didn't leave much when she died. "They all stole it from her in one way or another. She must've run through millions."[17]

Patrick loved the club visits better than any other part of his trip. His mom had had to go to confession to find out if it was okay for an almost-twelve-year-old to go to a night club. Once she had the go-ahead, the two of them were escorted by Tommy at least once a week.

The club, to young Patrick, was a playground, nothing more. He was unaware of liquor, money, women, cigarettes. Just fun times and the weekly chicken à la king that he liked to order. He thought the dancers were good and awfully pretty, and the comedians funny.

Sometimes Tex would include him in the show, gesturing from her piano to welcome the little nephew with a big hand. For his twelfth birthday party, he played leapfrog with the chorus line and was later told he had leaped over several famous bodies.

While Pearl might play the scrupulous Catholic, she loved the club as much as Patrick. She loved watching Tex greet the patrons with "Hello, Sucker!" and introduce the acts with the thirty gorgeous dancers led by Kitty O'Reilly and that Norma Taylor whom Tommy had his eye on. Pearl also loved listening to Jimmy Carr and his orchestra and Austin Mack. She'd been present when Max Schmelling the fighter had been the guest of honor and had seen Mae West the night she'd opened in *Diamond Lil*.

On Labor Day, Pearl and Patrick returned to the West Coast, smuggling some fine cognac for Pearl's husband George, and Tex left the roadhouse and began rehearsing for her *Broadway Nights* tour. The New York Police Department had not become any friendlier during Tex's absence from the city, and when the Shuberts offered her a role in their show and a chance to go on the road, she decided she would give the police more time to forget. Replacing the leading comedian Dr. Rockwell, and earning a salary of $5,500 a week, Tex was an immediate success as the show toured through the Midwest.

By mid-October, Chicago critics were praising her for that Guinan industry and vitality. Journalist Ashton Stevens called her a super saleswoman, who "sells first herself and then anything else around the place":

> She sold a pewter revue last night for platinum and made us like the bargain . . . But taking the good with the bad, it was Miss Guinan's indefatigable Guinanness that made the night a howling (I choose my words carefully) success.
> As an actress, this salty woman (the Wilson Mizner of her sex) may be a rhinestone, but as a Texas Guinan doing the stuff that has made not only the night club public her sucker, but the morning and afternoon press, she is a blue diamond. She has neither beauty nor youth, voice nor figure but O Egg Man, the personality! She is the human wisecrack with magnetism in it. She seems to think in flashes of electric light.[18]

Tex was in Chicago when the stock market crashed. There is little information on her involvement in the market. Some, like Heywood Broun, insist she lost prodigious sums in the market; others say she was smart and didn't toy with stocks at all. In her memoirs, Tex claimed that on the way to the West Coast to film *Queen of the Night Clubs*, "I did something smart just about that time. I bought Warner Bros stock at 103. Before I went back to New York I sold it at 123 and cleaned up $80,000. So I got spending money for that trip to the coast."[19]

Tex made this remark in May before the crash. It suggested that she was somewhat knowledgeable about the market and that she had invested in it. There is no way to know if she had been smart enough to get out while the going was good. Some time after the crash, she would comment in her syndicated column about Wall Street (no. 76) that "The only man who cleans up is the janitor."

Whether or not Tex lost money in the market, she was still determined to continue her road tour and tell jokes on stage every night. And somebody still had money, for the show continued to play to large crowds.

While passing through Chicago with the company, Tex caught the attention of a scheming couple, Mr. and Mrs. Harry O. Voiler. Harry Voiler was an ex-con who had been jailed for armed robbery with intent to kill. Although he had been sentenced on April 6, 1917 to serve from fifteen to thirty years in the Jackson (Michigan) penitentiary, by the early 1920s, he had found his way to Chicago on parole. Then he and his wife had gone seemingly "legit" and were running a small ticket brokerage at 72 Randolph Street. Both Voilers saw that Tex could lead them out of their small-time operation and into bigger and better things. They judged she would be susceptible to flattery and name-dropping, and they used both to convince her to work for them in a Chicago club.

Contrary to Mr. Shubert's orders, Tex had been moonlighting at the Club Royale on Wabash Avenue while the show was in Chicago. The people loved her. The tour was scheduled to end after two more weeks in Cleveland, and she was not sure what to do next. Voiler sent her flowers and gifts and followed her from Cleveland to Detroit until the show closed. He dropped the name Capone as if the man were his friend, and Tex began to think more seriously about his offers. She was attracted to the slippery Voiler.

Tex was not one to take advice when it came to love, and she quickly assigned Voiler the title of personal manager. Meanwhile Mrs. Voiler, described by Sam Cimman (soon to be one of the owners of Tex's new club) as "buxom and arrogant, like her husband,"[20] stayed quietly behind the scenes and egged on her husband.

Returning to Chicago, Tex opened at the Green Mill in mid-December when Paramount had just released the film *Glorifying the American Woman*, a musical revue drama about a girl (Mary Eaton) who dreamed she was in a Ziegfield revue. Tex, along with Helen Morgan, Rudy Vallee, Noah Beery, Eddie Cantor, and many others played themselves in walk-on roles.

The club almost didn't open on time. When Tex agreed to join the Green Mill, she had asked co-owner Sam Cimman if he could lower the thirty-by-sixty-foot dance floor, which was then six inches off the floor. Not wanting to tear up the interior while the club was active, Cimman engineered the whole project after hours in one day. He started the workers at 5:00 A.M. Because this was the Depression, an ad placed in the *Chicago Daily News* requesting six carpenters brought eight hundred applicants who began lining up at 3:00 A.M. Cimman hired twelve. It was odd, recalled Cimman, that there it was, December of the first year of the Depression and they were spending thousands on a silly dance floor. Still, some people must have money. Tex rehearsed the girls while the carpenters built their stage.[21]

After the new revue was set and the floor in place, Voiler informed Tex that he couldn't pay his share in the club, which amounted to $27,000. So Tex paid it for him. Though Voiler billed himself as her manager, he must have also been one of the owners of the club along with Cimman, Leon Sweitzer—a former policeman and nephew of a local politician, and Leonard Leon. Tex's contract with the four men included a guaranteed minimum of $1,500 a week plus 50 percent cover and 50 percent general profits.

The Green Mill opened to a December snowstorm. Tex's parents stopped by on an extended trip west, and they sent news to Pearl of the show's success. The Green Mill did fabulous business and was proud of the star attraction. Tex's energy seemed higher than it had ever been, and the suckers loved her. Cimman said she was by far the best emcee Chicago had ever seen.

Still the climate of Chicago made Tex uneasy. The streets frequently witnessed violent murders and other crimes. Tex dared to joke, "I heard of a fellow who was arrested in Chicago on the charge of vagrancy. He was carrying a machine gun, and it had no bullets."[22] Earlier that year, on St. Valentine's Day, there had been the massacre of seven members of the Bugs Moran gang, which ruled the north side of town. It was clear that Al Capone, Caesar of the south side and Public Enemy Number One, had engineered the killings, but nothing had been done to bring him to justice.

As a precaution, Voiler hired Tex a bodyguard who, though his official title was club bouncer, kept his eye on her and escorted her around the city. According to Stein, Leo "Buster" Brothers actually saved Tex from a kidnapping attempt during her stay in the Windy City. The unfortunate man would be framed two years later for the murder of *Tribune* writer Jake Lingle and would serve a long prison term for a crime he did not commit.

As time passed, Tex began to miss New York and grew more and more uneasy about guns that kept appearing at her club. The Green Mill rapidly gained a reputation as a gangster hangout and folks assumed Tex had an "in" with the underworld. Even her reporter friends Jim Doherty and Chesly Manly were asking questions. Like the time gambling concessionaire Ted Newberry disappeared—they wanted to know where he had gone. If Tex knew, she kept her mouth shut.

Tex was trying desperately to keep her nose clean and had her agent book her a stand in New York. She realized now that she had affiliated herself with the wrong kind of crowd. When she told the owners of the Green Mill that she had plans to leave, they tried to stall her. Tex was worth a tremendous amount of money to them. She threw farewell parties all through the end of March until the evening of March 23, when Sweitzer and Voiler had an argument and a shoot-out. The *New York Times* said that Voiler's bodyguard had shot and seriously wounded Sweitzer in an argument over money.

Other papers said the men had had a jealous quarrel over one of the chorus girls. In the *Chicago Herald and Examiner*, the recap of the fight went something like this:

> Sweitzer went to the cabaret with his own guard, "Solly" Marks and his sweetheart Lorraine Hayes, until last Wednesday employed in the show at the Green Mill and a protégé of "Tex" Guinan's brought here by the latter from New York. They arrived at the club. He tells her to wait in the car.
> "Just wait in the car for me. I'll only be a minute. I've got to see Voiler about the rent."
> Sweitzer said he saw Voiler and Reed [Voiler's bodyguard] sitting at a table and held this conversation with them.
>
> S: I want to talk with you, Voiler.
> V: Sit down, have some coffee.
> S: I hear you're going to close.
> V: Yes, this is Texas's last appearance here. We close next Saturday.
> S: Who is going to pay the rent for April?
> V: I'm not.
> S: No? Guess again. I'll be around for the receipts for tonight's business and you'd better see that they're here.
> V: Don't be like that. I'm not going to pay.
> S: We'll see.
>
> At this point someone called Voiler and he and Reed edged away, leaving Sweitzer seated. Next moment he felt a gun in his back and was told to walk quietly upstairs. Stepped into the private office and then there were shots.[23]

Tex was temporarily taken, along with other employees, to the old Summerdale police station. Ed Eulenberg, a retired reporter from the *Sun Times* remembered when she pulled up in her Rolls Royce, swept into the station, and said, "Well, boys, I've got the Rolls, who's got the coffee?" The policemen loved her. "Would've thought it was a party," reflected Eulenberg, instead of a serious investigation.[24]

Two days later Tex was on the train bound for New York. Sweitzer's shooting had given her much to think about, and all she could say was, Thank God the folks had left town before it had happened. They had only been there to witness a few nights of great business. Mike had written Pearl all the details about Tex: "She has done a fine business but spends money like a Drunken Sailor on strangers.

We went to the Scandals last night with a party of Tex's friends and Tex's secretary Jack Stein. After the show we all drove out to Tex's club the Green Mill. . . . Tex had so many places to go and of course we have a nice room at the Sherman House."[25]

When they returned to New York, Mike caught up on the shoot-out details and reported further: "Understand she is busy trying to get her ex-convict manager out of jail in Chicago. Walter Solinger [Tex's lawyer] says he ought to go to the chair. Tex sure got herself into a nice mess with this ex-convict Voiler."[26] Then "Texas arrived home yesterday. She says her ex-convict Voiler is coming to New York in two weeks. She is crazier over this bum than she was over Kerwin."[27]

The *Chicago Herald and Examiner* reported Tex's efforts to obtain Voiler's release mainly on the grounds that he "is a wonderful man." She offered bail, but it was refused on the grounds that the victim, Sweitzer, might die from the gun wounds, upping the charge to murder. Tex then telephoned a score of politicians for help—with little success. Her public was embarrassed for her. The papers said, "Notwithstanding 'the Guinan's' reputation for worldly wisdom, Voiler for a long time has been profiting handsomely as her 'manager.' He took over the lease to the Green Mill premises when Sweitzer moved out. To the flippant ones of the night life circles, 'Tex' was Voiler's 'meal ticket.'"[28]

Stepping off the train in New York City, Tex fingered the leopard fur collar of her coat and in answer to reporters' questions cooed, "Have I any plans? Say young man, I've got more plans than an architect."[29] She told them some of her plans included a club in New York City to open in the fall, a brief showing at the Capitol Theater, another season at the Show Place on Long Island, and a bit of freelance reporting for the *New York Journal*. Her first assignment was to review Mae West's trial over her scandalous play *The Pleasure Man*. West had been charged with writing many of the skits in the play that police and prosecutors declared were too shocking for the stage. Tex thought maybe a few more acts were needed. ("Mae's a good girl at heart," Tex had said earlier in one of her syndicated columns (no. 7), "but she's got a bad heart.")

The following month Tex could be seen fighting for women's rights at a rally protesting the Mastick Law. The Mastick Law advocated a forty-eight hour work week for women, thus limiting the amount of overtime hours. Protesters condemned the law, calling it discriminating legislation designed by political lobbyists to steal jobs from women. Tex, one of the speakers at the rally, urged that a test case be made of the law's constitutionality.

Tex was always regarded as a fair employer and was known to take particularly good care of her "girls." Two years later she would telegraph President Roosevelt her congratulations when he proposed the minimum wage of thirty dollars a week for chorus girls. She assured the President of her support and said she had never paid her girls less than thirty-five a week.

Everyone left the city in the summer, so did Tex. In late spring, Tex opened in Valley Stream in a club backed by Feets, Owney, Frenchy, and Tommy. It was a calm enough summer, another season living at the Nassau Hotel, zigzagging back and forth to the city to prepare for the opening of the Argonaut Club, sunning on the beach when there was time in her favorite red velvet bathing suit that oughtn't get wet, occasionally scribbling a word or two for her new syndicated column, "Texas Guinan Says," in the *New York Graphic*.

The Club Argonaut was located at 151 West Fifty-fourth Street, the site of the former 300 Club. On October 8, shortly after the club opened, a short circuit caused a fire that would cost $40,000 in damages. The club was rehabilitated by October 29, just in time for the police to raid it. They found no liquor, but plenty of ice, and argued that the club had been guilty of serving setups. The charge was dropped, however, due to insufficient evidence. The club continued to run through the winter and into the spring.

Tex, at age forty-seven, continued to hold the undisputed position of Queen of the Night Clubs. One columnist said,

> One sits and looks at her in amazement. How can she go through the ordeal, and it's nothing short of an ordeal, some three hundred nights in a year, from midnight until dawn, and retain her mental as well as physical balance, is an enigma; in fact, it is nothing short of a miracle. To stand on a chair and bellow forth songs and an endless line of witticisms for two or more hours night after night would break down the resistance of most normal beings, but Texas goes merrily on, apparently thriving on what would put another person of her age under the sod in a short time.[30]

The indefatigable Tex remained in the embrace of the public spotlight. Fans watched as, in January 1931, Tex, Belle Livingstone, and actress Fannie Ward pranced off to hear a rajah tell them what they were thinking. Then it looked as if Tex were returning to school. Was that her taking a course in advanced literature at Columbia University Extension School? It had something to do with becoming an evangelist. But these were little things. Tex had actually been playing with a grand, new, exciting idea. She saw that, for the meantime, New York City was not a comfortable place for a night-club entertainer. Chicago was too dangerous and Los Angeles too boring. It was time, then, to go abroad. Paris. It would be good for the girls to get a little bit of "cultuh," and she'd enjoy the rest. The money. Becoming internationally known.

That April as Tex was rehearsing her girls in the Savoy Theater in Brooklyn, a surly man came in and sat down to watch. After a while, he approached Tex and demanded a cut in the Paris trip's profits. Seemed his girl was in the line. Tex wasn't interested in his "offer." She called the police and had him thrown out of the theater. This might have been a mistake as Arthur Flegenheimer, better known as Dutch Schultz, didn't like the police knowing where he was. In fact, he'd been hoping they'd forgotten him.

Fifty Million Frenchmen Can't Be Wrong: We're Too Hot for Paris

The greatest toll gate is that of success.
—TEXAS GUINAN, QUOTED IN CHARLES SHAW'S LOWDOWN

As the boat moved slowly toward Plymouth, Tex paced excitedly back and forth on the deck. Here was England at last! Finally she could leave the S.S. *Paris* and stop rocking, for God's sake. It was the end of May and the weather was particularly fine. She noticed, with excitement, that a small boat full of reporters and photographers was coming their way, and she turned to tell her manager. He hadn't slept well the night before and was cranky. He told her to go below. He wasn't risking an encounter with the British press. They probably wouldn't understand Tex's brand of humor, and anyway he'd heard they were sure to be hostile. Tex wasn't convinced. However, she let him bully her into retiring to her cabin. She wanted to change into a more suitable outfit, perhaps the white riding suit with the rhinestone buttons that she'd bought especially for this trip.

After the unpleasantness with Dutch Schultz, the preparations for the trip had gone smoothly. Countless farewell parties had filled an entire week in May and left little room for nostalgia or pre–going-away panic. The finale, the very last of the celebrations, had been the greatest of successes, from the high caliber of the guests down to the refreshments. Someone had warned Tex that the government would have an agent at the party because they were sure she'd serve illegal drinks. With a little bit of imagination, she and her crew had devised a smorgasboard of colorful punches, whose far-from-lethal ingredients included fruit juice, spices, cordials, and club soda.

That last party had continued way past dawn and on into Reubens for breakfast. No one—not Joe Fejer, Helen Morgan, Maurice Chevalier, George White, Gloria Swanson, Fanny Ward, Belle Livingstone, not the reporters or the officers of the S.S. *Paris* who had thrown the damn thing—was willing to let go. It was almost as if New York City would be doomed to several months of boredom once Tex left. So they were stocking up on fun until she returned.

Tex was putting the final touches on her makeup when there was a sound of a struggle in the corridor: scuffling feet, bodies, loud, strident British voices. They'd gotten aboard and found her, anyway. Perhaps she'd have a chance to say a word after all! She brightened. But her manager slipped into the room and told her that though they had tracked her down to her cabin, she was still not "safe." "Safe from what?" she muttered. "Enjoying myself?" Though the trip across had been entertaining, she'd done most of it—the entertaining, that is—and hadn't had nearly enough time to talk to that genius Paderewski, who was also on board. Most of the trip had been work. Talking to reporters and posing—why that was play. She loved interviews. She loved being photographed. Once, when a photographer asked if he could take her picture when she stopped talking, she replied, "Can you wait that long? I'll be dead when I stop talking."[1]

Still, her manager had his way with her, and when the reporters burst into her cabin, she was safely in her bathroom. From her hiding place, she could hear the disappointment in the next room. Then a lovely British voice: "Come on boys, it must be true that she's over seventy."[2] This was too much.

"Who said I was seventy?" Cameras caught her smile and reporters' pads filled with her wisecracks, many of which the Englishmen didn't understand. Tex was quite charming until she learned that England would not permit her troupe to land on its shores. When the reporters asked her how she felt about that, she replied, "Why should you shut the door in my face before I knock?"

The Associated Press on May 29, 1931, wired the States of Tex's troubles and reflected her confusion over the restriction:

What has England against me? My parents were born in Great Britain and England was only too glad to welcome me when I worked for her during the war. . . .

I will gladly give a check for a hundred thousand dollars to any charity, if anyone can substantiate statements made against my character. . . .

Is it because I said I would ride down the Strand on a white horse that I've been barred from England? If you can find any statute in the laws of England which make it criminal to ride a white horse I'll make you my heir.

Tex also told the press, "I will come back, because England will want my company as does every civilized country. We are not out to make money. We want to make people happy."

Apparently, nobody believed her. The entertainers in Paris certainly didn't. They banded together and told the Minister of the Interior that if he issued Tex a permit to work, she would usurp their territory and profits.

Months later, Tex would explain that she was not permitted to enter France because she was considered dangerous. "Sort of a queen of an underworld. A female gangster and racketeer, because I had an armored car which at one time belonged to the King of Belgium, because 91 cafe managers signed a petition to keep me out so that I would not take the American tourist business into my madhouse.... All of the reasons which they gave me seemed as thin as my first husband's excuses."[3]

In public, Tex appeared more disappointed for her girls than for herself. "I don't mind for myself," she explained to the *New York Times* on May 30, "because I didn't expect to make any money in Paris anyway. But I did so want my kids to have the broadening influence of foreign travel. They're the prettiest kids in the world already and with just a little culture they'd be knockouts."

Everyone was sympathetic, even some of the French. Though the French Syndicate of Entertainers had long been protesting the hiring of foreign entertainers, Josephine Baker had been working there for quite a while and had never been asked to leave. However, Tex had a different kind of reputation. To non-Americans, she was *the* symbol of the twenties and American night-club entertainment.

In France, Tex and her crew were held at a third-class hotel to await deportation. The French may not have wanted to lose money in the tourist trade, but they would now have to foot the bill to send her home.

Also, France unwittingly gave Tex some wonderful publicity. Crowds hovered around le Havre hoping for a glimpse. Letters poured in, offering jobs all over the world, and few bold, young gentlemen offered proposals of marriage.

Still, quietly, Tex was sick at heart. Clearly, this was France's way of acknowledging how powerful a figure she had become in the night-club entertainment world. But even though Tex loved the publicity, she had wanted to stay and see France. It was all right for the girls, they were young and would have plenty of chances to visit again, but she was forty-seven. She might not have another chance.

Fame, she'd just told the public in her April 15 "Texas Guinan Says," "is like losing one's diamonds. Once possessed, you do not wish to be stripped of them. Your friends are apt to think that they were borrowed jewels. And so you hang to fame. It is a matter of public pride.

"Many people are supposed to wake up and find themselves famous. Don't let them kid you. Undoubtedly they were sleeping all the while with one eye open.

"I believe it was Andrew Carnegie who philosophized that fame is chiefly a matter of dying at the right moment."

She lifted her chin and told reporters that fifty million Frenchmen can be wrong. "I was a sucker to come 3,000 miles to go to jail when every jail in America is waiting for me. Oh well, you know me—an indiscretion a day keeps depression away."[4]

Tex and her girls sailed back to America, "the land of the free and the home of prohibition. Where liquor has been cut so much it has bled to death." It was June by the time they returned to New York and thousands of welcoming friends, along with the curious and the concerned. Within a week, Tex and her managers had devised a new revue in the form of a night-club show entitled *Too Hot for Paris*. The cast included Jack Osterman, Joe Frisco, Dick Lane, and the Neal Sisters. Several of the girls had left the company, and Tex had to hold an audition for new ones. Would there be another Ruby Keeler or a near-Claire Luce?

The day of the auditions, the theater filled with young hopefuls of all shapes and waist measurements. One fifteen-year-old, Nanon Gardener, had been talked into waiting by two of her friends. She was dressed all in blue—in blue coat, blue dress, and blue hat. As she stood wondering whether to stay or to go and what she was going to sing, a woman emerged from next door and looked around the room. Nanon thought she looked awfully old and wondered if this was the famous Texas Guinan she'd heard so much about. She said, "The little girl in blue, would you step up please?" "So I went up," Nanon would recall fifty years later, "and she said 'I would like to see you in rehearsal clothes at the Majestic Theater on Thursday.' So that was that. Thursday came and I went and then we found out she was looking to produce a show 'Too Hot.'"[5]

Nanon went home and recorded in her theater route book, "Joined Texas Guinan for her Broadway show 'Too Hot.' Rehearsed two weeks. Opened at the Brighton Theater, Brighton Beach, Brooklyn. Show was too smutty for Broadway. Shubert wouldn't buy it. Closed after one week at the Brighton Theater."

"It really wasn't that dirty," explained Nanon. "It was a regular revue—lots of girls. The costumes were brief but I think they were even prettier than the Ziegfield costumes and I was in the Follies, too."[6]

Too Hot ran from the sixth of July until the twelfth. Robert Garland of the *World Telegram* reviewed it and said, "And French government or no French government, Miss Guinan, in low white pants and high good humor, remains the queen of the night clubs.

"Even if there aren't any night clubs to rule over, Miss Guinan is every inch a queen, drawing down the rain of applause on those who don't deserve it as well as those who do; turning the spotlight of publicity on the papa and mama who, rising from their seats in a left stage box, do not seem to mind. . . . The point is that there is only one Miss Guinan."

Later that month, Tex took the *Too Hot* revue to Woodmansten Inn, right off the Pelham Parkway and Kingsbridge Road in Westchester. Woodmansten Inn was a big club, another roadhouse inn. A 1931 description said the inn attracted a "slightly higher hat clientele than the usual roadhouse commands, and (served) exceptionally good, expensive food."[7]

Playing at the roadhouse was something to do while Tex repaired the weaker parts of the show and prepared to take the girls on the road. By August, she told the newspapers she was going to tour the countryside in a motor bus with forty girls, a fourteen-piece band, and all the comforts of home that could fit inside.

Four weeks after she had installed herself in Westchester, a hand bomb exploded in the club early one morning after it had closed. Investigators could not discover any motives, and the bomb hadn't done much damage, but some thought the bomb had been a warning from Dutch Schultz. A few days later, before Tex had a chance to worry much about it, the inn was raided by federal agents and two bottles of what was alleged to be gin confiscated. The six hundred guests present were to be the last of the season.

Tex poured her energy into her road tour but worried about her status in the night-club world. If the bomb had really been planted by Schultz's men, then the Bronx Beer Baron was still angry about being ejected from the rehearsal hall. Perhaps Tex had made a serious mistake. Schultz was one of the most powerful underworld figures in New York. He not only ruled uptown, but supposedly controlled Tammany Hall through the pliable J. J. Hines. She wouldn't really know until she returned from the tour, but it seemed as if Schultz was doing his utmost to bar her from working at any club in New York. Her insomnia grew worse, and she phoned her manager Jack Naples at all hours of the morning to talk. Even the girls knew about this.

Tex and her busload were slated to bring a bit of nightlife from Broadway to Main Street, U.S.A., in the early fall. Described as "Whoopee on Wheels," their bus was fully equipped with resting quarters, bridge tables, and refrigeration. Tex told reporters of the *New York Times* that her show could be set up anywhere, on a prairie if need be. "We even carry our own applause."

Tex bade farewell to New York and proclaimed she was leaving "so's it can get a good, long sleep" while she and her girls embarked on their "anti-depression" tour. She hoped that the trip would lift her own spirits and wanted to explore how effective she would be in disseminating her personal gospel of happiness the only way she knew how—in true night-club fashion. She knew that folks had been hit hard by the Depression, especially in the Midwest, and she wanted to cheer them up. But cheering them up was not enough. She and her company would donate a portion of their earnings to local unemployment relief.

The show proved too hot for towns smaller than New York City and folded after a month. One mayor barred the revue before he'd even seen it. Too hot for Paris? It was certainly too hot for his town. Tex thought the mayor was so narrow-minded that his ears touched in back. "Whoopee on Wheels" journeyed on into Boston and played a benefit performance for the unemployed.

During the tour, Tex began to make other plans. She had learned that Aimee Semple McPherson Hutton was to be in Boston the following month and on September 26, the *New York American* carried the headlines "Texas Guinan Challenges Aimee to Debate in Boston Garden on Happiness."

"Resolved, that people are entitled to a bit of fun and happiness in these troublesome times," Tex declared.

From Portland, Aimee met the challenge. "I am an evangelist and my campaign in Boston will be a revival and not a side show."[8]

Tex thought perhaps Aimee was piqued at some of the things Tex had said about her in her syndicated column of September 19, 1931—about McPherson's recent marriage and perhaps the parting shot about California being God's country and Sister Aimee being the territory's little cashier. Couldn't she take a little joke?

On October 5, the *New York American* carried a mini-debate between the two ladies on "A Woman's Place in the World." Aimee contended that "Wherever men live, work, love and pray, there is woman's place in the world." Clearly, Tex's own life had not fit that pattern. Tex gave women a larger world. She was eloquent:

When Betsy Ross made the first flag of our U.S. I don't think she was by the side of the one person she loved. She stayed by the country she loved. . . .

If woman's place should be next to her man, then Peggy Hopkins Joyce would have to be an acrobat.

Woman's place is with her enemy if she can render humanity service. Aimee must have forgotten that part of the scripture which says, "love thy neighbor as thyself."

Woman's place in life is in the heart of the man and woman where she can do the greatest amount of good. Religion means service, and when we have served either our beloved or our enemy, we have made religion just another little dramatic incident.

Tex ended the argument with another challenge for the debate in Boston, followed by her Saturday column, "Texas Guinan Says," in the *Graphic* on October 10.

A public challenge to Aimee Semple McPherson Hutton: I have always been fond of talking. It's grand to gab. I like it. Here is an honest confession that is good for the soul. Aimee refuses to debate with me because she says that oratory in the form of debates is time wasted. Revival is the stuff—so says Aimee. Sister Aimee, have you forgotten the famous Lincoln-Douglas debates? The Webster debates? . . .

I challenge you to meet me in a public debate. You pick the subject and the place and I will be on hand.

If the proceeds of such an event can be distributed to the poor and needy and the unemployed, I fear that your revival meeting will not be a side show in vain.

Save all the souls you like, Aimee, but give man his substance to strengthen his body first. You might save a dozen souls and lose ten stomachs. Where's the gain? Feed them and save them.

I'm just as widely talked about as you and in no less degree than yourself. And for you to take issue with me is just one way of collecting cold cash that will give the unfortunate a little buttered toast.

Those who saw Tex as the Queen of the Outlaws found her affiliation with religion incongruous. Those who knew her well knew she had always been devout and generous. She took a practical approach to the spiritual, taking issue with such realities as hunger. She had a reputation for performing at benefits. Aimee, on the other had, had once said, rather flippantly, "I bring religious consolation to the great middle class, leaving those below to the Salvation Army and those above to themselves."[9] To many, it was always clear that Aimee had "a good deal more ham than halo about her,"[10] but she continued to fascinate Tex.

While Tex was discovering the holes in her *Too Hot* tour, Harry Voiler decided to complicate her life once more. He tried to seduce her back to Chicago with the story that Capone had loaned him the money to back the Planet Mars Cafe. Capone was by that time in prison for tax evasion, and the whole world knew that. Still, Capone might have been powerful enough to touch people even though he resided behind the walls of the penitentiary.

Tex knew that with New York closed to her, temporarily—though her brother Tommy was working on an agreement with Schultz—that Chicago was one of her only choices if she wanted to get back into the business. However, she was afraid that if she returned to Chicago she would take up with Voiler again.

It didn't matter what kind of moral debates Tex engaged in because Voiler was determined to win her back. Part of his determination was rooted in his situation with the underworld. Voiler had always played the loner and walked the fence between the north- and south-side gangs. Now he would be allying himself with Capone's gang by asking Capone for financing. And his agreement with the head of the Chicago underworld was that he'd get the money if he got the Guinan. There were no *ifs* for Voiler.

Stein tells how the *Too Hot* tour ended abruptly in Louisville, Kentucky, when "three rough gentlemen from Chicago" paid a visit to Tex's dressing room. If soft words had not had effect, real guns certainly did. An hour later, Tex was packed and off to join the Planet Mars. Later when National Touring Artists told her they would sue for breach of contract, those same gentlemen from Chicago would use their guns in her favor, and "talk" them out of it.[11]

Tex was uncomfortably deep into the places she'd avoided for years, the backdrop to her clubs, the activities she'd just played front to—and all because she'd fallen for the wrong type of man.

Voiler's bad health took him away from the club to Colorado Springs for a rest cure. Tex, who had begun work in late October, continued to do her three shows nightly: supper show at 7:00 P.M., midnight, and 2:30 A.M. The cafe was located on Randolph Street near Wells Street, opposite the Palace Theatre and the Bismarck Hotel. The manager, Leo Nelson, who took over while Voiler was away, watched Tex draw the crowds night after night. He was handsome, young, and ambitious. Perhaps—and this is what Stein thought—he had visions of forming his own night club. Whatever the reason, he made a play for Tex. Tex was flattered by his attentions and sought to shake off the cobwebs of the Voiler entanglement. As she did so, Sam ("Golf Bag") Hunt, one of Capone's henchmen, stepped in. And she fell for him instead.

Sam Hunt's middle name came from the machine gun he carried in his golf bag. He was rumored to have been one of the Valentine's Day Killers, though Tex never found out for sure.

Meanwhile Voiler's wife had been keeping an eye on Tex while her husband was away. She noticed Leo Nelson's advances and having found him attractive herself, had no doubts that Tex would succumb readily. Not wanting to jeopardize her cash flow, Mrs. Voiler phoned her husband, and he returned to Chicago. There, he rushed to Tex's hotel, burst into her room, and found her at dinner with Hunt. He was in a tight spot because Hunt was one of Capone's right-hand men and didn't have his nickname for nothing. Voiler reputedly turned to Tex and said, "All I want to know is whose woman are you?" She replied, "Certainly not yours."[12] After this encounter, Nelson was fired, just in case he decided to go after Tex again, and the romance with Hunt came to an end.

Christmas was coming, and Tex was anxious to return to New York to see the window decorations *and* her darling family. But Voiler still stood in her way. This time when the law showed its face at the club—it always did sooner or later—it proved a help, not a hindrance for Tex. The Queen of the Night Clubs laughed later to think that the day had finally come when she'd prayed for a raid. New Year's Eve with reservations all booked, the Feds took all the money, $85,000 worth of fixtures, ransacked the place, and arrested several employees, including some waiters. Voiler himself was arrested. Seems he had a revolver in his pocket.

New Year's Day, Tex reigned on the front page of the *Chicago Herald and Examiner*. It was reported that after making such a huge mess at the club, the Feds were not going to press any charges against the performer. Tex was obviously disappointed. She had gone down to the courthouse "all dressed up like the night before Christmas" because she said she had a date with "Clark Gable" down at the federal building. Unfortunately, "Mr. Gable" didn't show.

"Gable" was A. E. Aman, Deputy Prohibition Administrator in Chicago who had led the raid on the Planet Mars. Tex chatted to reporters about the raid. "Oh that lovely man! What a man! Why he can raid my place every night! I never was in such a nice raid and I never met such nice Prohibition agents. When they came I thought sure it was Clark Gable and a party, but they kept on their hats, so I knew it was a pinch. The suckers thought it was the best part of the show. It took two hours to chase them home."[13]

Tex was attired in typically conservative fashion, reported the paper.

> She wore a flaming red dress trimmed in leopard skin and carried a leopard coat and hat. On one arm she wore a tiny two-inch-wide bracelet and on the small finger of her right hand a ring—or was it two rings?
>
> About her neck hung a 4" diamond brooch and a string of pearls. And inside her satin pumps, she said, reposed her "mad money," just in case Uncle Sam wanted to send her to jail.
>
> She carried an amber-headed cane. "Because people will ask me when I was in an accident and I can tell them a raid isn't an accident, but an "act of God." . . . You know, there should be a new motto: "Now is the time for all good men to come to the RAID of their party."[14]

Voiler was held on liquor charges. Though he tried to pin part-ownership of the club on Tex, Tex's contract protected her once again. As soon as she could, she left Chicago, telegramming to New York on January 11, 1932, for advance press.

> Leaving the Windy City, where you never know where your next bullet is coming from. Here one has to talk louder than the radio. Keep off the gunny side of the street if you don't want to turn into a popgun. Suggest that a gas mask and a few trenches be built on the main drag of Chicago Stem so that the war of the little play fellows who take the north side and the south side of the city don't take you for a walk and lull you to sleep with that soothing melody bye bye baby. Arriving Tuesday morning with my famous gang, who have learned to jump through a .38 without getting burned. Returning to my New York night club as well as to do a drama of my new play, which is a life of Sister Aimee who believes in the hereafter, because I know what I am here after first.[15]

Tex had tried, when first arriving back in New York, to play up her Aimee idea. Once again she posed before cameras in her red ensemble with a jeweled lorgnette hanging from her neck—a costume apparently considered befitting one whose "life had run parallel," as she expressed it, to that of Aimee Semple McPherson. Tex told reporters of the *New York Times* that if one compared the lives of the two women, starting back when they were little girls, one would find that they ran parallel in many respects. "She, too, is a mighty clever woman."[16] However, after a bit of publicity, the play she had planned to star in was temporarily shelved.

Meanwhile, Schultz was attending to his feud with twenty-three-year-old Vincent "Mad Dog" Coll, known as New York's most ruthless killer. Coll, a former gunman with Schultz's gang, had left the fold in 1930 and gone out on his own. Through a series of acts, the worst of which was to raid Schultz's territory and steal his beer, Coll managed to antagonize his former patron and associated thugs like Owney Madden. By the middle of 1931, Schultz was out for blood. So was Coll. Among others, the cross fire killed Coll's brother and a five-year-old boy, while wounding four other children who happened to be playing on the sidewalk of East 107th Street when one of the bouts of shooting started. That incident became known as "the Baby Killing."

The feud continued. On the evening of February 6, 1932, Walter Winchell's column in the *Daily Mirror* read, "Local banditti have made one hotel a virtual arsenal and several hot-spots are ditto because Master Coll is giving them the headache."

Winchell, on good terms with several underworld figures, had often printed such blurbs. In the 1920s, reporters covering the nightclub beat needed to keep on top of the underworld gossip. But this was Winchell's first "prediction." The next morning at 12:45, Coll was shot by machine-gun fire while standing in a phone booth making a call.

Several versions of the story have it that Winchell had been tipped off by Tex herself. One of Winchell's biographers, Herman Klurfeld, wrote, "On February 6, 1932, Winchell made his nightly newsgathering visit to the club run by Texas Guinan. It was hardly a secret along Broadway that Tex was on intimate terms with the gangsters who financed her club. On the evening in question, she stopped at Winchell's table and whispered to him. . . . [Winchell] testifed that the Coll tip had come anonymously via the mail. The real source—whose friendship with Winchell was well-known—was ordered exiled by the mob czars for talking too much."[17]

Winchell had plenty of his own contacts with the underworld, and Tex had been in Chicago and out of the scene for a while. She didn't have a club of her own then, though she had been doing miscellaneous gigs around town. Could she have known about the murder plan? She might have heard the word from her brother Tommy or his buddy Owney.

Winchell said of Tex's relationship to gangsters: "Tex was the only ally of the gangster night spot–speakeasy–owners I ever knew who bulldozed them. They didn't dare raise their voices to her. She was their Big Front. And she hated them all."[18]

Schultz's mind relieved of Coll, he could vent his spite on Tex. As she went to different cafe owners, she received funny looks and no jobs. Some would even go as far as to offer her a contract, then never follow through. In the past, these people would have jumped at the chance to feature Tex in their clubs.

How could New York be closed to her? A man tells the night-club world that Tex is not to be employed and they listen? One lousy man? Wasn't she the Queen?

The worst part for Tex lay in her inability to work in New York City. Though Tex thrived on the night-club scene, it was New York she adored. Her life was there; her friends, her family, her beloved Eighth Street apartment. New York was *home*.

Schultz was powerful, but Tex had powerful friends herself. Why couldn't Tommy make any headway? Owney ruled midtown, and what about Frenchy? It would not be until April, when Tex was out at the Fox Theater in Detroit—having no other choice but to return to the road with her girls—that Tommy would telegram her with the news that things were okay. On June 15 she could open in Valley Stream at La Casa. What he forgot to tell her was that Schultz would be a silent owner of the club.

In May, before joining the new club, Tex took a trip to France. The *New York Times* was certain that she had journeyed there only to prove to the world "that the country that had rejected her coldly last year was waiting to receive her with open arms"[19] and that was true, in part. But she was also going over to have some fun. The government had invited her back as their guest, and she had a glorious time. The country was full of beauty and peace—they had no word for gangster there. France was also the heart and home of nightlife. Tex decided that when she turned fifty, she'd retire and return to the country where they really knew what having fun meant—and remain there for life.

La Casa opened upon Tex's return to New York, and to everyone's surprise, there was no cover charge. The absence of the cover charge signaled the end of Prohibition. Since the crash, the movement toward repealing the Eighteenth Amendment had been gaining strength. The economic depression aided the champions of the "wet" cause in pressuring the government about all the money spent on Prohibition enforcement, money that might better go for unemployment relief. Better yet, if the liquor industry were made legal again, hundreds of new jobs would become available, and the economy would rally. By June, the month Tex began working at La Casa, the Democratic convention had adopted a "repeal" plank outright.

La Casa was managed by Harry Lyons, one of Schultz's men. Although Tex was unaware of Schultz's ownership in the club, she was nervous about the arrangement and didn't trust Lyons. As it turned out, she lasted ten days at La Casa. The papers said that Lyons had fired two of her girls without her permission, and infuriated, she'd walked out on the show. Stein told a different story: Lyons had hired a girl whom Tex found to be "distasteful." She promptly fired her only to see her back at the club the next night in full costume. It seems she was Schultz's latest girl. Schultz turned sour and barred Tex from the club.

Tex went north to Montreal, the closest thing to France that she could think of. It was quaint and European—in some spots—and the folks spoke French. She settled there for the winter, worked the Frolics Club run by the Hill brothers, fell in love with a fellow called Eddie Baker. Schultz pursued her for a bit, threatened the owners, and found he had no power past the Canadian border. Tex was safe, for the time being.

Tomorrow and Tomorrow

> *It seems reasonable to regard the World's Fair as about complete, now that Texas Guinan has quit flirting with the Loop's numerous and neglected night clubs and moved out where the midnight crowds move.*
> —ASHTON STEVENS, CHICAGO AMERICAN, JULY 6, 1933

*T*he World's Fair—a circus, playground, night club, and educational arena all in one—a zoo! A place for kids of all ages to roam and watch fantasies become real, then evaporate before their very eyes. A place to be bamboozled out of all your spot cash, a place to spend for the sheer joy of it.

Four years had passed since the stock market had summoned the black cloud of depression. Jobs and cash remained scarce, but Americans were beginning to feel ready to play again. In Chicago, there was talk of a one-hundredth anniversary party in the guise of a world's fair. What an excuse to have fun!

Chicago's "Century of Progress" was planned to celebrate not only the city's first hundred years but human accomplishments over that period. Though the fair would look back over time, many of the instructive pavilions concentrating on the advances made in science and technology, "Tomorrow" was the main theme. For the many still concerned with the here-and-now, and still in tune with the twenties philosophy of living for the moment, there was also the midway, complete with roller coasters, games, jugglers, midgets, and sideshows. "Visit the place where daring youths dive into tanks and wrestle with alligators!" invited the official guidebook of the fair.[1]

The midway, city of a million lights. "Visit it by day and you might think of brilliant bands of color connecting two great sections of the Fair," said the guidebook. "At night, you might think of a gorgeous scintillating trinket."[2]

Tex could not observe a gorgeous scintillating trinket without wanting it on her wrist. She wanted a piece of the action on the midway.

Tex had been living in Chicago since her engagement had ended in Montreal. She had been a great success with the Canadians but hadn't made any money. Her bosses had promised to pay her at the end of her stay instead of each week, and since she was drawing huge crowds, she figured she would end up with thousands. Yet when the show closed, the owners told her the club was in debt and they could not pay her. This didn't sound quite right to Tex, but by then she was too tired to fight. She left town without a word.

Tex stopped off in Manhattan long enough to hear the shocking news that her former partner Larry Fay had been shot and killed by the doorman of his latest club. She attended the funeral, settled his unpaid hotel bill, and headed to the Windy City. It was January 1933.

That year, John Ashenhurst's *All about Chicago* described Jake Adler's Frolics, at 18 East Twenty-second Street, as "a gay rendezvous patronized for years by the highest and lowest classes. . . . For revelry and atmosphere no place in Chicago can compete with it." When Tex opened there, the place grew so popular that the management was anxious to keep her, at least until the fair opened. Indeed, they were hoping she'd stay even longer and attract the late-night fair crowds.

Fortunately, things on the underbelly of night life in Chicago had changed some since her last visit, and Tex didn't need to worry about being pressured into staying—nor about Voiler. Though Sam Hunt put in a nightly appearance at the club, it was soon apparent, after he eloped with a chorus girl, that he was no longer interested in Tex's affections. She was relieved, though a little disappointed. However, she was quite in love with her Eddie.

Eddie Baker was her latest "personal manager," acquired in Montreal. Though newspapers had managed to engage her to several different millionaires during her stay in Canada, they had missed the main item. A regular at the Frolics Cabaret in Montreal when the two met, Eddie caught Tex's eye immediately, with his big square jawline à la Julian Johnson. At one time, he had been a fight promoter and a race-horse bookie. He'd then begun toying with the bootlegging business on the Canadian side and eventually became part-owner of the Frolics, Tex's manager and attorney, and when the occasion called for it, "husband." Stein was disgusted with this latest infatuation and called Baker a "useless leech." He said Tex would advertise her affair by talking baby talk to Eddie and calling him "Oochie Boochie Boo." Tex had a pet Pekingese with the same name.³

In Chicago, if the gossip columns missed Mr. Baker, who was back in Montreal, they continued to keep a close eye on the queen's activities. Not knowing that she was barred from New York City, they were proud that she had parked herself in their city and were generous with their coverage. Their spotlight followed her from the benefits she arranged ("Wonder if anybody knew that Tex Guinan is one of the few stars who goes for benefits in a big way . . . wonder if charity isn't one of her middle names.")⁴ to her guest appearances at the Garrick Theater with other personalities like Jack Dempsey. They reported the parties she threw for friends like Mae West and Belle Livingstone. And when beer reappeared in America on April 6, eyes turned first to Tex.

In mid-February, both the Senate and the House had passed a motion to submit to state conventions the Twenty-First Amendment to the Constitution repealing the Eighteenth Amendment. Three-fourths of the states needed to agree. On April 3, Michigan had become the first state to ratify the amendment. Now, four days later, Tex predicted the death of the night club and welcomed the young successor to the throne—the beer garden. Beer was Chicago's drink, the working person's drink. Chicagoans cheered her answer.

With her prediction in mind, Tex considered her next move. That evangelism idea was haunting her. People listened to her, people had always liked what she said. She could be an Aimee, spread her personal gospel of happiness. She would practice by debating.

Louella Parson, infamous gossip goddess for the *Los Angeles Examiner*, grabbed this one on April 9, just as Tex knew she would and meowed, "You just won't believe this but it's the truth. Texas Guinan sent George Bernard Shaw a telegram while he was in California, saying 'I'd like to debate with you on any subject any place you say or in print if you prefer. I am sure we might become great friends. Signed Texas Guinan.' 'Who is this Miss Geenan?' inquired Shaw. 'What an amazing person!'"

To prove her seriousness about evangelism, Tex again attempted to stage, direct, and star in a play based on Aimee's life. *Sister Aimee*, written by Nancy Barr Mavity, was scheduled to open on May 15 in the Chicago Auditorium in time for the World's Fair. Tex would preach on the stage for several hours, then retire to the Frolics to put on, as the *New York Post* put it, "a somewhat different entertainment." Then Tex heard there might be a way for her to get her foot in the door at the fair.

The Dance Ship concession, located near the Twenty-third Street exit on the midway, had been having financial difficulties, and there was a possibility she could take over. Tex approached fair officials and waited while they debated about her show. Some argued that she would bring in money for the ailing Dance Ship and the fair itself. Others balked at the thought of including her infamous show.

To plead on her behalf, several friends wrote letters to the fair committee, including General Roy D. Keehan, a well-known Chicago attorney, and the writer Thornton Wilder, who was then on the faculty at the University of Chicago. They understood how it was for Tex, how she had to be part of the fair. Keehan sent a full description of the show, to prove how harmless it was, along with a contract that assigned Tex only one-quarter of the profits, unlike her usual 50 percent. Wilder defended the "legend" of Texas Guinan: " . . . built up by headlines and by a number of regrettable circumstances that have taken place independently in her circle, [they] give no idea of her real character. She a buoyant, energetic, hard working, sincere (sentimental) and four square, honest soul."[5]

Finally, negotiations were complete, and Tex was able to write and tell the family the good news. She sent a postcard from the Alligator Farm to her nephew Patrick. "Darling. Do you get the papers every day from Chicago—I have a great spot on the fair grounds. Texas Guinan Pirate Ship. love, Tex."[6]

Although opening night, June 29, was rained out, Tex's "Century of Whoopee,"—named in the anniversary spirit—appeared to be a great success. She wrote and told her parents she was "packing them in." Anyone who could afford the fifty-five-cent cover charge came to visit: all the Chicago columnists, and such varied personalities as William Walker, "who sells fish and plays golf"; Ira Fisher, butter-and-egg man; Mrs. Gertrude Vanderbilt, "a Follies toast a few years ago"; A. Steinson, envelope millionaire; and R. MacFarland, constructionist.[7] The club was in a large ship containing two dance floors, four dance orchestras that took turns playing, a bar, and a huge frieze of dancing pink elephants that seemed to mimic the antics of the customers.

Tex and her forty girls worked five shows daily, beginning as early as 4:00 P.M. and ending after 2:00 A.M. The show was a smorgasboard of acts ranging from costumed numbers like "The Brides," where the girls posed in bridal outfits from all over the world, to a Japanese ballet, a cowboy number, and a Mardi-Gras pageant. Interspersed with the group numbers were Tex's specialty acts, including the telephone routine in which Tex played the operator and the girls, the phoning parties.

Ashton Stevens of the *Chicago American* said it was a good and fast floor show, but as always, Tex was the star. Tex might have thought she was losing her touch, but to the crowds that swarmed the decks of the Pirate Ship, she was the Great Guinan. Stevens said,

> The old Guinan girl is both a persona and a personage, not only a great showman but a great show.
>
> I doubt if ever we have known another showman quite so spry in the bean as Texas Guinan, who is at her best and at her most when the unexpected happens and she is compelled to swap routine for invention. . . .
>
> It may be, to be sure, that she is not above capitalizing her flashes, making last night's repartee tonight's repertory. . . .
>
> I began to pray for bigger and better emergencies to arise for Miss Guinan as devout farmers pray for falls of rain. For it is the undesired and the unforeseen that exacts the best from this undebateable queen of the after-night.[8]

Tex was back to her old pirate tricks and dressed for the part as well. She surpassed herself with charm and ingenuity. She would note a banker with a long expression on his face and before anyone had noticed her disappearance, she would return with a hostage from the neighboring midget village and install the sweet two-footer upon his knee.

Even outside of the club, Tex entertained her fans. Wandering the "Streets of Paris" one July evening, she met a group of young people led by a twenty-year-old Fred Wittenmeier. He was entertaining his cousin, his cousin's fiancé, and a beautiful young girl whom he was trying hard to impress. They were proceeding down a passageway en route to the exit when they heard a group of rowdy people approaching. Wittenmeier recognized Tex among them, having seen her at her club, and decided he'd introduce her to his guests. He knew she was friendly, and what the hell—anything to impress his girl. "I asked my guests if they would like to meet Texas Guinan," he said years later, "and they thought I was kidding. So I went up to Tex and said, 'Tex, I would like you to meet some friends of mine.' She said, 'certainly Fred,' and I proceeded to introduce my amazed friends, and Tex kept calling me Fred. I think I was more startled than my guests. But later I realized Texas called every man she met 'Fred.'"[9]

The Pirate Ship had only opened its portals in early July, yet by mid-July, it was already rumored that Tex was leaving. For one thing, fair officials had suddenly decided to change the curfew laws and close admission gates at midnight. Tex's best customers usually came to her between midnight and 3:00 A.M. This decision angered Tex, who said fun shouldn't be put on a business schedule. Thanks to the shortened hours, business at the club was poor. In addition, the Ship was a large space to fill, and was costing too much to run. Tex decided to close the show.

Meanwhile, Tex had already received several telegrams discussing a movie contract out in Hollywood. The first had been from her dear friend Walter Winchell who wrote, "Dear Sucker, Zanuck [of Paramount Pictures] wants you to play yourself in my first picture which will include everybody that has meant anything to Broadway and would not be complete without you. Engagement will run only one week. Will consider it great personal favor if you give Darryl every consideration in this matter."[10]

Tex was flattered. Would they guarantee her $2,500? Zanuck okayed the contract, assuring her $2,500 net, round-trip fees, and drawing-room plus hotel expenses not to exceed $500 weekly. The film would be shot sometime in August. Tex thought she could work out a West Coast tour to follow in the fall. There was also some correspondence discussing the opening of a Texas Guinan Club on the West Coast.

Leaving the ill-fated Pirate Ship, Tex and the company were soon breaking house records throughout the Midwest. In Detroit and Indianapolis, theaters gave her trophies. By the time she arrived in Los Angeles and her suite in the Ambassador Hotel, she was ready for a rest. For some reason, she was finding her work tiring, and she seemed to be losing a lot of weight no matter what she ate.

Los Angeles welcomed Tex and didn't notice her condition. Parties were thrown in her honor, friends phoned and dropped by her hotel, and her sister and nephew were constant visitors. Tex thrived on the attention. Yet despite all the people around her, she was somewhat hurt that Mae West hadn't come by. She was also feeling quite low because after reviewing the script to Winchell's *Broadway thru a Keyhole*, she discovered that although she played herself, she wasn't the star. In fact, her role was minor. To cheer herself up, Tex took a trip to the Angelus Temple where Aimee reigned. Aimee was absent at the time, but her right-hand woman, Rhema Crawford, known to all as the "Angel of Broadway," was temporarily in charge.

Though she planned to wear her smallest diamonds and the simplest of picture hats, dress in black, and refuse photographs, Tex knew the press would not pass over her. However, she was thinking of her future. Better to show the world she was truly serious about all this evangelism stuff and what better time to invade Aimee's territory than when she was absent?

On September 10, 1933, Tex went and "got religion," according to the press. The newspapers watched her kneel at the altar, renounce her sins, and sing hymns in a loud voice. They observed, as devoted followers of Aimee surrounded her after the service. Was the great queen of midnight revelry about to become a convert? She told journalists, "I'm not good enough to save souls now. But I see the time coming when I will take the evangelistic trail when I retire from the show business."[11]

Tex had truly been moved by the experience. She found that when the photographers had inevitably caught up with her, she didn't want her picture in the paper. Afterward, in the solitude of her suite, she began composing her own gospel of happiness. After the film for Winchell was complete, as it seemed no one was really interested in setting up any kind of club for her, she would take one last vaudeville tour up the coast. But it wouldn't be just any tour, for she would use it to begin feeling her way along the evangelistic road. When it was over, she would return home to New York, which she missed desperately, retire from the nightlife for good—maybe—and take up preaching. If that didn't work, she'd move to France.

In the fall, Tex left Hollywood and headed up the coast to Oakland and San Francisco. While in 'Frisco she told the press of her intentions to hit the sawdust trail. "I'm not going in for money when I preach," she explained to reporters on the *San Francisco Rounder*. "Aside from my actual expenses and those of my troupe who will take part, every cent will be turned over by me to a worthy cause ... I want to invest my time and efforts in spreading sunshine, happiness and blessing to others ... I love people and that's why I am going to make a success of my evangelism of happiness, because I know how to reach them ... Happiness is the goal of all human achievement and that is what I intend to tell the world."[12]

As the tour continued, the four performances a day were beginning to wear Tex out. For the first time he could remember, Stein heard her complain of too much work. Yet when he begged her to take a rest, she told him she was too stagestruck to stop.[13] She had also begun to have severe stomach pains and her appetite had begun to fail.

By Portland she took herself to a doctor. The doctor said it was nothing, and she believed him. She continued to play four performances a day and continued to plan her preaching debut.

In fact, she decided it was time to experiment and preach a sermon on happiness. The more she thought about it, the more she liked the idea. She was really quite sincere and didn't mean to preach the word of God, just the word of happiness. She thought she knew enough about the art of giving audiences a good time to transform that into a gospel of sorts. Why everyone wanted to be happy. And she thought she knew what did the trick.

For one thing, the people who came to her clubs seemed to be the type who had everything—materially. Yet they were unhappy. Clearly money was not an answer, nor fame, nor power. It must be the simple things in life that counted. Because what the guests at clubs liked best were simple, childish antics and silly jokes. In her sermon, she thought she might talk about the natural happiness of children or about simple things, about a baby's smile being a simple bit of heaven here on earth, about the beauty of nature.

Then she would weave in her own personal theory on how to get the most out of life. The secret had to do with sacrificing one's best for others; it had to do with loving the unlovely.[14]

By the time she reached Tacoma, Washington, Tex had located a place to preach. She would take a regular Sunday off and attend mass at Dr. Henry Victor Morgan's church on North Eye Street. No one except Stein and Baker knew about the plan, and even the press, this one time, was not notified.

Tex was nervous. She looked down at the notes she'd typed out to prompt her as she spoke. Dr. Morgan was addressing the congregation. He was talking about her. He was convinced, he said, of her sincerity and thought the listeners would learn from her message about happiness. He spoke at length of other guest speakers and the rewards their lectures had brought. Then suddenly Tex found herself adjusting her glasses—she never wore them in public—and feeling quite unlike herself. She cleared her throat and began.

To the people in the audience, she looked like somebody's grandmother, taffy-colored hair falling over glasses haphazardly, sagging flesh of upper arms, kindly eyes. Yet her voice was terribly gruff, even when using gentle words. Was this the infamous Texas Guinan, the woman preached against on street corners? The audience found her a rare treat. Afterward, one girl came up and kissed her, and the rest of the congregation shook her hand.

Texas's experience proved to be both beautiful and moving. It is never quite clear what she said to her audience, beyond encouraging them to be happy, but Stein reported that early into her talk she grew confused, mixed up her notes, and started to cry. At one point, she must have thought she was in a club and began exhorting her customers to have a good time. She was bewildered by the kind faces of the people seated below her who were not making noise but listening quietly, who were not hitting the pews with wooden knockers but listening, listening to her.

Later she told Stein she had cried because she noticed a paper addressed to her, standing against the Bible in the pulpit. It read, "Remember, whatever you say this morning, God and your mother will be listening to you and they will be proud you have said it."[15] Later when Stein asked Dr. Morgan about the note, he claimed to know nothing about it.

Dr. Morgan came to the pulpit and taking Tex's hand, turned to the gathering and said, "All sorts of things have passed by this little pulpit. We have married people and sent them out into the world to meet their joys or woes; we have baptized the baby and started him on his way with God, and we have said the final rites over those who have left us for a world of eternal bliss, but rarely have we seen a soul bare itself as we have seen it today."[16]

Louis Sobol, in his book *The Longest Street*, borrowed a quote from the public Tex, who wrote him about the incident and said, "I wouldn't have minded if I could only have saved the situation by thinking up a wisecrack—even one. What a sap the pastor and the congregation must have thought me."[17]

Tex felt humbled by the experience, but she had learned a great deal. Being an evangelist would not be easy. Why, one stood naked before these people and what was worse, before God. Perhaps Tex had never really known what God meant to her until that day, and if she was ever to "get religion," she got it then. And put aside her plans to supplant her rival Aimee.

The experience also gave Tex a glimpse of her own mortality. In a moment of panic, she bought a $10,000 annuity policy for Pearl at Equitable Life Insurance. A week later, she was dead. The date was November 5, 1933.

After Words

> *The true wisecrack is the one that hits bottom—*
> *that touches fundamentals of human nature.*
> *Yet on the surface it seems superficial.*
> —TEXAS GUINAN, NEW YORK EVENING GRAPHIC,
> FEBRUARY 25, 1927

> *They will have to padlock my coffin*
> *if they expect to keep me in it.*
> —TEXAS GUINAN, PICTURES, SEPTEMBER 1926

*H*ello *there. How's the folks?*
   The queen was dead, but the sound of the kleeterklapper still echoed down Broadway, and wisecracks still bounced off bald customers' heads.
   Now this is a brand-new girl, just out of the shell. She's a little shy—
   Texas was dead, but none were willing to believe it. Wasn't that Tex, astride those two cane chairs posed back to back? Wasn't that the queen, walking her pet Peke down Eighth Street in the Manhattan dawn?
   Play that little girl's music . . .
   Her presence was everywhere, on street corners, in newspapers, even in the movie theaters. Death had proven her most efficient press agent, and at first, friends and fans hoped it was just another publicity stunt.
   After completing her engagements in Washington state, Tex had proceeded up the coast to the city of Vancouver. The abdominal pains she'd been experiencing in Portland had grown worse, yet she would not stay off the stage. She led four shows in a row at the Beacon Theatre and wore the mask of gaiety with her usual skill,

but by the next set of shows she could no longer pretend. The pain had grown unbearable. In the middle of the third show she was forced to stop. She asked to go to a hospital.

During her days in the hospital, Tex had no premonition of the end. She didn't have time for it. She was too busy planning a trip to Hawaii. When rumors of her death reached her, she sent a telegram to all the papers. "I'm not dying. Like the Blue Eagle, I'm on my way to recovery." But Tex was not herself. For the first time in her life, she complained to those around her of the noise.

Shut up, there, or I'll pick up a waiter and hit you with it. . . . Oh, there's my beau from Brooklyn . . .

Tex died quietly, without whispering any noteworthy, last-minute advice to the world. She had slipped from unconsciousness after surgery into death at the time she usually slipped into bed after a long night at the club. She was two months short of fifty.

The death certificate read that she had died of toxemia with shock, perforation of the cecum, and ulcerative colitis. Surgery had revealed an advanced state of peritonitis, possibly caused by amoebic dysentery, and part of her intestine had been removed. But she never recovered from the anesthetic. Friends and fans blamed her end on anything from dieting too much to poison, homesickness, and her forced exile from New York. At least now she could come home.

I'd rather a square inch of New York than all the rest of the world.

Death and the Queen of Midnight Revelry did not mix well. The queen had been too concerned with living and laughing, and besides, she never did take to hooking up with gloom. She had a strong belief in the afterlife, had been an aficionado of the séance, and had claimed she was really an old Oriental soul at heart. She insisted that after the body died, the spirit lived on. In fact, the spirit could enjoy the fanfare of the funeral procession, the grand turnout, and the crowded streets where the police were needed to hold back the masses. *I want my funeral to be the speediest ever, with a cop on a motorcycle to lead it.*

What a fuss they made over her body! Twelve thousand or more pushed and shoved outside Campbell Funeral Church on Broadway between Sixty-sixth and Sixty-seventh streets. *Tell them to put me in Campbell's. I want the suckers to get a last look at me without a cover charge.* How glorious to be in New York again, surrounded by friends, on view.

Flash. Mayme is four. While shopping with Bessie in a department store, unbeknownst to her mother, she has lingered behind and the store clerks, eager to lock up for the night and go home, don't notice her. In the darkened store, Mayme plays house, explores. When finally she grows too weary to play anymore, she stretches her arms, yawns, and climbs into the bed in the front window. The next morning, a rising sun reveals a sleeping Mayme on display.

When I kick off, I don't want 'em to bury me, I want 'em to put me back in Tiffany's front window.

Like Tiffany's window, the room at Campbell's that Tex lay in, where years before she'd taken her girls to visit Valentino, allowed the thousands to file by and browse, admire, observe. Tex wore her white chiffon gown. In her left hand, instead of a wooden kleeter-klapper, she held a rosary, which seemed at home beside a large diamond ring. The rest of her was tucked in under a blanket of mauve orchids and purple pansies.

Tex had requested to be buried at St. Malachy's, the actors' church, which she had attended regularly during her years on Broadway. But because of her night-club reputation, the clergy were not sure if she were a "good" Catholic. Ironically, on September 22, two months before her death, George W. Lynn of the *Santa Barbara News* had seen something "Catholic" in Tex that the clergy failed to see:

> Most unwittingly Texas Guinan is a hypocrite. She thinks she is what she is, but unintentionally she portrays a character who is not real. . . . Guinan professes to be the faith of the Roman Catholic Church, but she likes the world to see her as a hard, wisecracking, soulless woman who is paying off the mortgage on some debt that can never be fully cancelled.
>
> And it is in that role that she makes herself out a fakir of the most magnificent sort. At heart, Texas Guinan is real and sympathetic. She is a woman who has lived hard, but kept faith with humanity. She will make a sucker out of the wise guys but at the same time she still has a tear for the downfallen and destitute.

Unfortunately, the clergy had not read this short article. They'd read the countless clippings that spread her legend. In particular, they had read she'd been married many times, and wanted proof, beyond the protests of those close to her, that she had actually had only one husband. John Moynahan was contacted, and he sent the startling news that they had indeed been divorced in 1921, but that to his knowledge she had never remarried. The clergy said since no one had known about the divorce, how could they prove she hadn't remarried? Tex's most stalwart friends were furious. Tex had been a practicing Catholic all her life, attending mass regularly, contributing large sums to the church, and playing many benefits to help the poor and needy. While she was alive, the clergy had known her reputation, yet they had always accepted her contributions.

As the debate continued, the Board of Health interfered and said the body had been held too long. Tex finally went on view at Campbell's, but not before another, slight "emergency" arose, having to do with the condition of the body. Belle Livingstone was called in to help. As she told it in her autobiography, "Tex, determined to keep her chin up to the end, had several times had it lifted. The process of embalming had put everything into reverse and now Texas's chins were beginning to unroll. What to do? I sent out for tulle and swathed her decently and artistically."[1]

Be gay. It's too expensive to grow old. And have your hair bleached and your face lifted.

The crowds continued to file by the sleeping Tex, a strange mixture not unlike those who had sat at her clubs: girls with bright face paint, middle-aged men with hats pulled low to hide tears, elderly actresses laden with feather boas and heavy veils. Many people who had never met but had read of the famous night-club hostess stood in line for hours to catch a three-second glimpse.

Outside, newsreel cameramen set up their equipment and filmed the weeping and the curious as they passed the bier. Every now and again, attendants brought in flowers, mostly chrysanthemums, and wreaths. Radio newscasters kept listeners informed about the status of the crowd.

Outside Campbell's on every corner, young boys hawked newspapers containing her life story. Down the block the film *Broadway thru a Keyhole* was showing, where Tex played herself in her final role.

Fame is chiefly a matter of dying at the right moment . . .

The choreography of the event continued to be perfect, from the viewing to the funeral ceremony, an invitation affair marked by numerous tearful eulogies, to a final sounding of taps. The men who had carried her through life carried her in death: the press, the law, and select friends. The honorary pallbearers included journalists Heywood Broun, Mark Hellinger, O. O. McIntyre, Ed Sullivan, Louis Sobol, and Paul Yawitz, and lawyers Walter B. Solinger and Maxwell E. Lopin.

"All afternoon I had a strong feeling," wrote Heywood Broun in his November 8 column for the *New York World Telegram*, "that this was not so much a funeral for Texas Guinan as a funeral by Texas Guinan. All her own qualities of showmanship were evident." He continued,

> There was something grotesque about the funeral. It wasn't just the slightly florid character of the ceremony. It wasn't that any wandering eye met some eloquent mask which plainly said:— "I wouldn't have done this for anybody but you, Tex. And what wouldn't I give for a drink!" In fact, it seemed just a little silly to talk about Texas being dead. She remained a far more vital living force than numerous ones among haggard hundreds in the chapel.
> I didn't go to the cemetery. That seemed far less appropriate than anything else in the ceremony. They had to drive all the way to White Plains. I think it was Texas who said, "Once you leave New York any town you strike is Bridgeport." . . .
> I honestly believe that Texas saw the funeral and took a great pride in the performance. It was almost as big as Valentino's.
> The universe is intricate, and very nice adjustments are necessary to keep the planets from running into one another. It would be a fearful error in taste if by any stipulation Tex were barred from the knowledge that the police had to fight back the thousands.

At the cemetery, mobs of mourners had gathered to wave farewell to the queen. In a wild rush, they stampeded through the graveyard in an attempt to grab flowers, wreaths, whatever they could carry away that reminded them of Tex. It was an ugly scene, messy, insane, and somehow—appropriate.

I love crowds, whether I watch them on 42nd Street, First Avenue, Long Beach or Deauville. . . . My big kick in life is crowds of humanity. When I can get them with me, rooting for me, I am drunk with the joy of it.

That night, a more intimate gathering of one hundred or so of Tex's night-club friends gathered in the cemetery to bid their own farewells. Entertainers, bon vivants, and columnists stood in a tight, sad semicircle around the doorway to the mausoleum under a starless, moonless sky. Slowly Helen Morgan reached into her pocketbook and pulled out a book of matches. She began lighting them, creating brief stars of matchlight within the circle of standing friends. Soon all her companions joined her. She said, "It's dark now. This is just when Tex would be starting to live."[2]

Come on, folks, and give this little girl a hand. . . . I am some-

times called the 'Queen of Clubs,' but I want people to know that I have a heart . . . as big as a miniature golf course. . . .

Listen, Suckers, as I said to my friend Mark here, why take life so seriously—in a hundred years we will all be gone or in some stuffy book . . . give me plenty of laughs and you can take all the rest.

So don't hook up with gloom. In other words,—step out!

Broadway friends marked the end of the Roaring Twenties with Tex's death, but as in life, her timing was perfect. One month later, Prohibition was repealed and the suckers were free to drink in the daylight once more.

Notes

Introduction: Hello, Suckers!—A Glimpse

1. Richard Milne, *Boston Sunday Post,* June 14, 1931.

Waco: Home on the Ranch?

1. Texas Guinan, "My Life—AND HOW!" *New York Evening Journal,* April 29, 1929–May 25, 1929 ["MLAH"]. The quote is from the April 29 column.
2. Ibid., April 29, 1929.
3. Waco Immigration Society, *Immigrant's Guide to Waco and McLennan County, Texas,* p. 20.
4. "MLAH," April 29, 1929.
5. Ibid., May 4, 1929.
6. Ibid., April 30, 1929.
7. Texas Guinan, "Texas Guinan Says," February 11, 1931. Tex wrote a syndicated column for the [New York] *Graphic* from September 15, 1930 to October 17, 1931, entitled "Texas Guinan Says." Columns ranged from her thoughts on the price of gasoline, the modern girl, and football to Albert Einstein and *Lysistrata.* Many have been collected in a scrapbook at the Billy Rose Theatre Collection, New York Public Library for the Performing Arts.
8. Interview with Mrs. F. A. Kling and Mrs. W. Harrison (Eaton's granddaughters), February 7, 1981.
9. Interview with Sarah Hopkins Muhl, *Baylor Lariat,* December 8, 1967.
10. Interview with Mrs. Evelyn Sharp (daughter of Sarah Hopkins Muhl), February 5, 1981.
11. Ibid.
12. Letter from Mrs. A. Cowper Smith (Kathleen Gorman's younger sister Mary), May 29, 1981.
13. "MLAH," April 30, 1929.

Did She or Didn't She?

1. "MLAH," April 29, 1929.
2. Ibid., April 30, 1929.
3. Ibid.
4. Ibid., May 3, 1929.
5. Ibid., May 6, 1929.
6. "Texas Guinan Says," May 6, 1931.

There's a Sucker Born Every Minute

1. "MLAH," May 9, 1929.
2. Ibid.
3. Ibid.
4. John S. Stein and Hayward Grace, "Hello Sucker!" p. 27.
5. "MLAH," May 10, 1929.
6. Letter from Hollins' archivist Anthony Thompson, December 3, 1980.
7. Letter from Hollins' president Matty Cocke, Hollins College, Hollins, Va., August 14, 1929, to Henry Luce, Editor of *Time*.
8. Letter from Luther Greene of the Virginia Drama League to Susie Blair, assistant professor of drama at Hollins College, March 3, 1931.
9. Letter from Jos. A. Turner, business manager and secretary to the Board of Trustees at Hollins, as well as founder of the Texas Guinan file at Hollins, to Luther Greene, Hollins College, March 5, 1931.
10. Texas Guinan file, Hollins College.
11. Interview with Katy Hoban, *Rocky Mountain News*, October 5, 1945.
12. Lowell Thomas, *Good Evening Everybody from Cripple Creek to Samarkand*, pp. 34–35. (Also in letter from Lowell Thomas, August 10, 1981.)
13. Lowell Thomas, *Good Evening Everybody from Cripple Creek to Samarkand*, p. 35.
14. Leslie D. Spell and Hazel M. Spell, *Forgotten Men of Cripple Creek*, pp. 125–26.
15. Obituary for Texas Guinan, *Denver Post*, November 6, 1933.
16. *Denver Post*, February 21, 1927, 10–11.
17. Interview with Charlotte Wright, September 6, 1981.
18. "MLAH," May 11, 1929.

Marie

1. "MLAH," May 11, 1929.
2. Ibid.
3. Ibid.
4. Stein and Grace, "Hello Sucker!" p. 37.
5. Ibid., p. 52.
6. Charles G. Shaw, *The Lowdown*, p. 30.

Notes to Pages 42–60

7. "MLAH," May 11, 1929.
8. Letter from Marshall Field Historian Herman Kogan, January 15, 1981.
9. Lothrop Stoddard, *Luck, Your Silent Partner*, p. 13.
10. Interview with Texas Guinan, *San Antonio Evening News*, May 16, 1922.
11. "MLAH," May 11, 1929.
12. Ibid.
13. Mark Hellinger, "All In A Day," [*New York*] *Daily News*, November 7, 1933.

Everything West of New York Is Just Bridgeport

1. *New York American*, November 12, 1933.
2. "MLAH," May 13, 1929.
3. *Detroit Journal*, January 3, 1913.
4. Ibid.
5. "Texas Guinan Says," September 17, 1931.
6. Gordon Leland, ed., *Peppe's Diary*.
7. Review of DeKoven's *Girls*, unmarked clipping, Robinson Locke Collection, Billy Rose Theatre Collection, New York Public Library for the Performing Arts.
8. "MLAH," May 13, 1929.
9. Itemized bill for costumes, *The Snow Man*, March 8, 1907, Shubert Archive, New York.
10. "MLAH," May 14, 1929.
11. Allen Churchill, *The Great White Way*, p. 43.
12. Review of *The Hoyden*, May 18, 1908, Robinson Locke Collection, Billy Rose Theatre Collection, ser. 2, p. 3.
13. Elsie Janis, *So Far, So Good*, p. 91.
14. Stein and Grace, "Hello Sucker!" p. 50.
15. Louis Sobol, "The Voice of Broadway," *New York Evening Journal*, November 7, 1933.
16. *New York Telegram*, November 22, 1908.
17. Obituary for Texas Guinan, *Chicago Tribune*, November 6, 1933.
18. Stoddard, *Luck, Your Silent Partner*, p. 12.
19. "MLAH," May 14, 1929.
20. *Denver Times*, November 3, 1909.
21. Stein and Grace, "Hello Sucker!" p. 60.
22. Ibid., p. 61.
23. "MLAH," May 14, 1929.
24. Ibid., May 15, 1929.
25. Ibid.
26. Robinson Locke Collection, Billy Rose Theatre Collection, ser. 2, p. 6.
27. Ibid.
28. Stein and Grace, "Hello Sucker!" p. 63.

29. Letter from Oliver Morosco to Lee Shubert, October 23, 1912, Shubert Archive.
30. Stein and Grace, "Hello Sucker!" p. 65.
31. Ibid., p. 66.
32. "MLAH," May 15, 1929.
33. Stein and Grace, "Hello Sucker!" p. 66.
34. "MLAH," May 15, 1929.
35. Ibid., May 16, 1929.
36. Stein and Grace, "Hello Sucker!" p. 49.
37. Robinson Locke Collection, Billy Rose Theatre Collection, ser. 2, p. 35.
38. *Detroit Journal*, September 18, 1913.
39. Letter from Julian Johnson to Lee Shubert, July 22, 1913, Shubert Archive.
40. Ibid.
41. Telegram from Texas Guinan to Julian Johnson, August 3, 1913, Shubert Archive.
42. *St. Louis Globe-Democrat*, January 16(?), 1915, Shubert Archive.
43. Ad for weight reducer, *Variety*, September 12, 1913, p. 23.

Texas Guinan—Quack, Actress, or Saleswoman?

1. *Journal of the American Medical Association*, 61 (December 13, 1913): 2174.
2. Unmarked clipping, Texas Guinan clipping file, Museum of the City of New York.
3. Review of *Hop O' My Thumb*, *Dramatic Mirror*, November 26, 1913.
4. Affidavit, U.S. Post Office, as quoted in the "Memorandum for the Post Master General Recommending the Issuance of a Fraud Order," January 14, 1914, file 3617, Fraud Orders, National Archives, Records of the Post Office.
5. Ibid.
6. "MLAH," May 16, 1929.
7. Review of *Whirl of the World*, *New York Review*, January 16, 1915.
8. Review of *Whirl of the World*, *Milwaukee Journal*, Easter week 1915, Robinson Locke Collection, Billy Rose Theatre Collection, ser. 2, p. 8.
9. *Pictures*, September 1926, p. 69.
10. *New York Evening World*, April 10, 1929.
11. *Chicago Illinois Examiner*, February 27, 1933.
12. Texas Guinan, "The Modern Cinderella," *Photoplay*, April 1915, p. 128.
13. Advertising advice for *The Gun Woman*, *Triangle*, January 1918, p. 17.
14. *Triangle*, August 25, 1917, p. 8.
15. "Belle Bennett As a Clever Business Adventuress," *Triangle*, November 3, 1917, p. 10.

16. Review of *The Fuel of Life, Exhibitor's Trade Review* (*ETR*), November 18, 1917, p. 2005.
17. *Triangle*, November 3, 1917, p. 10.
18. *The Moving Picture World* (*MPW*), November 24, 1917, p. 3665.

Never Jilt a Woman Who Can Shoot

1. Line introducing Tex's character in *The Gun Woman* by Alvin Neitz, Triangle Corporation, 1918.
2. Plot summary of *The Gun Woman* for advertising purposes, *MPW*, February 2, 1918, pp. 718–19.
3. *ETR*, August 23, 1919, p. 981.
4. Advice to exhibitors "For the Program," *MPW*, February 2, 1918, p. 719.
5. Ibid.
6. Advice for exploitation, *Motion Picture News* (*MPN*), June 21, 1919, p. 4222.
7. *MPW*, February 2, 1918, p. 719.
8. "Studio Gossip," *Triangle*, December 1, 1917, p. 63.
9. Johnstone Craig, "Texas, the State of Excitement," *Photoplay*, August 1918, p. 77.
10. "MLAH," May 16, 1929.
11. Review by Lawrence Reid, *MPN*, August 23, 1919, p. 1683.
12. *South of Santa Fe*, screenplay by Archer McMackin, Frohman Amusement Corp., 1919.
13. John Morrell, review of *The She Wolf*, undated clipping from Cheseboro file, Billy Rose Theatre Collection.
14. Adela Rogers St. John, "Guinan of the Guns," *Photoplay*, August 1919, p. 60.
15. "Texas Guinan Says," no. 50.
16. Interview with Irving Caesar, January 28, 1981.
17. Louis Sobol, "The Voice of Broadway," *New York Evening Journal*, November 7, 1933.
18. Nils T. Granlund, Sid Feder, and Ralph Hancock, *Blondes, Brunettes and Bullets*, p. 63.
19. *MPN*, October 30, 1920, p. 3375.
20. Lawrence Reid, *MPN*, November 12, 1921, p. 2599.
21. *ETR*, October 29, 1921, p. 1523.
22. "MLAH," May 22, 1929.
23. *Atlanta Georgian*, April 28, 1922.
24. United States Department of Justice, FBI files, "Journal Memorandum re: Case of Texas Guinan and Gilbert Salmon, Victim," December 11, 1922.
25. Ibid.
26. Letter from Texas Guinan to J. J. Shubert, November 27, 1922, Shubert Archive.

Birth of a Hostess

1. "Texas Guinan Says," June 26, 1931.
2. Granlund, Feder, and Hancock, p. 120.
3. Rian James, *Dining in New York*, p. 79.
4. "MLAH," May 20, 1929.
5. Colgate Baker, *New York Review,* July 9, 1927.
6. "MLAH," May 20, 1929.
7. Granlund, Feder, and Hancock, p. 125.
8. Ben Finney, *Feet First,* p. 147.
9. Interview with Ben Finney, March 12, 1981.
10. Ibid.
11. "MLAH," May 21, 1929.
12. Granlund, Feder, and Hancock, p. 124.
13. Interview with Finney.
14. Granlund, Feder, and Hancock, p. 127.
15. Jack Lait, *Los Angeles Herald Express,* August 21, 1945.
16. Richard Milne, *Boston Sunday Post,* June 14, 1931.
17. "Texas Guinan Says," June 30, 1931.
18. Walter Winchell, *Winchell Exclusive,* p. 49.
19. Interview with Finney.
20. *Brantford [Ontario] Expositor,* January 6, 1933.
21. Winchell, p. 51.
22. Ibid., p. 42.
23. Herman Klurfeld, *Winchell,* p. 54.
24. Jim Bishop, *The Mark Hellinger Story,* p. 86.
25. *Pictures,* September 1926, p. 89.
26. Interview with Ruby Keeler, September 17, 1981.
27. Granlund, Feder, and Hancock, pp. 59–60.
28. Texas Guinan, one of her standard sayings, appeared many places.
29. Interview with Keeler.
30. Interview with Doris Vinton, February 26, 1982.
31. Program for *Too Hot For Paris,* June 1931, author's collection.
32. Interview with June Carroll, *New York Mirror,* October 14, 1934.
33. Interview with Keeler.
34. Interview with Claire Luce, June 11, 1981.
35. Ibid.
36. Ibid.
37. Interview with Vinton.
38. Granlund, Feder, and Hancock, p. 129.
39. Obituary for Texas Guinan, *New York Daily Mirror,* November 6, 1933.
40. Leslie F. Catten, undated clipping, Texas Guinan file, the Theatre Collection of the Free Library of Philadelphia.
41. Finney, p. 151.
42. "MLAH," May 22, 1929.

Where the Bread-And-Butter Men Roam

1. Oscar Wilde, "The Harlot House," in *The Portable Oscar Wilde*, ed. Richard Aldington, p. 587.
2. Interview with Meyer Weintraub, January 7, 1982.
3. Interview with Frances Schwab Hewick, April 22, 1984.
4. Shaw, *The Lowdown*, p. 30.
5. Interview with Lou Rigler, May 4, 1981.
6. From Tex's show *Padlocks of 1927*, libretto, Library of Congress.
7. Stephen Graham, *New York Nights*, p. 107.
8. Interview with Rigler.
9. *New York Post*, July 17, 1941.
10. Ibid.
11. *Pictures*, September 1926, p. 69.
12. Letter from Spencer Clark, October 29, 1981. Mr. Clark played in the band at the Forty-eighth Street club as well as in the pit band for *Padlocks*.
13. Letter from Elizabeth Lawton, October (?), 1981.
14. Heywood Broun, "It Seems To Me," *New York World Telegram*, November 8, 1933.
15. Ibid.
16. Interview with Rigler.
17. Robert Sylvester, *No Cover Charge*, p. 173.
18. Ibid., p. 172.
19. Ibid., p. 173.
20. Interview with Rigler.
21. Graham, p. 95.
22. *New York Times* (*NYT*), December 22, 1926.
23. "Impossible Interview Number 14," *Vanity Fair*, January 1933, p. 36.
24. *NYT*, February 17, 1927.
25. *New York Evening Post*, February 17, 1921.
26. *New York American*, February 18, 1927.
27. *Denver Morning Post*, February 19, 1927.
28. Carey Williams, "Sunlight in My Soul," in *The Aspirin Age*, ed. Isabel Leighton, p. 51.
29. *New York Evening Post*, February 19, 1927.
30. Louis Sobol, "The Voice of Broadway," *New York Evening Journal*, November 7, 1933.
31. Belle Livingstone and Cleveland Amory, *Belle Out of Order*, p. 270.
32. Ibid., p. 271.
33. Ibid., p. 303.
34. Ibid.
35. Ibid., p. 334.
36. "Texas Guinan Says," January 9, 1931.
37. Livingstone and Amory, p. 267.
38. Alison Smith, review of *Padlocks of 1927*, *New York World*, July 7, 1927.

39. Bushnell Diamond, Review of *Padlocks of 1927*, *Denver Post*, July 18, 1927.
40. *NYT*, July 6, 1927.
41. *New York World*, July 7, 1927.
42. Letter from Aubrey Hastings, October 11, 1981.
43. Program advertising Tex's Century Club, October 21(?), 1927, Harvard Theatre Collection, Harvard University, Cambridge, Mass.
44. Lew Ney, *Satire Day Night* 1, no. 1 (October 8, 1927).
45. Interview with Rigler.
46. "MLAH," May 22, 1929.
47. Gilbert Maxwell, *Helen Morgan*, p. 58.

On Trial

1. The trial account in this chapter is based on Maxwell Lopin's manuscript, "The Trial of Texas Guinan," a retrospective account of the trial based on the stenographer's minutes (*United States v. Texas Guinan*, New York, April 9–11, 1929), his own notes, material and recollections. It may be noted that much of this material also appeared in the New York dailies on those dates (see note 2).
2. All of Tex's remarks to the press on the days of the trial, April 9–11, 1929, were picked up by the following New York dailies on those dates: *The Telegraph, World, Sun, Herald Tribune, Evening Graphic, Daily Mirror, Evening Post, American,* and *Times*.

Homecoming

1. Description of party from Maxwell Lopin, "The Trial of Texas Guinan."
2. Ibid.
3. *New York Evening Post*, April 12, 1929.
4. Lopin, "The Trial of Texas Guinan."
5. Ibid.
6. Ibid.
7. [*New York*] *Daily News*, April 12, 1929.
8. Ibid.
9. Lopin, "The Trial of Texas Guinan."
10. *New York Journal*, April 13, 1929.
11. Mark Hellinger, "All in a Day," *Daily News*, April 15, 1929.
12. *New York Sun*, April 17, 1929.
13. Bishop, *Hellinger Story*, p. 106.
14. Interview with Patrick Smith, December 28–29, 1981.
15. Ibid.
16. Ibid.
17. Ibid.
18. Ashton Stevens, *Chicago American*, October 20(?), 1929.
19. "MLAH," May 24, 1929.

20. Interview with Samuel Cimman, October 15, 1981.
21. Ibid.
22. "Texas Guinan Says," *Milwaukee Leader*, May 10, 1931.
23. *Chicago Herald and Examiner*, March 24, 1930.
24. Interview with Ed Eulenberg, retired reporter for the *Chicago Sun Times*, October 15, 1981.
25. Letter from Michael Guinan to Pearl Guinan Smith, March 13, 1930, Pearl Guinan Smith family papers.
26. Letter from Michael Guinan to Pearl Guinan Smith, March 26, 1930, Smith family papers.
27. Letter from Michael Guinan to Pearl Guinan Smith, March 31, 1930, Smith family papers.
28. *Chicago Herald and Examiner*, March 24, 1930.
29. *New York American*, March 31, 1930.
30. Unmarked clip about Club Argonaut, Texas Guinan file, the Theatre Collection of the Free Library of Philadelphia.

Fifty Million Frenchmen Can't Be Wrong

1. *New York Telegram*, August 6, 1928.
2. Stein and Grace, "Hello Sucker!" p. 303.
3. Texas Guinan, quoted in the program for *Too Hot for Paris*, June 1931, author's collection.
4. *NYT*, June 4, 1931.
5. Interview with Nanon Gardener Sanderson, February 28, 1981.
6. Ibid.
7. Rian James, *Dining in New York*, p. 250.
8. *New York American*, September 26, 1931.
9. Lately Thomas, *Storming Heaven*, p. 114.
10. Joseph C. Furnas, *Great Times*, pp. 115–16.
11. Stein and Grace, "Hello Sucker!" p. 344.
12. Ibid., p. 346.
13. *Chicago Herald and Examiner*, January 1, 1932.
14. Ibid.
15. *New York Sun*, January 11, 1932.
16. *NYT*, January 14, 1932.
17. Klurfeld, *Winchell*, pp. 60–62.
18. Winchell, *Winchell Exclusive*, pp. 50–51.
19. *NYT*, June 27, 1932.

Tomorrow and Tomorrow

1. *Official Guidebook of the Fair, Chicago*, p. 121.
2. Ibid.
3. Stein and Grace, "Hello Sucker!" p. 371.
4. *Chicago Herald and Examiner*, March 2, 1933.

5. Letter from Thornton Wilder to Dr. Moulton, June 21, 1933, Hull House Collection, University of Illinois at Chicago Circle.
6. Postcard from Texas Guinan to nephew Patrick Smith, June 15, 1933, Pearl Guinan Smith family papers.
7. Review of show on Pirate Ship, "A Century of Whoopee," *Chicago American*, July 1, 1933.
8. Ashton Stevens, *Chicago American*, July 6, 1933.
9. Letter from Fred Wittenmeier, October 12, 1981.
10. Telegram from Walter Winchell to Texas Guinan, July 13, 1933, Billy Rose Theatre Collection.
11. Obituary for Texas Guinan, *New York American*, November 5, 1933.
12. *San Francisco Rounder*, September 30, 1933.
13. Stein and Grace, "Hello Sucker!" p. 379.
14. *San Francisco Rounder*, September 30, 1933.
15. Stein and Grace, "Hello Sucker!" pp. 384–88. Louis Sobol also mentioned this in his autobiography, *The Longest Street*.
16. Stein and Grace, "Hello Sucker!" pp. 384–88.
17. Louis Sobol, *The Longest Street*, p. 65.

After Words

1. Livingstone and Amory, p. 333.
2. Dorothy Kilgallen, *New York Journal American*, July 27, 1945.

A Bibliographic Note on Major Sources

New York City is the best place to look for the famous Tex of the Roaring Twenties, and it is where her heart belonged from the first day she arrived in 1906. Here one can see where her night clubs stood, where she performed on stage, and where the building she lived in still stands on Eighth Street.

The richest assortment of memorabilia can be found at the Billy Rose Theatre Collection at the New York Public Library for the Performing Arts, Lincoln Center, and clippings range from her early stage career to her funeral. Much can be learned about her film and stage careers in such periodicals as *Variety* or *Motion Picture News* as well as in the scrapbooks from the library's Robinson Locke Collection. There are programs of most of the shows Tex appeared in (or claimed to have appeared in), biographies and name files of actors and actresses, film trade books, scripts. The collection also owns several of Tex's personal scrapbooks along with photographs, clippings, telegrams, and a few letters she wrote as well as ones she received (especially from the Paris trip of 1931). This is the only place I ever saw letters aside from the postcards in her nephew's personal collection. Also of importance in the collection is the unpublished manuscript of John Stein and Hayward Grace. It is not clear what role John Stein played in Tex's life. We know that he worked with her for the last seven years of her life. Although Stein said he was her manager, Tex's father, in his correspondence to Tex's sister, called him Tex's secretary/publicity man, and a 1931 contract from the Shubert Archive lists him as publicity man for the company and Tex's personal representative. Stein's book is valuable for information on such things as Tex's kleptomania, which is never mentioned elsewhere. Unfortunately, he seems to have swallowed her phony autobiography since he repeats much of it, and the inaccuracies of that memoir (dates, incidents, etc.) also appear in his text.

The Shubert Archive contains Shubert correspondence, playbills, cast lists, contracts, and other materials connected to their productions.

The New York Public Library on Forty-second Street and the Annex on Forty-third Street are also great "New York" resources, particularly for their collections of the New York dailies. These papers are the best source of information on New York nightlife in the 1920s.

The New York Historical Society has street files for locating where the clubs stood and what New York looked like when Tex lived there.

The Museum of the City of New York has a Texas Guinan file with photos and clips. Also, the museum provides good background information on old New York.

The Queens Public Library owns former Broadway columnist Louis Sobol's clipping collection.

The Sherman Grinberg Film Library and Twentieth Century Fox Movietone have small amounts of footage, mostly newsreel, about Tex.

In New Jersey, John Allen, Inc., has Tex's films *The Girl of the Ranch, The Night Rider,* and a Dutch translation called *De Bank Roovers (The Bank Robbers).*

In Los Angeles, the Library at the Academy of Motion Picture Arts and Sciences has files on various film people associated with Tex, film trade journals, and a few stills of Tex. The film collection at the University of California–Los Angeles has the films *Broadway thru a Keyhole, Glorifying the American Girl,* and *A Moonshine Feud.* It also has the 1945 biopic, *Incendiary Blond,* starring Betty Hutton as Tex.

The American Film Institute in Washington, D.C., is the other major repository of Tex's films, and these, housed at the Library of Congress, include: *South of Santa Fe, The Gun Woman, The Stampede, Letters of Fire,* and a fragment from a silent western. (Note: The George Eastman House also has *Letters of Fire* as well as *The Boss of the Rancho.* They have nitrate prints of *The Night Rider* and *My Lady Robin Hood,* which cannot be projected. The author owns *The Desert Vulture,* a gift from Ivan B. Berger.)

Also in Washington, the National Archives has ample information on World War I and the Post Office records relating to the weight-loss fraud case.

Chicago is another city of significance in Tex's later years. The Chicago Historical Society has a useful collection of memorabilia from the 1933 World's Fair, including the official guidebook and the souvenir guide as well as photos and even a file of photos of Tex. The library at the University of Illinois has much original material relating to the fair, including a file of the business negotiations and correspondence relating to Tex's Pirate Ship concession. Included among the letters is the letter of recommendation for Tex from Thornton Wilder.

Colorado and Texas are connected to Tex's early (and most elusive) years. Public records and daily papers were somewhat useful in following those years. In Denver, the Colorado Heritage Center and the Denver Public Library's Western History Department are helpful in tracking down information on Tex's possible involvement in theater and her cousins in Cripple Creek.

Waco, Texas, where Texas was born, is the location of the Texas Collection, a specialized library on the campus of Baylor University, having one of the largest Texana collections in the world. This is a good place for the student of Waco and Texas in general; it is a repository of local dailies and phone directories as well as pamphlets, photos, microfilm, and other local and regional materials. I learned much about Tex's early life here—what little there was—and got a good sense of what local life must have been like when she was growing up at the turn of the century.

Also of note are the Hoblitzelle Theatre Arts Library and the Journal American morgue at the Harry Ransom Humanities Research Center, University of Texas at Austin.

Bibliography

Books

Allen, Frederick L. *Only Yesterday.* New York: Harper, 1931.
———. *Since Yesterday.* New York: Harper, 1939.
Allsop, Kenneth. *The Bootleggers.* London: Hutchinson, 1961.
Amory, Cleveland, and Frederic Bradlee, eds. *Vanity Fair: Selections from America's Most Memorable Magazine.* New York: Viking Press, 1960.
Asbury, Herbert. *The Gangs of New York.* New York: Knopf, 1927.
———. *The Great Illusion.* Garden City, N.Y.: Doubleday, 1950.
Ashenhurst, John. *All about Chicago.* Boston: Houghton Mifflin, 1933.
Atkinson, Brooks. *Broadway.* New York: Macmillan, 1970.
Bahr, Robert. *Least of All Saints: The Story of Aimee Semple McPherson.* Englewood Cliffs, N.J.: Prentice-Hall, 1979.
Bishop, Jim. *The Mark Hellinger Story: A Biography of Broadway and Hollywood.* New York: Appleton-Century-Crofts, 1952.
Blum, Daniel. *A Pictorial History of the American Theatre, 1860–1960.* New York: Chilton, 1950.
Cantor, Eddie, and David Freedman. *Ziegfield, the Great Glorifier.* New York: Alfred H. King, 1934.
Churchill, Allen. *The Great White Way.* New York: E. P. Dutton, 1962.
———. *The Improper Bohemians.* New York: E. P. Dutton, 1959.
———. *Over Here! An Informal Re-Creation of the Homefront in World War I.* New York: Dodd, Mead, 1968.
———. *Remember When.* New York: Golden Press, 1967.
———. *The Theatrical Twenties.* New York: McGraw-Hill, 1975.
———. *The Year the World Went Mad.* New York: Thomas Y. Crowell, 1960.
Coffey, Thomas M. *The Long Thirst: Prohibition in America, 1920–1933.* New York: W. W. Norton, 1975.
Cohen, Lester. *The New York Graphic.* New York: Chilton, 1964.
Conger, Robert N. *A Pictorial History of Waco, Texas.* Waco: Texian Press, 1972.
Connable, Alfred, and Edward Silberfarb. *Tigers of Tammany: Nine Men Who Ran New York.* New York: Holt, Rinehart, and Winston, 1967.

Dedman, Emmett. *Fabulous Chicago.* New York: Random House, 1953.
Dos Passos, John. *Mr. Wilson's War.* Garden City, N.Y.: Doubleday, 1962.
Dulles, Foster R. *America Learns to Play.* New York: D. Appleton-Century, 1940.
Durante, Jimmy, and Jack Kofoed. *Nightclubs.* New York: Knopf, 1931.
Erenberg, Lewis A. *Steppin' Out: New York Nightlife and the Transformation of American Culture, 1890–1930.* Chicago: University of Chicago Press, 1984.
Everson, William K. *American Silent Film.* New York: Oxford University Press, 1978.
Everson, William K., and George N. Fenin. *The Western: From Silents to the Seventies.* New York: Grossman, 1973.
Finney, Ben. *Feet First.* New York: Crown, 1971.
Fowler, Gene. *Schnozzola.* New York: Viking Press, 1951.
Furnas, Joseph C. *Great Times: An Informal Social History of the United States, 1914–1929.* New York: G. P. Putnam's Sons, 1974.
———. *The Life and Times of the Late Demon Rum.* New York: G. P. Putnam's Sons, 1965.
Gauvreau, Emile. *My Last Million Readers.* New York: E. P. Dutton, 1941.
Gibson, Charles Dana. *The Gibson Girl and Her America.* New York: Dover, 1969.
Gloag, John. *Victorian Comfort: A Social History of Design, 1830–1900.* New York: St. Martin's Press, 1974.
Graham, Stephen. *New York Nights.* New York: George H. Doran, 1927.
Granlund, Nils T., Sid Feder, and Ralph Hancock. *Blondes, Brunettes and Bullets.* New York: David McKay, 1957.
Green, Abel, and Joe Laurie, Jr. *Showbiz, from Vaude to Video.* New York: Henry Holt, 1951.
Green, Stanley. *World of Musical Comedy.* New York: A. S. Barnes, 1974.
Haskell, Molly. *From Rape to Reverence: The Treatment of Women in the Movies.* New York: Holt, Rinehart, and Winston, 1974.
Howe, Daniel Walker, ed. *Victorian America.* Philadelphia: University of Pennsylvania Press, 1976.
James, Rian. *Dining in New York.* New York: John Day, 1931.
Janis, Elsie. *So Far, So Good.* New York: E. P. Dutton, 1932.
Jobes, Gertrude. *Motion Picture Empire.* Hamden, Conn.: Archon, 1966.
Klurfeld, Herman. *Winchell: His Life and Times.* New York: Praeger, 1976.
Kobler, John. *Ardent Spirits: The Rise and Fall of Prohibition.* New York: G. P. Putnam's Sons, 1973.
———. *Capone: The Life and World of Al Capone.* New York: G. P. Putnam's Sons, 1971.
Lahue, Kalton C. *Dreams for Sale: The Rise and Fall of the Triangle Film Corporation.* New York: A. S. Barnes, 1971.
———. *Winners of the West.* New York: A. S. Barnes, 1970.
Lee, Henry. *How Dry We Were.* Englewood Cliffs, N.J.: Prentice-Hall, 1963.
Leighton, Isabel, ed. *The Aspirin Age, 1919–1941.* New York: Simon and Schuster, 1949.

Leland, Gordon M., ed. *Peppe's Diary.* N.p., 1937. (In the collection of the Museum of the City of New York.)
Livingstone, Belle, and Cleveland Amory. *Belle Out of Order.* New York: Henry Holt, 1959.
McDonald, Archie P., ed. *Shooting Stars: Heroes and Heroines of Western Film.* Bloomington: Indiana University Press, 1987.
McKelway, St. Clair. *The Life and Times of Walter Winchell.* New York: Viking Press, 1940.
Mallen, Frank. *Sauce for the Gander.* White Plains, N.Y.: Baldwin Books, 1954.
Masters, Edgar Lee. *The Tale of Chicago.* New York: G. P. Putnam's Sons, 1933.
Maxwell, Gilbert. *Helen Morgan: Her Life and Legend.* New York: Hawthorn Books, 1974.
Mayer, Harold M., and Richard C. Wade. *Chicago: Growth of a Metropolis.* Chicago: University of Chicago Press, 1969.
Merz, Charles. *The Dry Decade.* New York: Doubleday Doran, 1931.
Morgan, H. Wayne. *Victorian Culture in America, 1865–1914.* Itasca, Ill.: F. E. Peacock, 1973.
Morris, Lloyd. *Incredible New York.* New York: Random House, 1951.
———. *Postscript to Yesterday.* New York: Random House, 1947.
National Archives. Records of the Post Office Department. "Memorandum for the Postmaster General Recommending the Issuance of a Fraud Order," January 14, 1914. File 3617.
O'Connor, Richard. *Hell's Kitchen.* Philadelphia: J. P. Lippincott, 1958.
Official Guidebook of the Fair, Chicago: A Century of Progress, 1933. N.p.: Cuneo Press, 1934.
Parish, James R. *Film Directors: A Guide to Their American Films.* Metuchen, N.J.: Scarecrow Press, 1974.
Parish, James R., and Steven Whitney. *The George Raft File.* New York: Drake, 1973.
Robertson, M. S. *Rodeo: Standard Guide to the Cowboy Sport.* Berkeley: Howell-North, 1961.
Roscoe, Burton. *We Were Interrupted.* New York: Doubleday, 1947.
Sann, Paul. *The Lawless Decade.* New York: Crown, 1957.
Seldes, Gilbert. *The Seven Lively Arts.* New York: Sagamore Press, 1924.
Shaw, Charles G. *Guide to New York After Dark: Vanity Fair's Intimate Night Life.* New York: John Day, 1931.
———. *The Lowdown.* New York: Henry Holt, 1928.
Sinclair, Andrew. *Prohibition: The Era of Excess.* Boston: Little, Brown, 1962.
Skolsky, Sidney. *Times Square Tintypes.* New York: I. Washburn, 1930.
Smith, Cecil. *Musical Comedy in America.* New York: Theatre Arts Books/Robert M. MacGregor, 1950.
Spell, Leslie D., and Hazel M. Spell. *Forgotten Men of Cripple Creek.* Denver: Big Mountain Press, 1959.
Sobol, Louis. *The Longest Street.* New York: Crown, 1968.

Stagg, Jerry. *The Brothers Shubert.* New York: Random House, 1968.
Stevenson, Elizabeth. *Babbitts and Bohemians: The American 1920s.* New York: Macmillan, 1967.
Stoddard, Lothrop. *Luck, Your Silent Partner.* New York: H. Liveright, 1929.
Stone, Jill. *A Pictorial History of Times Square.* New York: Macmillan, 1982.
Sullivan, Mark. *Prewar Americans.* Vol. 3 of *Our Times: The Turn of the Century.* New York: Charles Scribner's Sons, 1930.
———. *The Twenties.* Vol. 6 of *Our Times: The Turn of the Century.* New York: Charles Scribner's Sons, 1935.
Sylvester, Robert. *No Cover Charge: A Backward Look at Night Clubs.* New York: Dial Press, 1956.
Thomas, Lately. *Storming Heaven: The Lives and Turmoils of Minnie Kennedy and Aimee Semple McPherson.* New York: William Morrow, 1970.
Thomas, Lowell. *Good Evening Everybody from Cripple Creek to Samarkand.* New York: William Morrow, 1976.
Thompson, Craig, and Allen Raymond. *Gang Rule in New York.* New York: Dial Press, 1940.
United States Department of Justice. Federal Bureau of Investigation. "Journal Memorandum re: Case of Texas Guinan and Gilbert Salmon, Victim," December 11, 1922.
Waco Immigration Society. *The Immigrant's Guide to Waco and McLennan County, Texas.* Waco: Lambdin and Furman, 1884.
Walker, Alexander. *Rudolph Valentino.* New York: Stein and Day, 1976.
Walker, Stanley. *Night Club Era.* New York: Frederick A. Stokes, 1933.
Weaver, John T. *Twenty Years of Silents, 1908–1928.* Metuchen, N.J.: Scarecrow Press, 1971.
Weiner, Ed. *Let's Go to Press: A Biography of Walter Winchell.* New York: G. P. Putnam's Sons, 1955.
Willebrandt, Mabel Walker. *Inside of Prohibition.* Indianapolis: Bobbs-Merrill, 1929.
Wilde, Oscar. *The Portable Oscar Wilde.* Edited by Richard Aldington. New York: Viking Press, 1969.
Wilson, Clarence T. *The Case for Prohibition.* New York: Funk and Wagnalls, 1923.
Winchell, Walter. *Winchell Exclusive.* Englewood Cliffs, N.J.: Prentice-Hall, 1975.

Manuscripts

Lopin, Maxwell E. "The Trial of Texas Guinan." MS. 1963. Author's collection.
Stein, John S., and Hayward Grace. "Hello Sucker! The Life of Texas Guinan." MS. 1941. Billy Rose Theatre Collection. New York Public Library for the Performing Arts, New York, N.Y.

Films of Texas Guinan, 1917–1933

1917   Triangle Company
        Fuel of Life, dir. Walter Edwards
        The Stainless Barrier, dir. Thomas Heffron (walk-on part)

1918   Triangle Company
        The Gun Woman, dir. Frank Borzage; with Francis McDonald; 5 reels
        The Love Brokers, dir. E. Mason Hopper; with Alma Rubens

1919   Frohman Amusement Corp.
        (All two reels; dir. Cliff Smith, unless otherwise indicated; all with George Cheseboro)
        The Boss of the Rancho
        The Call of Bob White
        The Dangerous Little Devil
        The Dead Man's Hand, dir. Julian Johnson
        The Girl of Hell's Agony
        The Heart of Texas
        Just Bill
        Little Miss Deputy
        The Sacrifice
        The She Wolf
        Some Gal
        South of Santa Fe
        The Spirit of Cabin Mine

1920   Reelcraft Film Co.
        (All two reels; dir. Jay Hunt; with TNT Harvey)
        The Desert Vulture
        Fighting the Vigilantes
        Girl of the Rancho
        The Lady of the Law
        Letters of Fire

        A Moonshine Feud
        My Lady Robin Hood
        The Night Rider
        Not Guilty
        Outwitted
        The White Squaw
        The Wild Cat

1921 Victor Kremer Productions
      (Dir. Francis Ford)
        I Am the Woman
        The Stampede

1921 Texas Guinan Productions
      (With David Townsend)
        The Code of the West
        Texas of the Mounted

1929 Paramount
        Glorifying the American Girl (talkie; walk-on part)

1929 Warner Bros.
        Queen of the Night Clubs (talkie)

1933 United Artists
        Broadway thru a Keyhole (talkie)

Index

Acker, Jean, 4, 94, 95
Adler, Jake, 182
Aitken, Harry, 74
Aitken, Roy, 74
Alda, Frances, 4
Aman, A. E., 176
Arbuckle, Fatty, 74
Ashenhurst, John, 182
Astaire, Adele, 52
Astaire, Fred, 52
Atterbury, W. W., 4

Baer, Arthur "Bugs," 147, 152
Baker, Colgate, 93
Baker, Eddie, 180, 182, 183, 188
Baker, Josephine, 170
Barrymore, John, 94, 109
Barrymores, 47
Bayes, Nora, 50, 62, 94, 109, 139
Beazell, S. David, 137, 138
Beery, Noah, 162
Bennett, Belle, 75
Bennett, Richard, 136
Berlin, Irving, 70
Bernhardt, Sarah, 48
Berryman, Albert, 114
Bey, Rahmin, 116
Bierbower, Mrs., 53, 54
Billingsley, Sherman, 101, 111
Bishop, Jim, 157
Bissing and Sloman, 55
Blair, Nick, 112, 116
Blair, Susie, 32
Bodenheim, Max, 49
Boole, Ella, 118

Borzage, Frank, 76
Boulden, Alice, 106
Boyd, Paul, 143
Boyer, Hannah, 54, 110, 152
Brice, Fannie, 52
Briggs, Clare, 125
Brothers, Leo "Buster," 163
Broun, Heywood, 2, 99, 115, 143, 151, 152, 161, 193, 194
Buckley, George, 125
Buckner, Emory R., 106, 117

Caesar, Irving, 83
Campbell, Maurice, 129
Cantor, Eddie, 52, 162
Capone, Al, 162, 163, 175
Carr, Jimmy, 160
Carroll, Earl, 96, 103
Carroll, June, 103
Cather, Willa, 49
Chaplin, Charlie, 52, 74
Cheseboro, George, 80, 81
Chevalier, Maurice, 169
Cimman, Samuel, 162, 163
Cocke, Matty L., 31
Codyre, Pat, 126
Coll, Vincent, 178, 179
Cowan, A. J. (combined pseud. for J. K. Cowen and J. A. Edson), 30, 31
Cowan, Sarah (pseud. for Sarah Cowen), 30, 32
Cowen, J. K. (pseud. A. J. Cowan), 30, 31
Craig, Johnstone, 78

Crane, Stephen, 49
Crawford, Rhema, 186
Cunningham, Walter, 65–69

Darrow, Clarence, 133
Davidson, John, 158
Davis, H. O., 74, 75
Dean, Priscilla, 136
De Koven, Reginald, 42–44, 46, 47, 50
de Langpre, Paul, 70
Delroy, Irene, 97, 98
De Mange, Frenchy, 112, 113, 166, 179
Dempsey, Jack, 183
De Remer, Ruby, 83
Diamond, Bushnell, 126
Dillingham, Charles, 53
Doherty, Jim, 163
Dos Passos, John, 49
Drew, John, 47
Duffy, Mary, 33
Duffy, Richard, 7
Durante, Jimmy, 114

Eaton, J. C., 9, 14
Eaton, Mary, 162
Edison, Buster, 144
Edson, Hyman "Feets," 112, 116, 159, 166
Edson, J. A. (pseud. A. J. Cowan), 31
Edward, Prince of Wales, 105, 106, 110
Edwards, Julian, 56
Edwards, Walter, 75
Edwin, Willie, 51
Eulenberg, Ed, 164

Fairbanks, Douglas, 48, 74, 79
Farnum, Franklin, 52, 53, 90, 92
Fay, Larry, 96–98, 103, 104, 106, 107, 112, 182
Fejer, Joe, 90, 92–94, 168
Field, Marshall, 42
Fields, W. C., 52
Finney, Ben, 89, 97, 99, 105

Fisher, Ira, 184
Fiske, Minnie Maddern, 47
Flegenheimer, Arthur. *See* Schultz, Dutch
Ford, Francis, 84, 85
Fox, William, 154
Foy, Bryan, 158
Foy, Eddie, Jr., 158
Frisco, Joe, 92, 140, 171
Frohman, Charles, 53

Gardener, Nanon, 171, 172
Garland, Hugh, 17–19
Garland, Robert, 172
Gervasini, Emile, 92, 93
Gest, Mrs. Morris, 92
Getz-Rice, Lt., 93
Giannini, Tony, 114
Gibson, Charles Dana, 55
Gibson, William, 70
Goldburg, J. J., 85
Goldman, Emma, 49
Gordoni, Arthur, 132, 133, 139, 141
Gorman, Kathleen, 16, 17
Gorman, Mary, 17
Granlund, Nils T. (NTG), 84, 92, 96–98, 103, 104
Greene, Luther, 32
Greenwald, John, 36
Griffith, D. W., 74, 86
Guinan, Bridget "Bessie," 7–11, 14, 15, 18, 20, 22, 26, 29, 33, 34, 37, 51, 52, 62, 109, 159, 163, 164, 191
Guinan, Joseph, 7
Guinan, Michael, 7–10, 14, 15, 20, 22, 24, 26–29, 52, 123, 159, 163, 164
Guinan, Pearl, 11, 23, 37, 158–160, 164, 189
Guinan, Tommy, 11, 17, 52, 109, 110, 112, 121, 159, 160, 166, 175, 178, 179
Guinan, William, 10, 11, 159

Harder, Harry, 113, 114, 119
Harding, Mrs. Warren G., 83

Index

Harding, Warren G., 83, 84, 87, 130
Hart, William S., 74, 76, 77, 80, 84
Harvey, TNT, 83
Hastings, Aubrey, 126, 127
Hawkins, Iris, 68
Hayes, Grace, 140
Hayes, Lorraine, 164
Held, Anna, 52, 53
Hellinger, Mark, 2, 44, 99–101, 143, 155, 157, 193
Hill brothers, 180
Hines, James J., 106, 172
Hitchcock, Raymond, 48, 79
Hoban, Katy, 33, 35
Holcolmb, Wynn, 123
Holtz, Lou, 104
Hoover, Herbert, 130
Hopper, De Wolf, 67, 79
Hopper, E. Mason, 78
Hoyt, Julia, 94, 95
Hunt, Jay, 83
Hunt, Sam, 176, 182
Hutton, Aimee Semple McPherson, 121–123, 173–175, 178, 183, 186, 189

Ince, Thomas H., 74, 75

Janis, Elsie, 53, 54, 72
Joffre, Joseph Jacques Césaire, 72
Johnnidis, John, 129, 133, 141, 144
Johnson, Julian, 59–62, 64, 68, 69, 73, 74, 80, 87
Johnson, Martin, 136
Johnson, Mrs. Martin, 136
Jolson, Al, 79, 83, 104
Jones, Bobby, 118
Joyce, Peggy Hopkins, 95, 111, 116

Kaufman, George S., 101
Keaton, Buster, 52
Keefe, Zena, 83
Keehan, Roy D., 184
Keeler, Ruby, 102, 103, 111, 140
Kellog, Shirley, 64
Kern, Jerome, 129

Kerwin, Al, 127, 128, 143, 165
Kirkwood, W. W., 63
Klurfeld, Herman, 178
Kremer, Victor, 84–86

La Guardia, Fiorello H., 151
Lait, Jack, 98
Lane, Dick, 171
Langtry, Lily, 48, 57
Lardner, Ring, 100, 125, 126
Lawton, Elizabeth, 115
Lee, Lila, 158
Lee, Walter Tug, 98
Leister, Mortimer K., 138
Leon, Leonard, 163
Lewis, Sinclair, 109
Libbey, Laura Jean, 17, 23
Lingle, Jake, 163
Livingstone, Belle, 123–125, 129, 166, 169, 183, 193
Longcope, James Walter, 119
Lopin, Maxwell E., xi, xii, 133–136, 138–142, 144–149, 151, 154, 155, 157, 193
Luce, Claire, 103, 104
Luce, Henry R., 31, 32
Lyman, Tommy, 129
Lynn, George W., 192
Lyons, Arthur, 154
Lyons, Harry, 180

McCabe, Mary, 7
McCourt, Col. Peter, 35
McCutcheon, Wally, 90, 93
MacFarland, R., 184
McIntyre, O. O., 193
Mack, Austin, 160
McLauglin, G. V., 117
McPherson, Aimee Semple. *See* Hutton, Aimee Semple McPherson
Madden, Owney, 96, 112, 159, 166, 178, 179
Manley, Chesly, 163
Manners, Lady Diana, 111
Mansfield, Richard, 47

Marks, "Solly," 164
Martin, John S., 32
Mason, Jack, 56
Mavity, Nancy Barr, 183
Maxwell, Gilbert, 129, 130
Menjou, Adolphe, 121
Michelena, Vera, 50, 51, 57
Millay, Edna St. Vincent, 49
Miller, Hank (pseud. for Zach Miller), 24–29
Miller, Zach (pseud. Hank Miller), 25
Milne, Richard, 98
Mitchell, John J., 138
Mix, Tom, 111
Mizner, Wilson, 98, 161
Moran, Bugs, 163
Morgan, Helen, 114, 129, 130, 132, 139, 141, 162, 168, 194
Morgan, Henry Victor, 188, 189
Morosco, Oliver, 60
Morrison, Norman J., 131–133, 136, 138, 140–149
Mountbatten, Lord Louis, 105
Moynahan, John J., 35–44, 49, 50, 60, 61, 192
Muhl, Sarah Hopkins, 15, 16
Murray, Mae, 80

Naples, Jack, 173
Nazimova, 48, 94
Neal Sisters, 171
Nelson, Leo, 175, 176
Nerida, 125
Newberry, Ted, 163
Newman, Joseph, 36
Ney, Lew, 127
Normand, Mabel, 74
Norworth, Jack, 158
Novak, Eva, 80

O'Keefe, Walter, 104
O'Neill, Eugene, 48, 49
O'Neill, James, 48
O'Reilly, Kitty, 140, 149, 160
Osterman, Jack, 171

Pani, Joe, 94
Parsons, Louella, 183
Peggy and Cortez, 93
Pickford, Mary, 79, 83, 109, 138
Prounis, Nick, 129, 132, 141, 144
Putnam, Katie, 24

Raft, George, 4, 104, 116, 158
Rambova, Natacha, 94, 95
Reed, John, 49
Reid, Lawrence, 77, 80
Ridenour, Ruth, 120
Rigler, Lou, 111, 127
Riley, Ed, 4
Ring, Blanche, 93
Roland, Ruth, 80
Romberg, Sigmund, 70, 93
Roosevelt, President, 166
Rubens, Alma, 53, 74
Runyon, Damon, 100, 105
Runyon, Mrs. Damon (Patrice Gridiere), 104
Russell, Dorothy, 62
Russell, Lillian, 62, 65, 110

Salmon, Gilbert, 88
Schmelling, Max, 160
Schultz, Dutch (pseud. of Arthur Flegenheimer), 167, 168, 172, 175, 178–180
Schwab, Franny, 109
Sennett, Mack, 74
Shaw, George Bernard, 183
Sherman, Lowell, 94
Sherrill, Jack, 80
Sherrill, William, 80
Shubert, Jake, 89, 162
Shubert, Lee, 60, 64
Shubert brothers, 50, 62, 64, 126, 171
Silverman, Sime, 55
Sister Clara, 16, 22
Slocum, John P., 56–60
Smith, Al, 129, 130
Smith, Cliff, 80, 82
Smith, Patrick (Tex's nephew), xii, 37, 158–160, 184

Index

Sobol, Louis, 2, 55, 189, 193
Solinger, Walter B., 133, 134, 145, 165, 193
Stein, John, 2, 29, 40, 41, 50, 51, 54, 57, 58, 61, 80, 87, 165, 175, 180, 182, 187–189
Steinson, A., 184
Steuer, Max, 134, 151
Stevens, Ashton, 161, 185
Stewart, Roy, 74
Sullivan, Ed, 99, 193
Sullivan, Wallace, 157
Swanson, Gloria, 74, 83, 121, 169
Sweitzer, Leon, 162–165

Tanguay, Eva, 52
Taylor, Norma, 160
Taylor, William Desmond, 74
Thaw, Harry, 111, 115
Thomas, Edwin C., 138, 141, 142, 145, 148
Thomas, Lowell, 33
Thomas, Olive, 74
Thompson, Anthony, 31
Thorpe, Sam, 97, 114
Townley, George E. (pseud. of David E. Townsend), 87
Townsend, David E., 86, 87
Trout, Emma, 22, 23
Tucker, Sophie, 52
Turner, Jos. A., 32
Turner, Wesley, 143

Valentino, Rudolph, 4, 94, 95, 116
Vallee, Rudy, 162
Vanderbilt, Gertrude, 184
Vanderbilt, Mrs. W. K., 94
Vechten, Carl Van, 109

Vinton, Doris, 102, 104
Voiler, Harry O., 161–165, 175–177, 182
Voiler, Mrs. Harry O., 161, 162, 176

Walker, Charlotte, 40
Walker, James, 111
Walker, William, 184
Walter, Eugene, 40
Ward, Fannie, 166, 169
Warren, Jack, 50, 53
West, Mae, 52, 160, 165, 183, 186
Whalen, Grover, 154–156
White, George, 103, 169
White, James L., 132–139, 141, 142
White, Pearl, 90, 93, 94
Whiteman, Paul, 123
Wilder, Thornton, 109, 184
Wilkenson, Laura, 122
Willebrandt, Mabel Walker, 129, 130, 132, 152–154
Wilson, Margaret, 94
Wilson, Woodrow, 3, 71, 73, 79, 82, 109
Winchell, Gloria, 100
Winchell, Walter, 2, 4, 99–101, 112, 143, 178, 179, 186, 187
Wittenmeier, Fred, 185
Wright, Charlotte, 35
Wynn, Ed, 79

Yawitz, Paul, 193

Zanuck, Darryl, 186
Ziegfield, Florenz, 48, 62, 96, 102, 103
Zittell, Harry, 151